PREPARING YOUR TEENS — for — COLLEGE

FAITH, FRIENDS, FINANCES, AND MUCH MORE

ALEX CHEDIAK

Tyndale House Publishers, Inc.
Carol Stream, Illinois

Visit Tyndale online at www.tyndale.com.

TYNDALE, Tyndale's quill logo, *The One Year*, and *One Year* are registered trademarks of Tyndale House Publishers, Inc. The One Year logo is a trademark of Tyndale House Publishers, Inc.

Preparing Your Teens for College: Faith, Friends, Finances, and Much More

Copyright © 2014 by Juan Alexander Chediak. All rights reserved.

Cover photograph of sweatshirt and pennant taken by Katie Fore. Copyright © by Tyndale Houe Publishers, Inc. All rights reserved. All other photographs are the property of their respective copyright holders and all rights are reserved: spiral notebook, note card, and sticky note © Elena Schweitzer/Shutterstock; stacked paper © kyoshino/iStockphoto; tablet © rvlsoft/iStockphoto; pointing finger © PhillDanze/iStockphoto.

Author photograph by Stephen Vosloo. Copyright © 2010 by Tyndale House Publishers, Inc. All rights reserved.

Designed by Mark Anthony Lane II

Edited by Jonathan Schindler

Unless otherwise indicated, all Scripture quotations are taken from *The Holy Bible*, English Standard Version® (ESV®), copyright © 2001 by Crossway, a publishing ministry of Good News Publishers. Used by permission. All rights reserved.

Scripture quotations marked NASB are taken from the New American Standard Bible,® copyright © 1960, 1962, 1963, 1968, 1971, 1972, 1973, 1975, 1977, 1995 by The Lockman Foundation. Used by permission.

Scripture quotations marked NIV are taken from the Holy Bible, *New International Version*,® *NIV*.® Copyright © 1973, 1978, 1984, 2011 by Biblica, Inc.™ Used by permission of Zondervan. All rights reserved worldwide. www.zondervan.com.

Scripture quotations marked NLT are taken from the *Holy Bible*, New Living Translation, copyright © 1996, 2004, 2007, 2013 by Tyndale House Foundation. Used by permission of Tyndale House Publishers, Inc., Carol Stream, Illinois 60188. All rights reserved.

Library of Congress Cataloging-in-Publication Data

Chediak, Alex.
 Preparing your teens for college : faith, friends, finances, and much more / Alex Chediak.
     pages cm
 Includes bibliographical references.
 ISBN 978-1-4143-8312-5 (sc)
 1. Christian college students—Religious life. 2. College student orientation. 3. Christian education—Home training. I. Title.
 BV4531.3.C4825 2014
 248.8′3—dc23   2013045357

Printed in the United States of America

20   19   18   17   16   15   14
 7   6   5   4   3   2   1

TO MARNI:

Excellent wife, loving mother, faithful friend, fabulous research assistant, skilled editor, and much more

Contents

Foreword by Tedd Tripp

ALEX CHEDIAK HAS done it again! This book is a needed addition to the universe of parenting books. Chediak brings his many years of experience both as a student and as a college professor to the task of preparing teens for college and for a useful future.

As a young man I spent a couple of years working as a resident director for a men's dorm at a Christian college. From that post I observed young people who were not prepared for college. They refused to accept responsibility for their lives. They lacked the foresight to postpone immediate gratification for the sake of future benefit. They did not understand how to internalize their faith and live as people of conviction. They made bad choices of companionship, not understanding that "the companion of fools suffers harm." They failed to comprehend the biblical truth that moral purity is essential to flourishing spiritually. Confronted with our consumer culture, they were tempted to squander money with high-interest credit cards. They did not understand how to be stewards of God's gifts to them. They lacked self-consciousness about their own talents and natural abilities.

I remember watching teens like those just wasting their years at college. I would try to counsel them, but more often than not the die was cast. The character issues and lack of maturity that drove their daily choices kept them from receiving wise counsel. As I read Alex's book, I thought that the sacrifice parents make to *keep* kids in college would be more wisely invested in *preparing* them for college in the ways this book outlines.

Preparing Your Teens for College is a clarion call to parents to be people of influence in the lives of their teens. Alex proposes a wide-ranging series of conversations for parents to have with their teens: conversations about being responsible, making good decisions, forming good friendships, understanding faith, learning how to live as a Christian in ways that are wise and gracious, being smart with money, maintaining personal purity, developing convictions, living from convictions, discerning gifts and talents, working diligently as to the Lord, and many other topics. Teens need these engaging conversations with their parents. They are at the point in their life when they are forming opinions on a whole range of issues: identity, personal values, career goals, relationships, how to live as Christians in our culture, and understanding their gifts and talents, to name just a few. They need parents who have maturity, wisdom, and life experience to engage them in serious conversations. This book will equip you to do just that.

Alex identifies the important topics, outlines the content of the conversations, and even walks parents through possible approaches to these much-needed conversations. The importance of these conversations is simply impossible to overstate. Too many parents want to have these conversations but are not sure what to say. Sometimes, they haven't taken the time to work through the range of topics they want to cover and plan those conversations.

In each chapter, you will find a discussion of the spirit of the age and how young people think in our culture. Alex provides a biblical critique of modern thought as well as the Christian truths you will want to emphasize with your teens. At the end of each chapter, there is a series of discussion questions that will lead to fruitful conversations. Parents who take the time to engage their teens in the ways Alex recommends will accomplish things that cannot be achieved through any exercise of parental authority.

One of the most humbling truths we know as parents is that we cannot save our children. God must work in their hearts. There are limits to what we are able to do. It is encouraging to remember that God works through means. One of the means he uses is parents who diligently shepherd their children. I am happy to recommend this book as a sharp tool for *Preparing Your Teens for College.*

Introduction

The Questions Every Parent Is Asking

MY BOOK *Thriving at College: Make Great Friends, Keep Your Faith, and Get Ready for the Real World* came out in April 2011. One afternoon that summer I was sitting in my office waiting to do a radio interview. I had done a few by then, and I felt I was getting the hang of it. But the first question that day brought on a momentary glaze: "Alex, we know college is a big deal. So how can parents get their teens ready?"

I thought, *Wait. That's not what the book is about!* I had written *Thriving at College* to help *students* get the most out of the college experience. I didn't write it for parents.

A week later it happened again: "We've talked a lot about the challenges college students face. But how about the parents? How can *they* do a better job getting their teens ready?" At least I wasn't caught off guard this time.

A few weeks later I received an e-mail about an upcoming conference. Would I give a seminar on how parents can prepare teens for college?

Since then, it seems I've been answering questions about

how to prepare teens for college as much as I've been talking about the college experience itself. At conferences, at churches, and in everyday conversations, it seems every parent is asking questions like these:

- Will my children's Christian faith be strong enough to withstand the tests of college—the party scene, the atheistic professors?
- Will they manage their time well or be overwhelmed with the amount of freedom that awaits them?
- Will they form solid, healthy friendships or be lonely and get in with the wrong crowd?
- Will they be happy, successful, and persevering in their studies, or will they wander aimlessly from one major to the next?

Those questions led to this book—a comprehensive manual for parents, pastors, guidance counselors, or anyone else getting teens ready for college. *Preparing Your Teens for College* is the overflow of my personal experience, both as a kid who once went to college and, more significantly, as a college professor who for the past eight years has worked every day with the "end products" of your labors—the students who leave home and head to college in search of professional preparation, a deeper sense of purpose, and a greater awareness of their place in God's world.

In the time since you and I have embarked on our adult lives, both the *cost* and the *importance* of college education have dramatically increased. But high school graduates have also changed. Just as Gen Xers are different from Boomers, teens today are in a whole new category. Let me unpack the challenges that we, and they, are up against.

THREE ECONOMIC REALITIES

Preparing teens for college has never been more crucial, due to three economic realities that don't seem to be going away anytime soon: the importance of post-secondary education, the escalation of college tuition, and the sluggish state of the global economy.

First, the importance of college attendance. As recently as 1980, only half of high school graduates chose some form of college after high school. In recent years, that figure is in the 65 to 70 percent range.[1] Combine that with general population growth over a 30-year stretch, and you've got a massive upswing in college enrollment (an over 80-percent increase from 1980 to the present).[2]

Why all this growth? Because we're fast becoming a skill- and knowledge-based economy. Between 1973 and 2007, 63 million jobs were added to the US economy, while the number of jobs held by people with only a high school degree fell by about two million.[3] And the "earnings premium"—the additional money earned by college graduates as compared to high school graduates—has been steadily rising for the last three decades. You're probably reading this book because you've gotten the memo: a college degree will give your child the greatest shot at getting and keeping a good job.

But the word *college* means different things to different people. While the highest-paying jobs (on average) are accessed with a bachelor's or an advanced degree (doctors, lawyers, engineers, business consultants), economists predict that nearly half of future job openings to be filled by workers with post-secondary education will go to people with an associate's degree or an occupational certificate[4]—think electricians, construction managers, and dental hygienists. These may not strike you as prestigious lines of work, but our economy needs them, and they pay better than most people think. They have the added benefits of not requiring a quarter of a million dollars in educational costs and of being difficult to outsource.

Which brings us to the second issue: college tuition. The annual price tag at a four-year, public university (the most common destination for college-bound teens) has risen three and a half times faster than the rate of inflation over the last 30 years.[5] Yet despite this steep increase, enrollment in these and other four-year schools continues to dramatically rise. Why? Because if it gives our kids a better shot at a successful career, we're willing to foot the bill.

But that's not *quite* true. Amid economic weakness, parents have actually been shelling out *less* for kids in college (covering 27 percent of costs in 2012–2013 versus 37 percent in 2009–2010).[6] What's picking up the slack? Subsidies (such as grants and scholarships) and loans. For the 2009–2010 academic year, six out of ten public four-year college students graduated with an average student debt load of $22,000. Student borrowing that year was deeper and more widespread at private schools: two out of every three students graduated with an average of $28,100 in student loans.[7] Loans to parents have jumped 75 percent since the 2005–2006 academic year.[8] And it seems to get a bit worse each year: approximately seven out of ten 2013 graduates accrued some form of debt (including money owed to family members), totaling an average of $35,200.[9] About $30,000 of this was student loan debt.[10] Even after adjusting for inflation, student loan debt has increased by over 300 percent in the last decade.[11] As a nation, we owe over one trillion dollars in student debt, more than we owe in credit cards.[12] Add to this the fact that graduation drops students into a sluggish economy—one in which many bachelor's degree holders under the age of 25 are either unemployed or underemployed (as of April 2012).[13]

Which brings us to the third issue: the lackluster state of the global economy. Folks with 10 to 20 years of experience, laid off in the economic downturn, are now applying for jobs normally filled by new college graduates. And they're often willing to work for lower wages (since they have no alternative). Employers, given their options, are understandably going with the more mature, experienced applicants, leaving lots of new grads out in the cold.[14]

It's a perfect storm. More people are going to college than ever before, it costs a fortune, we're borrowing crazy amounts of money to go, and the newer graduates are competing with experienced candidates for precious few job openings. Oh, and one more thing. The maturity of students going into college is often woefully low—as are graduation rates.

KIDS THESE DAYS

Lots of freshmen haven't gotten the memo that college is a lot of work. They seem to think it's an expensive vacation funded by you (along with student loans). Roughly one out of four freshmen does not make it to their sophomore year, often due to immaturity or lack of focus.[15] Other students get by, but never really grasp the purpose of the academic enterprise—they don't become lifelong learners; clearheaded thinkers; well-rounded, flexible, honest, hardworking, self-starting, responsible, mature, humble men and women. They never develop strong communication, problem-solving, or people skills—the very qualities employers are looking for.[16]

College Graduation Rates Are Terribly Low

According to the Organization for Economic Cooperation and Development, the United States now has the highest college dropout rate in the industrialized world. While we send as many as 70 percent of high school graduates to college, as of 2010 only 42 percent of 25- to 34-year-olds have a post–high school degree of any sort. At four-year colleges and universities, only 56 percent of students graduate in *six* years. At two-year schools, it's even worse: only 29 percent graduate in *three* years.[17]

Moreover, these traits equip us to love and honor God with all our minds and to do good works in the marketplace, in the laboratory, in the library, in the classroom, in the hospital, in the law courts, on the mission field, or wherever God leads us.

Many teens today are more dependent on their parents than we were at their age. They're more distracted by media and technology. They're less willing to discipline themselves and work hard. And they expect success to come more easily than is realistic. In a survey of more than 2,000 high school seniors in the Chicago area, sociologist James Rosenbaum found that almost half of them (46 percent) agreed with the statement: "Even if I do not work hard in high school, I can still make my future plans come true."[18]

Yet studies have shown—ironically—that overconfidence leads to underperformance. Those whose self-esteem is more reinforced, apart from objective accomplishment, exhibit declining performance over time and are most likely to quit.[19] It makes sense. If you think you're better at something than you really are, you expect it to come easily. This makes you less likely to work at it, less likely to succeed, and more likely to be surprised and disappointed when you don't. As a professor, I have seen this happen many times.

I'm happy to say that some students are well prepared, get over the inevitable hurdles, and come out on the other side just fine. Others who start off poorly respond well to correction. They learn their lesson and graduate with a high degree of maturity and skill.

THE PARENTING ROLE IS IRREPLACEABLE

Training matters. Not just what we professors do on campus but what you do before your teens ever get to us. Thriving at college begins in the home. What you model and impart to your teens, day in and day out, makes a huge difference.

Thriving at college begins in the home.

I've seen this play out countless times in the lives of my students, for good and for ill. Some students from churched backgrounds leave the faith while at college, either temporarily or permanently. Many fail to adjust to the rigors of college-level academics—even some of our most gifted students. And beyond academics, "failure to launch" is not uncommon—students preferring to linger in the no-man's-land of adolescence rather than complete the journey to full-orbed adulthood.

Each of these topics is the subject of countless books in recent years. And while there may be disagreement on the best remedies for spiritually apostate, professionally wandering, or developmentally stunted twentysomethings, there's strong agreement on what can mitigate these ailments: godly, involved parents who intentionally and wisely invest in their children, in word and deed, at all stages, but particularly in the teen years. There's no doubt about it—what you and I do as parents, before our teens leave home, has the greatest likelihood of preventing these kinds of decline.

Shepherding your children in the direction of responsible Christian living in every sphere of life prepares them for the tests of post–high school life like nothing else can. "Train up a child in the way he should go; even when he is old he will not depart from it" (Proverbs 22:6). "Like arrows in the hand of a warrior are the children of one's youth" (Psalm 127:4)—to be released with care and intentionality into the world to make a difference for the glory of God and the good of others.

So while *Thriving at College* is for students, *Preparing Your Teens for College* is for you. When I get to know college freshmen, I recognize that the worldview and character they bring to college are the result of 18 or 19 years of living with their parents. Their *worldview* (how they think) and their *character* (who they are) impact their *attitude* (what they think) and their *behavior* (what they do). Their attitude and behavior, in turn, give rise to their habits and their destiny, as they (like we) reap what they sow (see Galatians 6:7).

Worldview & Character ➞ Attitudes & Behaviors ➞ Habits & Destiny

And all of this is true whether our children become medical doctors or ultrasound technicians, engineers or electricians, businesspeople or beauticians. A four-year college is but one of several possible launching pads into a responsible, fruitful life.

THE STRUCTURE OF THE BOOK

The heart of this book is 11 conversations you'll want to have with your teens before they head off to college. The conversations deal with issues of character, faith, relationships, financial discipline, academics, and finally the college decision itself. To help you facilitate these conversations, I've included "Conversation Starters" at the end of each chapter. I know that talking to teens can be difficult, and it's not always easy to catch them at the right time. Sometimes you have to take time with them when you can get it—even if it means dropping what you're doing, or staying up until 1:00 a.m. to make yourself available when they're able to open up. But these open-ended conversation starters will help you to broach the topics in this book in a nonthreatening way.

Here's a short preview of the conversations in this book.

Character

We've all seen it: young people with enormous potential who flame out because of poor decisions. Perhaps it's substance abuse, reoccurring impulsiveness, or too much freedom before they're ready. As parents, we want to protect our children from turning out badly. And yet we cannot completely control what they choose. Their accountability is ultimately to God.

How can we help our teens develop critical thinking skills and an internal moral compass before they leave the home?

In conversation one, we'll talk about the dangers of "over-parenting" and "under-parenting." God expects us to shepherd their hearts. This involves instruction, correction, and admonition—delivered in love to influence them for their good.

In the second conversation we'll tackle the importance of delaying gratification, persevering, and building a life of integrity. The ability to say "no" to one pleasure (sinful *or* legitimate) for the sake of something later—something *greater*—is very important. Many fail for lack of it (Proverbs 25:28), and no one reaches their potential apart from it.

Faith

When I speak to parents about getting their teens ready for college, I've found this to be the most acute concern: Will my children's faith be strong enough to withstand the tests of college? Will they come out on the other side with their faith intact? We'll divide this section into two parts: internalizing the faith (conversation 3) and developing a winsome posture toward those with other beliefs (conversation 4).

The process of internalizing Christian convictions is sometimes messy. But it's one that must occur, at some point, for those raised in Christian homes. Some teens never see Christianity lived out and conclude it's not real. Other teens are raised in stern homes where they fear expressing any religious questions, doubts, or struggles with sin. Consequently, their faith remains dwarfed—more external than internal, more their parents' than their own. Our goal is to help them see, for themselves, that Christianity truthfully and satisfyingly explains reality.

In conversation 4, we'll talk about how Christians can engage those who think differently with true tolerance—and without compromising their convictions. In engaging others, your teens need to remember that each person bears the image of God and is thus worthy of dignity, respect, and honor. They ought not to demean or belittle those who think differently. At the same time, humanity is fallen, and sin impacts even our minds. That means some pretty smart people—including college professors—can believe some pretty dumb things.

Relationships

Your teens' close friendships will profoundly shape how they turn out as adults. "Whoever walks with the wise becomes wise, but the companion of fools will suffer harm" (Proverbs 13:20). As parents, we must help our teens realize that because friendships are so influential, they need to be chosen wisely. There's a place for friendship evangelism, but a Christian teen will generally not do well if their closest friendships are with non-Christians. They need the "iron sharpen[ing] iron" (Proverbs 27:17) benefit of those who share and reinforce the value system by which they aspire to live. In conversation 5, we'll discuss how you can help your teens be wise in their selection of close friends—being proactive and making relational choices, not reactions.

In conversation 6, we'll tackle relationships with the opposite sex. We live in an "if it feels good, do it" culture, yet the sexual arena is one in which, as Christians, we're called to go against the flow, to delay gratification so that we can say yes to God's best for us. In a day when the majority of adults cohabit before marriage and 40 percent of all children are born out of wedlock, we must raise our children to understand that God intends intimacy to be associated with marriage. Our teens must control their strong desires for physical and emotional intimacy and channel them into the identification and pursuit of a quality, lifelong partner.

Finances

In conversation 7, we'll deal with the enormously important (and often neglected) task of helping our children internalize wise financial habits and disciplines. Though credit card usage among college students may have decreased since 2009,[20] the majority of card owners fail to make full payments on a monthly basis, racking up needless consumer debt.[21] Other students take on excessive student debt with little regard to their future ability to make repayment.

While college students have little control over the global economy, they are responsible for their unbiblical attitudes toward money and for their inappropriate spending habits. Against this cultural tide, parents must teach their children the value of money. Raising children with a biblical perspective of money will go a long way toward short-circuiting the common financial mistakes young adults make during and after their college years.

Academics

In conversation 8, we'll talk about modeling the goodness of work to our teens so that they develop a biblical motivation for their academic pursuits. The work of students is to develop their intellectual capacities, understanding that well-trained minds prepare them for all that God has in store for them in the future. Because all truth originates in God, teens should approach all of their schoolwork with an attitude of worship.

Helping our teens to see their schoolwork as a God-assigned responsibility and to find joy in the learning process is the first stage of their academic preparation for college. The second stage, which we'll take up in conversation 9, is helping our teens discover their specific areas of academic interest and talent. We want our teens to become accurately and confidently aware of what they're naturally good at (talents) and love (interests). Wisely selecting a college major—one that taps into the intersection of their God-given talents and interests—is also of practical value if we hope they'll graduate in a timely manner.

The College Decision

In conversation 10, we'll discuss how to find a four-year college or university where a student can receive a high-quality education, excellent preparation for the job market, and vibrant Christian community on and off campus. We'll talk about the importance of a four-year college having a strong program not just in the area of your teen's major but in its liberal arts (or general) education as well. When done well, a liberal arts education teaches a student how to think critically, communicate clearly, and solve complicated problems. These are foundational competencies not just for a particular job but for *life*.

In conversation 11 we'll talk about a few overlooked paths to a rewarding career: trade schools, apprenticeships, and associate's degrees. Though less appreciated than in the past, being mechanically inclined is important for many lines of honorable work—ones in which millions of jobs are currently unfilled, as employers cannot find enough skilled workers (or people willing to make the effort to become such workers). God doesn't view skilled labor as less important, and neither should we.

LET'S GET STARTED

So there's the layout for the book. My aim is to provide a comprehensive handbook on getting teens ready for college (in all its forms). Although the six sections build on each other, feel free to read the book in whatever order you find most helpful.

Are you ready to help your teens develop responsibility and a work ethic that will persevere into their college years? Are you ready to coach them through smaller failures so they succeed over the long haul in the crucial areas of life?

Are you ready to help your teens internalize their faith and engage a lost world with conviction and compassion?

Are you ready to help your teens discern the character qualities to look for in friends and to embrace God's plan for purity?

Are you ready to help your teens cultivate a biblical perspective on money and draw up a plan to avoid the vortex of debt that captures so many college students?

Are you ready to help them assess academic interests and

talents so they can make an informed decision regarding a college major?

Are you ready to help your teens ask the right questions about prospective colleges so that they get the best value for their dollar?

Then let's get to work on preparing your teens for college.

PART 1
CHARACTER

CONVERSATION 1
Teaching Responsibility

A HUGE SIGH broke the awkward silence as Frank pulled up at another red light. In the passenger seat sat Matthew, a red-faced teen, staring out the window.

"Dad, the plan *was* to hang out at Johnny's Pizza. I'm not lying! I had no idea Josh was going to insist that we go to his house instead."

Frank's eyes didn't move. He was afraid to look at Matthew, who had alcohol on his breath. Frank's mind was racing: What had happened to the innocence of Matthew's childhood? Frank remembered Matthew's first year in Little League and how much fun they'd had going to his games. Ever since Matthew had turned 14, things had taken a turn for the worse. He was hanging out with the wrong crowd, neglecting his homework, and often seemed to have a chip on his shoulder.

It's not that Frank had been unconcerned. He and his wife, Mary, took Matthew to church every week and encouraged him to attend the youth group's activities. They just didn't want to dictate his every move. That's why they let him make his own choices. *But look where that led*, Frank thought.

With a pained expression, Frank glanced at his son. "What happened, Matthew? How could going over to Josh's lead to my getting a call from the police?"

More awkward silence. Then Matthew replied, "Josh insisted we all come over. Once we got there, he disappeared and came back with a few bottles and a flask with a weird shape. It was Jim's 16th birthday, he announced, and we needed to celebrate. Soon there were probably 30 people in the house.

"Look, I wasn't going to drink anything. Seriously. But once everyone got there, they started playing a game that involved sampling the bottles. *What could go wrong?* I figured. It wouldn't hurt to try a little. I never felt out of control. Not until Josh started getting on my nerves. Next thing I knew, he was going after me in the backyard, screaming. He tried to fight me, Dad. What was I supposed to do? The neighbors must have heard something and called the cops."

Frank was speechless. He stared at the road ahead. He didn't know if he wanted to scream or cry. *Something has to change.* He replayed the last few years in his mind. He had never talked to Matthew about the temptations of teenage life. Not just alcohol, but also the desire to fit in. To not only be accepted, but respected. He just figured it would all work out. Matthew had been such a sweet kid. Frank wanted his little boy back.

Slowly, Frank realized that he and Mary were parenting Matthew as if he were still a boy. This incident would give him a chance to begin a new kind of conversation—one about freedom, choices, responsibility, and accountability. But Frank felt overwhelmed. He had no idea where to start.

AUTHORITY AND INFLUENCE

As Christian parents, we must always seek to shape the character of our children, to set them on the right course, with an internalized, biblically informed moral compass. That's our duty: "Train up a child in the way he should go; even when he is old he will not depart from it" (Proverbs 22:6). In the early years, this often comes with a high degree of structure. "Eat your vegetables." "Brush your teeth." "Get to bed." And discipline. Children must know that we're in charge and that God, for their good, has put us in authority over them.

As our children grow into the teen years, their ability to do things we disapprove of increases, and like Matthew's parents, our ability to control them decreases. They can lie to us, hide things from us, and even live double lives. We can't spank them; they may even be bigger and stronger than we are! If we're banking solely on positional authority, we're in trouble. What we need is moral authority: *influence* in their lives, at the deepest level—a level we can't reach without their consent.

Positional authority is God-given; moral authority must be earned over time. Think of moral authority as the permission to speak into the inner core of someone's heart—to shape the person's heart and, in turn, life (see Proverbs 4:23). We must win the hearts of our teens so that they *want* us involved in their lives, leading them into adulthood, interpreting the fast-paced biological and social changes they're experiencing, helping them process their shortcomings and insecurities, and encouraging them that with God's help they can do great things.

But how? By seeing the hard moments as God moments—opportunities rather than irritations. When our teens make sinful choices or are caught in a web of deception, we have to fight the temptation to give them a piece of our minds. It's easy to show them "who's in charge around here." It's harder to remember that *God* is ultimately in charge and that he has put us in their lives to prepare them for adulthood. Their failures are opportunities to come alongside them, helping them to understand cause and effect and that (as a college mentor once told me) we never really get away with anything. It's a chance to remind our teens that the greatest happiness always lies in the sometimes hard path of obedience and to let them into our own lifelong discovery of this principle.

Please don't misunderstand. The quest for moral authority doesn't mean we abrogate positional authority. I'm not saying we turn household rules into mere suggestions for our teens

The Foundational Importance of Conversion

One possibility is that Matthew is not yet a Christian. Jesus said, "A good tree produces good fruit, and a bad tree produces bad fruit. A good tree can't produce bad fruit, and a bad tree can't produce good fruit" (Matthew 7:17-18, NLT). In other words, the fruit doesn't define the tree; the tree defines the fruit.

Matthew's dad should consider that Christian behavior can only flow from someone who has experienced the miracle of being born again (see John 3:3-6). The new birth makes us alive to God. A dead tree withers in the sunlight, but one that's alive grows in the sunlight. A non-Christian naturally chafes at Christian teachings— he has no desire to please God. A true Christian longs to please God, even though temptation and sin remain a lifelong struggle.

The first thing we must aim for in our parenting is the conversion of our children. Godly character traits will naturally flow from an authentic conversion experience. That said, a well-behaved, orderly, non-Christian teen is more tolerable in the home and a better influence on his siblings than one who is rude and disorderly. We can and must maintain propriety in our homes, even if our children are not yet saved. But as we do so, let's not forget that good behavior can never save anyone. We need to remind them of their need for Jesus even as we seek to preserve a sense of order, dignity, and respect in our homes.

to consider. We're still in charge in our homes. And while spanking is no longer an option as our children get older, there are other consequences that can prove instructive, such as curtailing certain expressions of freedom (e.g., driving a family car) until they've demonstrated an appropriate degree of maturity. But the *demeanor* of our authority must increasingly be one that appeals to their consciences. We have to go beyond our teens' external behavior to the internal motivations of their hearts.

> The goal is to shepherd our teens' hearts while recognizing that their ultimate accountability is to God, not us.

We *are* in charge, but we're not just bosses. We're coaches and mentors to guide our teens into the years when they'll be on their own. Our deepest desire is that they internalize godly principles and the Christian faith from which they originate so that they're obedient in our presence *and* in our absence, and not just to us, their earthly parents, but to God, their heavenly Father.

What does all this have to do with preparing teens for college? It's simple: the character of your teens is as determinative of their success in college as their intelligence, if not more so. I've seen this play out in countless students over the years: some come in with excellent ACT or SAT scores and solid high school GPAs, but their inner lives are a mess. They got by because high school was too easy. They lack self-control. They make reckless decisions. Before too long, they're in serious academic trouble. Thankfully, I've also seen the opposite: students whose academic ability is at best average but who through discipline and consistent effort have a seriousness about them that inevitably results in improvement. They find their niche and flourish academically and socially. Success in college really is more perspiration (discipline and effort) than inspiration (talent).

Because character is so important, we'll cover it first. This chapter and the next are devoted to helping you shape the character of your teens so that they leave your home college ready. To do that, we have to grapple with a tension—one that Frank was thinking about as he drove Matthew home: If we give our kids too much freedom and space, how do we know they won't go off the deep end and make some really bad choices? On the other hand, if we don't loosen the reins, how will our children learn to exercise critical thinking skills and make moral judgments for themselves? If we don't allow them to exercise greater freedom, even if it means the occasional blunder, how will they become more responsible?

Was Matthew's problem too much freedom? Or was it too little preparation? We need to think hard about the goal of our parenting and living between the extremes of under-parenting and over-parenting. The goal is to shepherd our teens' hearts while recognizing that their ultimate accountability is to God, not us.

UNDER-PARENTING

There are various ways to sidestep the struggle of parenting teens, all of which I'd put under the umbrella of under-parenting. I read an article recently about a man who was embarrassed by his wife's behavior. Since their daughter had turned 13, Mom had changed. She began to shop with her teen daughter and to buy the same clothes, preferring to both look and act like a high school girl. Why? She thought it would develop a special bond with her daughter, make her a more approachable mom, and prevent them from being drawn apart during the pivotal teen years. If you think about it, it's the same kind of fear Matthew's parents had—a fear of being too preachy and coming across as fuddy-duddies. We're afraid our teens will turn against us, preferring the acceptance of their peers to the wisdom of their parents.

When we as parents act like teens, we send a clear message that being an adult is less interesting than being a teen. Adulthood, and the responsibilities that come with it, are to be avoided for as long as possible. When we simply put off difficult conversations for fear that our teens will reject us, we send the message that we lack either the wisdom or the interest to help them transition into adulthood.

I have adult friends who tell me that when they were in high school, their dads would grunt and walk away if they disapproved of something. That sent the message, I suppose, but spared Dad the stress of uncomfortable conversations.

We get in trouble when we pursue friendships with our teens by becoming their peers and when we limit our involvement to clucks or grunts of disapproval. Either way, we're failing to provide what we alone can: preparation for entering the adult world. We're abdicating our God-given role as authority figures in the lives of our children. What teens really want from their parents is structure, wisdom, and guidance. Even secular psychologists recognize that this kind of authority gives a teen security.

Teens today spend the majority of their time with their peers, people who (whatever their strengths) are not in a

Rehoboam's Folly

King Solomon's son Rehoboam ascended to the throne and was immediately confronted with a thorny situation (see 1 Kings 12:1-11). He wisely sought counsel from a cluster of older men who had advised his father over a 40-year reign. He also checked in with a group of young men who had grown up with him. Their recommendations diverged, and Rehoboam was forced to issue a make-or-break decision that would determine the trajectory of his administration and the nation of Israel itself. Rehoboam foolishly sided with the ego-boosting advice of his peers ("show the people who's boss!"), rejecting the judicious, seasoned perspective of the older men who looked to the future and to the greater good ("take care of the people, and they'll serve you forever"). It was downhill from there. Rehoboam lost his moral authority and soon had an insurrection on his hands.

position to lead them into responsible adulthood. If we don't take the initiative to prepare them, our teens are left vulnerable to the powerful voices in their social scene, for better or worse. Either through impulse or ignorance, they'll probably make some regrettable choices, possibly with long-lasting, even devastating, consequences. Many would testify that parental abdication of leadership in the teen years can swell into a source of deep resentment between adult children and their parents.

Under-parenting can be subtle. Matthew's parents, from a distance, appear to be good and honorable people. They take their children to church every week. But on another level, they're actually taking the easy way out. They want to respect Matthew's space, so they choose to "let him make his own decisions." But what's their real motivation? They have no idea where to start the conversations. They've under-parented by default. It was easier to treat Matthew like a child even though he had begun the journey to adulthood.

The book of Proverbs assumes that parents are to be regularly teaching their children the lessons that will equip them for adulthood. It speaks of the need to heed parental wisdom (e.g., Proverbs 2–4) and of the fool who refuses to do so (see Proverbs 10:1; 15:5, 32). In the long run, the fool pays for it. My wife and I still have young children. When they're disobedient and I discipline them, I try to explain that the pain of discipline, though real, is much less than the pain that comes with habitual violation of God's standards. The way of the wicked is hard (see Proverbs 13:15). The undisciplined, in the end, wish they had heeded instruction (see Proverbs 1:20-33). In contrast, "it is good . . . [to] bear the yoke in . . . youth" (Lamentations 3:27) because that's when character is formed and when correction, discipline, and instruction are most crucial. In the words of J. C. Ryle, as true for young women as they are for young men:

> Youth is the seed-time of full age, the molding season in the little space of human life, the turning-point in the history of man's mind.
>
> By the shoot we judge of the tree, by the blossoms we judge of the fruit, by the spring we judge of the harvest, by the morning we judge of the day, and by the character of the young man, we may generally judge what he will be when he grows up.[1]

Many teens who disregard loving authority may wind up paying the price their entire lives. You can go to prisons all across the country and ask inmates to recount their regrets. In many cases, the earliest regret you'll hear is this: "I wish I had listened to my mom." (And the fact that many prisoners don't even know their fathers ought to tell us something.)

As parents, we need to *be* parents. We need to teach, model, encourage, and train. We must intentionally shape our teens into the kind of adults we hope, with God's help, they become. The last thing our teens need is for us to try to be cool or hip, to wear the same clothing, or to engage in the same sorts of conversations in the same way as their peers. If we do, we're more likely to look foolish than to impress them. And deep down, parents trying to be peers are not even what teens really want.[2] Offer your teens what they cannot get elsewhere, and you'll lay the foundation for a deep, lifelong relationship.

This parental instruction doesn't always have to be something formal. It can be listening to an update on your teen's life while working in the yard and then relating the things you've learned from your parents, someone else, or the "school of hard knocks." It can be taking your teen out for ice cream after a basketball game and talking about how character (good and bad) was exhibited on the court that night. It's in drawing your teens out, taking the time to get into the nitty-gritty of their lives, listening and looking for those opportune moments when they're most teachable. (From working with students, I've learned that these moments can come without warning. But we need to take them when we get them.)

And there's something to be said for persistence. What you say may sometimes seem to fall on deaf ears. But you'll be surprised at what your teens remember.

OVER-PARENTING

Over-parenting controls teens instead of coaching them. It's too much positional authority and too little moral authority. It tells teens what to do but not why to do it. It conveys the message, "You need me to do things for you. I'm afraid you'll blow it if you do it yourself." The "helicopter parent" falls into this category.

What kind of teens are we trying to produce—the kind who will continue to depend on us like children? Or the kind who can one day relate to us as competent, functionally independent friends? If I check my daughter's math homework every night, whether she asks for it or not, I'm telling her that she's incapable of finishing anything on her own and that she doesn't need to check it herself. Instead, if I first *show* her how to check her homework, and then *expect* her to do it, she often will (not just now, but also in college). She'll be both empowered and motivated to take ownership for this area of her life.

It's a common misconception that high performance comes from high self-esteem. "If you believe, you'll achieve." It's true that extremely low self-esteem can lead to failure as a self-fulfilling prophecy. But it does not follow that high self-esteem guarantees high achievement. Plenty of people think they're good at math but aren't. And others think they're not good at math when in fact they are.

What I've found more commonly is that high performance comes from high expectations, and high performance, over time, gives rise to healthy, objectively justified self-esteem. Confidence and self-esteem grow in proportion to the expectations of others and actual accomplishments.[3]

But what about the consequences of failure? Shouldn't we want to protect our kids from the emotional or physical repercussions?

Yes and no. Playgrounds didn't always have foam padding below the equipment. They do now. Kids used to have sleepovers and ride their bikes alone in the neighborhood, often without a helmet (if you can believe it). Not anymore. Bombarded with headlines of child abductions and sexual predators, we have a deep-seated sense that the world has become a more dangerous place. As parents, we've become more safety conscious, and in some cases, for good reason.

High performance comes from high expectations, and high performance, over time, gives rise to healthy, objectively justified self-esteem.

But occasional failure is inevitable. Everyone who has ever achieved any level of greatness in life knows that failure is one of the best teachers. Knowing what doesn't work is crucial. Henry Ford, who failed twice in business before building the Ford Motor Company, said that failure is an opportunity to begin again more intelligently. Thomas Edison tried thousands of materials before he found one that would work as the filament in the lightbulb.

The only kind of self-esteem that failure shatters is the unhealthy, unsubstantiated sort. In Romans 12:3, Paul writes, "By the grace given to me I say to everyone among you not to think of himself more highly than he ought to think, but to think with sober judgment." In other words, we ought not to entertain exaggerated notions of our status or abilities. If failure shatters unjustified self-esteem, so much the better.

When I was a teen, my father used to ask me to bring in firewood from our garage to our living room fireplace. Sometimes, eager to resume my prior activities, I'd try to do it all in one trip. My dad would watch as all the wood fell out of my hands. Then he'd say, "*El vago trabaja doble*" (Spanish for "the lazy guy ends up working twice as hard"). His words would ring in my ears as I collected the scattered logs. At the time, I didn't give him the satisfaction of knowing I was listening. Your kids might not either. But I remember what he said now, more than 20 years later.

Learning from failure—and picking ourselves up after failure—often leads to future success and enhances healthy self-esteem. In raising teens, there's another angle: small mistakes made while they're *in* our homes are often far less consequential than the larger mistakes they can make when they *leave* our homes. And while they're still with us, we can help them process what happened and why.

NOT ALL PROTECTION IS OVER-PARENTING

But aren't there some kinds of failure that are so serious we should do everything in our power to prevent them from happening? Absolutely.

We should prevent our children from developing sinful habits.
It would be irresponsible to allow our children to practice habit-forming behavior that clearly violates God's commands. There are plenty of things that our teens don't need to do to know they're dumb (recreational drugs, drunkenness, being

romantically involved with non-Christians, pornography, and so on). I'm not claiming any of us can provide continuous, 24-7 vigilance on the actions of our teens, but we can and must forbid things that God says are wrong.

Of course our teens might do those things when they leave our household (or even now, behind our backs). That's why mere dos and don'ts aren't enough. We have to come alongside them and be as winsome as possible—helping them to see the benefits of a godly life and to want to grow in grace. But "you won't do that in my house" is by no means unfair, especially if we consider the impact of sinful behavior on siblings.

We should protect our teens from excessive temptation.
As Paul Tripp writes in his excellent book *Age of Opportunity*, the instruction to Timothy to "flee youthful passions" (2 Timothy 2:22) presupposes that certain desires are more acutely felt in our youth.[4] One temptation is certainly sexual immorality. For example, leaving teen boys with an Internet-accessing device in the privacy of their bedrooms is giving them access to unlimited pornography (unless you have software to stop it). It's at least worth a serious conversation or two (the average child is first exposed to Internet pornography at the age of 11, in most cases unintentionally), if not a more overt limitation on their freedom until they are older.[5]

Again, it's true that when our teens leave our homes, either to college or elsewhere, they'll have unfettered access. But we have until they leave to train them. Personally, I'd rather they not have additional opportunity for sexual sin at the time when they are first coming to know themselves as sexual beings. And there is plenty of research to show that early exposure to pornography can be particularly damaging and addictive.

We should prevent our teens from failures that would have long-lasting and far-reaching implications.
Teens sometimes act impulsively. (You might consider that an understatement.) Their ability to perform a risk-reward assessment is often highly skewed: they are motivated by thrills but underestimate risks. When I got my driver's license, a friend and I thought it'd be fun to race down side streets at night in "stealth mode" (no headlights). What were we thinking? We weren't. A kid I knew accepted a dare to jump out a window. He broke a leg, and not in a figurative sense.

As parents, we should consider the severity of the consequences when allowing our teens to make decisions with which we disagree. It's one thing to let your 14-year-old son spend most of his life savings on a skateboard that you *know* will be collecting dust in about three months. That can serve as a memorable object lesson on the perils of impulse purchases. It's quite another to let your daughter quit school at the age of 16.

An unwise purchase won't mess up your 14-year-old for life. It might even make him a *better* money manager when he leaves home. Quitting high school, in contrast, would have long-lasting, far-reaching, life-changing implications, almost certainly for the worse. If your teens still hate school when they graduate two years later, that's different. There are plenty of nonacademic careers they can pursue. What matters is that while they're under our authority, we prevent them from making impulsive decisions that can truly put them at a long-term or even permanent disadvantage.

TWO CASE STUDIES: AMANDA AND CHRISTOPHER

Amanda and Christopher had very different experiences at home and therefore at college. Their stories exemplify the differences between over-parenting and good, solid preparation.

Amanda's parents really wanted her to be academically successful. So from the time she first started school, they had done her homework with (and occasionally *for*) her. They had planned her extracurricular activities around her schoolwork to make sure she got everything done. They set up strict schedules for her. And their efforts paid off! Amanda graduated high school with a 3.8 GPA and was accepted to a moderately selective college on a full scholarship. She began college eagerly, but by her second semester, she was barely scraping by with Bs and Cs. Soon afterwards she lost her academic scholarship. Amanda learned that she had no idea how to manage her schedule or her workload, especially under the rigors of college.

Christopher's parents took a different approach. He brought home all Cs his first semester of high school. His parents were disappointed but not defeated. They decided to use this occasion to draw closer to their son and teach him responsibility. They asked Christopher if those grades reflected his true abilities. Christopher said they didn't, but he wasn't sure how to improve. So they talked about it. Christopher walked his parents through a typical school day and how he went about his assignments after school. It became apparent that Christopher needed help taking notes in class, so his mom taught him some strategies. When Christopher would get home from soccer practice, his dad would have him quickly write a list of which assignments had to be completed that evening and which needed doing later that week. They would review this list over dinner, and Christopher would knock out the assignments one by one in order of importance.

If Christopher did poorly on a test, his parents would help him assess what went wrong and determine how he could do better. They also talked to him about what kinds of things he could see himself doing after high school. Christopher was interested in architecture, so his parents found ways to connect him with friends from church who worked with or for architects. Christopher's motivation grew. By the time he graduated, his GPA had risen to a respectable 3.4. His first year in college, he earned a 3.5 GPA, maintaining the discipline his parents had encouraged.

What was the difference between Amanda and Christopher? Amanda's parents had ensured her high school success through a high degree of external structure and control. Christopher's parents had given him the freedom to fail and to learn from it. But they didn't stop there. They motivated him at the heart level and empowered him to take steps that, over time, facilitated earned success.

The irony is that over-parenting, in seeking to protect teens from failure, often makes future failure more likely. Scary as it may seem, the day is coming when our teens will be on their own. Resilience is formed in the crucible of experience, even—and perhaps especially—failure.

CULTIVATING RESPONSIBILITY

Mindful of the dangers of under-parenting and over-parenting, how should we cultivate responsibility in our teens? In the words of Stephen Covey, we ought to begin with the end in mind.[6] Our long-term goal is to work ourselves out of a job. We want our teens to take their places in society as responsible adults, never independent from God or isolated from others, but no longer needing us to provide structure and management for their day-to-day lives.

As we think about preparing our teens for college (or whatever comes next), are there specific character traits we ought to be aiming for? Our children need to learn how to exercise discernment, make choices for themselves, and accept responsibility for the outcome of those choices. Matthew, for example, needs to learn what led him down the path to his dad getting a call from the police: identification with his friends and a fear of disappointing them or being ridiculed for his scruples. Frank should draw his son out so that Matthew can see his actions and motivations objectively, against the backdrop of biblical standards. If Matthew rejects those values, that needs to be discussed honestly (and we'll talk about internalizing faith in conversation 3).

When we think about raising teens who accept responsibility, what related character traits should we seek to instill?

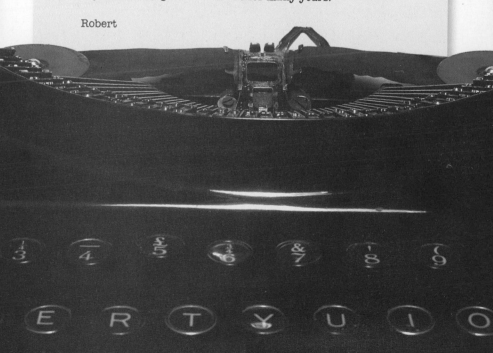

Each of our boys at some point during high school was a weekly Sunday school teacher. At first they were under the supervision of an adult, and later they each became the lead teacher for their group. They had to show up on time, know the lesson, teach it, and show genuine interest in their group. To me it was important that neither Kim nor I was in the classroom so they could observe and serve under other Christian adults. This was part of a larger strategy: we wanted them to make connections with other Christian adults who could serve as examples and mentors. Each of our boys loved doing this and did so for many years.

Robert

Two big ones, in my view, are taking initiative and accepting correction.

Taking Initiative

I first heard the buzz word *self-starter* when I was an undergraduate looking for summer jobs. The staff person in the career office of my college told me to put it on my résumé. Apparently, prospective employers were looking for people who didn't need to be told that they should start doing something. They wanted interns who had an internal motivation and drive to contribute to the team's efforts. (I suppose it would have been more "self-starting" if I had thought to put that descriptor on my résumé myself.)

We want our teens to have a sense of purpose that animates them to useful activity. We want them to get off their duffs and make things happen rather than sit back and watch them happen. True servants (and servant-leaders) don't sit around waiting for a command; they anticipate needs and respond to meet them.

The teen years are often a time of identity crisis because boys and girls are becoming men and women. The "Who am I?" question is wide open. They're coming to a greater awareness of their abilities, intellectually and otherwise, but they're doing so in a cultural milieu that regards pleasure, popularity, and power (be it social, athletic, or academic) as ideals to be pursued—and responsibility and work as punishments to be minimized or avoided. This faulty perspective must be confronted and replaced. Teens need to learn that work is a gift of God and that with greater *ability* comes greater *responsibility*. In a world where God is supreme over everything, freedom and opportunity are never divorced from accountability to others and (ultimately) to God. On the contrary, "to whom much [is] given, of him much will be required" (Luke 12:48).

Start with the natural goodness of work. God himself is a worker, and being made in his image, it's not surprising that we find dignity and satisfaction in the use of our faculties and skills in productive labor. The Fall did not create work; it distorted our relationship with work. It made it often painful and sometimes tedious and frustrating. Nevertheless, for Christians, work is a sphere in which we're to bring glory to God and good to others. As Dorothy Sayers wrote in her classic essay "Why Work?":

[Work] should be looked upon, not as a necessary drudgery to be undergone for the purpose of making money, but as a way of life in which the nature of man should find its proper exercise and delight and so fulfill itself to the glory of God. . . . It is, or should be, the full expression of the worker's faculties, the thing in which he finds spiritual, mental and bodily satisfaction, and the medium in which he offers himself to God.[7]

Our teens need to know that transitioning to adulthood is a good thing, a normal thing, a necessary thing. God intends their burgeoning intellectual, athletic, and musical skills to be developed through regular effort, so that they might be equipped for a lifetime of good works for which he's preparing them (see Ephesians 2:10).

Okay, but how? Here's where modeling comes in. Teens are *listening* to the way we talk about our workloads, our bosses, and our responsibilities—and they're *watching* the way we respond to them. If we have the attitude that "a bad day fishing is better than a good day at work," they'll take away the lesson that work is drudgery to be avoided. We should be honest. Yes, work is hard and sometimes unpleasant. But it's also an avenue by which we can serve others and experience the joy of using our skills. Work is a big part of our lives, so it's important to pursue work that we both enjoy and have the potential to do well.

> *Teens are listening to the way we talk about our workloads, our bosses, and our responsibilities—and they're watching the way we respond to them.*

With regard to the principle that "from those to whom much is given, much is expected," the Parable of the Talents (see Matthew 25:14-30) is instructive. We're told of three servants, each of whom is entrusted with a different amount of money. Apparently, their master regards them as having different levels of ability (see verse 15). No detailed instructions are given; the master expects each to take personal initiative to invest the funds wisely.

Q: *How can we prepare teens for college responsibilities? Is there an area where they typically fall short?*

A: College involves far more homework and many more recreational options than high school, especially if a student lives on campus. Freedom is a powerful feeling for first-semester freshmen. But if they don't use their time wisely, it quickly leads to another powerful feeling: stress!

Parents can prepare teens by developing their time-management skills. Encourage them to use a calendar or planner to track assignments. They should begin by recording when papers and projects are due or when tests will be given. Next, they should schedule adequate time to complete each task before the deadline. Third, they need to regularly look at their schedule to make sure they're following it. Just as a budget helps our spending reflect our financial priorities, a schedule helps us to be good stewards of our time. But the only way to learn this skill is by doing it.

The 2006 High School Survey of Student Engagement of over 81,000 students found that 90 percent of respondents studied five hours or fewer *per week*. If your teens are planning to be full-time students at a reputable college, they'll only be in class three to four hours per weekday, but to be successful, they'll need to put in about 30 hours per week of out-of-class work. That's five hours *per day* (taking Sunday off). Adjust their expectations.

The first two servants get to work immediately—they take personal initiative. And it pays off, literally—each reaps a 100-percent return on investment and receives identical praise from the master: "You have been faithful over *a little*" (Matthew 25:21, 23, emphasis mine). The similarity of this praise is interesting, considering that one servant had earned more than twice what the other had (not to mention that biblical scholars regard even one talent as representing a considerable amount of money). What mattered to the master, however, was not how much they had, but what they *did* with what they had.

And then there's the last servant. He buried his talent in the ground, earning nothing with it. It doesn't seem *that* bad; it's not like he spent it or lost it. But the master calls him "wicked" and "slothful" (Matthew 25:26). He's wicked because he received something of value and didn't put it to good use. But he's also slothful because with minimal effort he could have at least earned some gain.

Our teens need to "remember . . . [their] Creator in the days of [their] youth" (Ecclesiastes 12:1)—when they first come to recognize themselves as talented in particular ways, in ways that differ from others in kind and degree. God made them that way, and he did that so they might develop those talents and use them to serve others and glorify him. As the apostle Paul says, "None of us lives to himself, and none of us dies to himself. For if we live, we live to the Lord, and if we die, we die to the Lord. So then, whether we live or whether we die, we are the Lord's" (Romans 14:7-8).

Youth is the time to learn this—as our teens' bodies and minds are coming into maturity. We were not made to live for ourselves. We're to love God and love others, by serving them with the gifts he has entrusted to us. This gives birth to initiative, to a sense of personal responsibility, to a fire in the belly to do great things—not for worldly reasons but for God's glory and the good of others.

So how do we help our teens catch this vision? By encouraging them to process the events and opportunities in their lives as chances to give rather than get. Student government is a chance for teens to serve their classmates; being captain of the volleyball team is a chance for them to motivate their teammates to excel. And watch out for a common youth idol: popularity. Teens naturally angle for praise, but taking initiative must have a higher aim. Encourage them to pursue faithfulness, service, and doing the right thing even when nobody is looking.

Of course, don't expect them to always seek out your wisdom. And if they won't talk at the dinner table, don't give up. Tell them how you've learned that "it is more blessed to give than to receive" (Acts 20:35). They'll be listening better than you think.

Accepting Correction

I'm often asked in interviews if there are any differences between what college students are like today and what they were like when I was a student. At first I thought my critical answer proved only that I was getting older. When has it *not* been true that the older people get, the more disappointed they become with "kids these days"? It seems that pastors and leaders of every age have offered many protestations about the laziness, rudeness, arrogance, and carelessness of teens.

But perhaps we're on to something if the young people themselves affirm the shift. And they do. In a June 2009 national poll of over 1,000 college students, two out of three agreed with the statement "My generation of young people is more self-promoting, narcissistic, overconfident, and attention-seeking than previous generations."[8] Related traits such as assertiveness, dominance, brashness, arrogance, and lack of empathy are likewise on the rise.

Narcissism is self-esteem on steroids and divorced from actual accomplishment or even ability. Many of our young people feel great about themselves even while they fall behind the rest of the world in academic metrics. I once surveyed incoming freshmen at a nonselective college. The majority *expected* to go on to graduate school and become leaders in their fields. The chest-thumping of our day is in stark contrast with the humility, restraint, valor, and obvious accomplishment of previous generations.

We all want our teens to have a healthy self-confidence, to not cower in fear at the social complexities of teen life or the many pressures of high school. We want them to have a strong sense of personal initiative, since it's so closely tied to taking responsibility for their lives. But if we don't simultaneously cultivate humility and a willingness to accept correction, they'll be unprepared for the real world, a world in which everyone must be deferential to someone (see 1 Peter 2:13-17).

Of course, teens can get defensive when confronted. They often interpret concerns as personal attacks, which leads to blame shifting or making excuses to deflect the issue. So we need to be gracious and winsome—ready to model humility by apologizing for our shortcomings. And by asking questions and listening, we can hopefully neutralize the impact of their (often) short attention spans, keeping them engaged in the conversation.

We want them to feel our love for them—and that our correction is an overflow of that love. For every time we catch them doing something wrong, we should catch them 10 times doing something right. If every "talk" we have with them is a rebuke, they'll learn to run the other way when they see us coming.

I often do a midsemester survey with my students. I bring a stack of paper and a cardboard box with a slot in the top, encouraging them to submit anonymous feedback. One time I had a student who went ballistic, slamming me for a hundred things. At the end of the next class period I made a public offer to buy a Coke for anyone who was willing to offer me significant criticism face-to-face. Everyone cleared the room except the offended student. We had a great conversation in which I acknowledged his concerns and pledged to work harder to earn his trust. He felt he was heard. A few weeks later he told me he was enjoying the course. That conversation, I think, was the start of a stronger relationship.

Modeling humility for our teens will go a long way toward developing it in them. We also need them to persevere in their commitments, even if something better comes along. This requires delaying gratification—a quality in short supply among many teens. And delaying gratification requires a future-orientation, the subject of conversation 2.

SUMMARY

- Teaching responsibility to our teens is a marathon, not a sprint. Cultivate a long-term perspective.
- Positional authority is effective when our children are young, but we must work to earn moral authority as they grow older. As our *control* decreases, we must aim for increasing *influence*.
- We should strive to protect our teens from catastrophic mistakes with long-term consequences while still allowing them some freedom to mess up in smaller ways in the short term.
- It's good to help our teens assess their mistakes and learn from them. It's bad to shield them from all negative consequences. The prodigal son "came to his senses" when he was broke and hungry (Luke 15:16-18, NLT).
- To become responsible, our teens must learn to take initiative for their lives and to accept (and, even better, *solicit*) correction and instruction.

CONVERSATION STARTERS

1. Describe under-parenting and over-parenting to your teens. Then be vulnerable: ask your teens how they think you're doing at avoiding these extremes. Discuss expectations going forward.

2. Identify an area of strength in your teens' lives— perhaps an area of responsibility that they are managing well, or maturity in relating to siblings, or diligence with homework, or cheerfulness in completing household chores. Let your teens know you appreciate them.

3. Identify a growth opportunity in your teens' lives— an area in which they need to take more initiative, ownership, and responsibility. Describe it, and then listen. Offset defensiveness, aim for winsomeness, and try to make wisdom sweet.

4. Confess any ways you may have sinned against your teens. Remind them that you have their best interests in mind, even though you sometimes fall short.

CONVERSATION 2
Training Teens to Be Future-Oriented

IN THE LAST CHAPTER, we talked about the importance of training teens to assume responsibility for their lives, taking initiative in appropriate ways, while also accepting occasional correction. And we talked about how we as parents can promote personal responsibility in our teens with a balanced parental approach, one that avoids the dangers of both under-parenting and over-parenting.

In this chapter, we'll talk about the importance of training teens to be future-oriented. Teens often live in the moment, but this can get them in trouble if they make foolish decisions with long-term consequences. The common temptations teens face—either to overt sin (sexual promiscuity, cheating on a test) or to mere folly (spending too much on a shopping binge, playing video games instead of studying)—offer immediate gratification. As parents, we've probably developed strategies to overcome such temptations in our own lives (such as shutting off e-mail alerts while finishing an important report). At the heart of such victory is a *future-orientation*: a recognition that actions have consequences and a willingness to consider our options accordingly. "The prudent carefully consider their steps" (Proverbs 14:15, NLT).

Future-orientation is a major part of personal maturity. It results in a willingness to, when necessary, delay gratification and to persevere when the going gets tough. But training our teens to be future-oriented will require that we first give them an overarching vision for teen life. Because we have fierce competition from the wider culture.

The prevailing view—even among some Christians—is that teenagers are impetuous, irresponsible, incompetent, and rebellious. It's just who they are. This stereotype is relentlessly propagated by media outlets—television, popular movies, even news programming and magazines. We're told that teens aren't yet capable of being future-oriented. That won't be possible until they pop out the other side of adolescence as adults, whenever *that* happens—and don't hold your breath.

We must first debunk this myth, because our teens will rise only as high as our expectations for them. It's up to us to give them a big vision for teen life as a season in which self-control, good manners, spiritual growth, personal accountability, and academic diligence are the norm. Yes, it is possible! Internalizing this kind of vision leads to future-oriented teens—teens who are preparing for all that goes with responsible Christian adulthood. And future-oriented teens thrive as adults, in college and beyond.

THE POWER OF VISION

Don't underestimate the power of a positive vision. When I was 19 to 20 years old, I took a semester off school and worked for eight months at a national laboratory in Oak Ridge, Tennessee. A group of coworkers would run every day at lunch, and I joined them. I bought a road bike and took some long-distance rides. Although I had never been much of an athlete, a coworker convinced me to train for a triathlon. He helped me make a training schedule. Soon I was timing myself running different courses and logging those times into a journal. I started watching my diet in a way I never had before. I would go to bed early, because I knew I needed energy to exercise the next day.

While I usually ran with the others, I would swim and bike mostly on my own, building up my endurance for the big day. I can still remember double workouts, usually on Saturday mornings: I'd swim a mile and then bike for 20 miles. Or I'd ride my bike for 20 miles and then run 6 miles, just to see how my body held up. I didn't always feel like doing it. But the vision of successfully completing the triathlon and meeting my time goals propelled me to keep training.

A positive vision animates our lives and focuses our efforts like nothing else can. In Nehemiah 4:6 we read, "So we built the wall. And all the wall was joined together to half its height, *for the people had a mind to work"* (emphasis added). The book of Nehemiah describes the various obstacles Nehemiah and his team encountered, but they pressed forward with a vision to complete the wall.

Likewise, a student determined to get into medical school is willing to study long hours, losing all track of time. Legendary Dallas Cowboys football coach Tom Landry used to say, "Coaching is making men do what they don't want, so they can become what they want." Teens need to be willing to do things that don't give an immediate payoff so that they can eventually become what they deeply want to be. It helps if they understand that no successful person always does what he or she wants to do in the moment. There's a deeper reservoir of "wanting" that overpowers any surface-level "not wanting."

> No successful person always does what he or she wants to do in the moment.

A vision can produce focus and even delight in the midst of intense work. It's a joy that overwhelms the pain of struggle and propels us to go farther. It's when you're so absorbed in what you're doing that you forget yourself. Runners speak of "runner's high"—that delightful sensation they achieve *after* they've already been running for some time. Musicians feel this ecstasy when they're playing or singing their hearts out. A pastor experiences this in the pulpit or perhaps in his study. Think about it: When do you feel most alive? Probably when you're doing something you feel you were made to do, something that's consistent with your life's vision.

Those who lack vision, by contrast, seek only comfort and pleasure, and they want it *now*. But deep down what they really want is escape. They want to dull the pain of their (apparently) meaningless existence. And they seek company, because nobody wants to be meaningless *and* lonely. Sadly, this characterizes a lot of the partying found on college campuses. That's why we have to give our teens something better.

A VISION FOR TEEN LIFE

What kind of vision for teen life is depicted by Hollywood and other media outlets? The popular view seems to be that teens are inherently irresponsible, self-centered, rebellious, incompetent, and sexually promiscuous. And of course, many teens fit this description. They regularly argue with and disobey their parents. They experiment with drugs and alcohol. They sleep around. They get in trouble with the law. The peak age for arrest in the United States for many crimes is roughly 18. The high school dropout rate in some cities is as high as 50 percent among minorities.[1] Depression, eating disorders, and attempted suicide are, sadly, not uncommon among teens. And we're all aware of the tragic stories of gang violence and deadly shootings.

But is such behavior in the teen years unavoidable? At least once a year, it seems, the major news magazines run a cover story saying it is, and their usual reason goes like this: the teen brain is undeveloped and is going through a variety of major changes in those critical years. As a result, teens experience massive mood swings, irrationality, and occasional depression. This leads to irresponsibility, reckless-ness, and all-around incompetence.

The problem with this theory, as Dr. Robert Epstein, con-tributing editor for *Scientific American Mind* and a former editor in chief of *Psychology Today*, has persuasively argued, is that "if the turmoil-generating 'teen brain' were a universal developmental phenomenon, we would presumably find tur-moil of this kind around the world."[2] And we don't:

> In 1991 anthropologist Alice Schlegel of the University of Arizona and psychologist Herbert Barry III of the University of Pittsburgh reviewed research on teens in 186 preindustrial societies. Among the important conclusions they drew about these societies: about 60 percent had no word for "adolescence," teens spent almost all their time with adults, teens showed almost no signs of psychopathology, and antisocial behavior in young males was completely absent in more than half these cultures and extremely mild in cultures in which it did occur.[3]

Add this to the fact that throughout most of recorded human history the teen years have been "a relatively peace-ful time of transition to adulthood. Teens were not trying to break away from adults; rather they were learning to *become* adults."[4]

We see this in the life of biblical characters like David. When he was told he was too young to take on Goliath, he responded by recounting his activities as an anonymous shepherd (duties given to him, notice, by his parents):

> David said to Saul, "Your servant used to keep sheep for his father. And when there came a lion, or a bear, and took a lamb from the flock, I went after him and struck him and delivered it out of his mouth. And if he arose against me, I caught him by his beard and struck him and killed him. Your servant has struck down both lions and bears, and this uncircumcised Philistine shall be like one of them, for he has defied the armies of the living God." (1 Samuel 17:34-36)

In recounting this story with our children, we rightly contrast David's faith in a big God with the Israelites' fear of a big man. That is the heart of the story. But it's also a testimony to *preparation*: David spent his youth preparing for adulthood. And when the opportunity for adult-sized responsibility presented itself, he was ready to seize it. Similarly, Daniel was a young man receiving elite training in Babylon, but at the risk of ridicule or worse, he resolved to follow Yahweh's dietary laws. At the end of the training, he and his God-fearing friends were found to excel over all the others (see Daniel 1:19-20). As a young man, Joseph fled from sexual temptation in Potiphar's house. When unjustly thrown in jail, he remained faithful to God, exhibiting competence, impressing the warden, and being put in charge of the other prisoners (see Genesis 39). And Mary was probably

As a youth pastor, I see teenagers becoming increasingly busy and overcommitted. They're trying to become well-rounded, but they end up exhausted and burnt out. In high school, I said yes to things until my parents said no for me. But in college I was on my own. And I found I had never learned to say no.

I was a pre-med major who had just made it onto the varsity golf team. I picked up a minor in political science for fun, accepted a role on the orientation committee for the following year, and was in the midst of trying to join a fraternity. My social life was hitting all-time highs, and the amount of pizza and video games I consumed was astronomical. But I was always tired, my GPA fell to 2.6 (not exactly med school quality), and rather than enjoying things, I just felt frazzled all the time.

That year I learned an important lesson about being diligent about setting priorities. If I try to do everything, I end up unable to enjoy anything. I'm still learning self-control, but I'm glad for the lesson I learned my freshman year. I only wish I had learned it in high school.

Bob

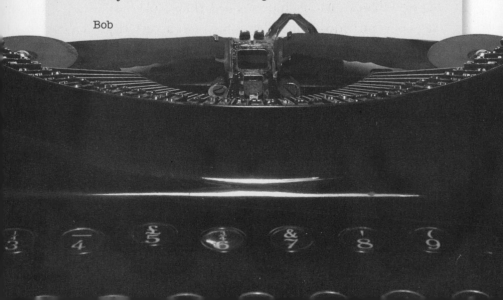

a teenager when she gave birth to Jesus at the end of a long, uncomfortable journey to Bethlehem with her husband, Joseph (see Luke 2:1-7).

I'm not suggesting that teenagers behaved perfectly in preindustrial societies. Sin is as old as the human race, and parents and pastors complaining about "kids these days" is nothing new. But the reluctance to enter adulthood, the avoidance of responsibility, the "failure to launch" all seem more pronounced in our day than in previous eras. Never before have *ability* and *opportunity* been so decoupled from *responsibility* and *obligation*. More than half of parents today have continued to provide financial support for their adult children, even after college graduation, on expenses such as housing, groceries, and transportation costs.[5] Marriage is increasingly delayed—the average age in 2012 was 28.6 for men and 26.6 for women[6]—as more couples prefer to cohabit, enjoying a sexual relationship while avoiding the responsibility that comes with a permanent commitment. More than half of all births to American women under 30 now occur out of wedlock.[7] Meanwhile, in 2011 alone, $24.75 billion was spent on video games, hardware, and accessories. The average age of the most frequent game purchaser is 35. And perhaps contrary to the stereotype, 47 percent of game players are women. In fact, women over the age of 18 represent 30 percent of the game-playing population, while boys age 17 or younger represent only 18 percent.[8]

What happened? About a century ago, separating teens from adults for the purpose of schooling became increasingly common. Nothing wrong with that, per se. But this separation led, over time, to teens socializing almost exclusively with other teens, rather than with the adults whom they were supposedly training to become. This, combined with Hollywood's messages, which relentlessly promote a teen vision of perpetual frivolity and crass vulgarity, has left young people trapped in a culture of low expectations.

Put simply, teens rise only as high as the expectations of those who most influence them. The problem is not that teen brains cause turmoil, but that our cultural milieu has messed up our teens' brains, and corrupt behavior is the natural output. Teens in the United States find it more difficult to transition into adulthood because 1) they don't really know what adulthood is supposed to look like, and 2) the message they're getting is "Responsibility and commitment are a pain—stay young and carefree as long as you can." The good news is that whenever a culture has *high* expectations for teens and regularly exposes them to adults who actively mentor them into responsible adulthood, those teens generally rise to the challenge. They actually *want* to grow up. Even in their teen years, they take the bull by the horns.[9]

But our problem today is twofold. On the one hand, our young people are in a rush to grow up—to have more freedom, to spend more time with their same-age friends, to solidify their identities. But on the other hand, they're picking up the cultural message that they're "just teenagers" and therefore not yet capable of taking on "real" responsibilities. To make matters worse, teen employment has taken a massive hit in our struggling economy. In 2013, just under a third (32 percent) of 16- to 19-year-olds held summer jobs (down from just over 52 percent in 1999).[10] And many schools have dumbed down academics so that teens can feel better about themselves and get good grades with less effort.

It's imperative that our teens embrace adulthood as a positive, even thrilling, thing. It's what they were made to do. They are capable of it, and we must hold them accountable to it. Yes, they should enjoy their lives. Some leisure, recreation, and downtime are important at every stage of life. But teens should not *just* have fun; they should be busy preparing for adulthood. This overarching purpose of preparing our teens for responsible adulthood should animate all our parenting as we shepherd them in their academic, extracurricular, athletic, and social pursuits.

COMMUNICATING THIS VISION TO YOUR TEEN

Pastor Crawford W. Loritts tells a story of when he was 12 years old and his dad asked him to help with a painting job. Loritts tried to escape by asking his mom to let him go out and play instead. His father intervened with these words:

> That boy one day is going to have to be somebody's father, somebody's husband, and that boy is going to learn today that he has to do the things he doesn't feel like doing, but has to do. Son, you take your hindparts upstairs and paint till I tell you to stop.

That might seem a little harsh for a 12-year-old, but several decades later, Loritts recalls this as a defining moment in his life. "He was pulling me out of impulse behavior. He was calling me up to a vision, he knew it was time for me to make a transition."[11]

This occasion proved memorable for Loritts because his dad spoke about his intention: he was training his son to be "somebody's father, somebody's husband." What about us? Are we doing the same for our sons? And are we training our daughters to be "somebody's mother, somebody's wife"?

Maybe you're reading all this and thinking, *Yeah, this vision thing sounds great. But how do I get my kids to believe any of it? I'm lucky to get a grunt when I ask them about their day.* It's true that telling your teens over the dinner table that you have a new, all-encompassing vision for their lives might get you a blank stare. So consider a little mood setting. Some cultures have coming-of-age ceremonies, like bar mitzvahs. You don't need to throw a big party, but communicating to your teen a vision of embracing adulthood is worth at least a piece of pie. Piggyback on something you already like to do together, just the two of you. Maybe it's shopping, coffee, ice cream, or catching a baseball game. You could turn it into an overnight trip—a special venue to facilitate a special conversation. What kind of conversation do I have in mind? Something like this:

Going forward, I view you as a young man/woman. Our interactions will have a different tone than in the past, when you were a child. Being a kid is great, but it's time for you to start taking on the mantle of adulthood. Adulthood is a wonderful thing, a glorious thing, and I'm here to help equip you for it, and to help you embrace it.

Maybe you're reading this book when your teens are juniors or seniors in high school. While the "now you're an adult talk" can happen when they're 12 or 13 (right around puberty), it's truly never too late to have this conversation.

Paul wrote in 1 Corinthians 13:11, "When I was a child, I spoke like a child, I thought like a child, I reasoned like a child. When I became a man, I gave up childish ways." Our teens must also give up childish ways. We motivate them to do so when we winsomely convey this countercultural, God-glorifying, future-oriented vision for responsible teen life.

This conversation should get into the nitty-gritty: What kind of adults do you hope your teens will be? What kind of adults do they want to become? Convey to your teens that, as we discussed in the last chapter, with adulthood comes greater liberty, but with greater liberty comes greater responsibility and accountability. Do your teens need to start carrying the burden for getting their own homework done without your prompting? Is it appropriate for your teens to pay for some of their clothing? Or prepare dinner once in a while? Or do their own laundry? By the same token, should your teens have more input in determining their curfew? Or whether they should invest more time in piano or in finding a job related to a possible college major?

Delaying Gratification and Persevering in Commitments

Think of gratification-delay as the short-term response of a future-oriented teen. For example, she turns off her cell phone so that she can finish her homework before catching up with her friends. And think of persevering in commitments as the long-term posture of a future-oriented teen. He makes the soccer team, only to find himself riding the bench. But he sticks with it, showing up to practice every day, working hard, being cheerful, encouraging his teammates, and not complaining.

Now that you've talked about the vision of adulthood and how that changes your expectations of each other, let's flesh out two practical expressions of this future-oriented vision: the maturity to delay gratification and the resolve to persevere in commitments.

ADULTS DELAY GRATIFICATION

In the story above, what Crawford Loritts's father was teaching him was that adults delay gratification. Sure, on any given day we might prefer to play rather than work. But responsible men and women pay their dues first. We resist misdirected impulses. And if we don't, we reap what we sow—which is why it's so important that we don't shield our teens from experiencing natural consequences.

And what might those consequences be? Real-world consequences include failure to advance in a profession, or in an extreme case, failure to hold a job. It could be a loss of relationships, as others find us to be undependable. We might gain excessive weight or become prone to illness because we fail to control our desire to eat and refuse to exercise. Or maybe we become mired in consumer debt, the fruit of easy credit and impulsive spending.

I passed by the field of a sluggard, by the vineyard of a man lacking sense, and behold, it was all overgrown with thorns; the ground was covered with nettles, and its stone wall was broken down.

—PROVERBS 24:30-31

The biblical pattern our teens must learn is this: dominate your responsibilities, or they will dominate you. Work is easier to manage if we don't let it get away from us. But that requires delaying gratification until the necessary work has been completed. It means owning our playtime rather than letting it own us.

In the 1960s, Dr. Walter Mischel initiated a study at Stanford University that would become known as the marshmallow test. Four-year-olds were given the choice of eating one marshmallow now, or of receiving a second marshmallow if they waited for the tester to return. The kids squirmed, one pulled on her pigtails in agony, another stroked the marshmallow like a pet. One kid broke into the desk drawer looking for more sweets! Some immediately ate the marshmallow. Only a third of those who tried to wait it out actually survived the entire 15 minutes before the tester returned.

But the study didn't end there. Researchers followed the four-year-olds into their teen years to see if there were any emotional, social, or academic differences between those who grabbed for the one marshmallow and those who had the restraint to wait for the greater reward. It turned out the differences were dramatic. Those who had resisted temptation at age four went on to become more socially competent, personally effective, and appropriately assertive and better able to cope with life's frustrations. They were less likely to freeze or panic in stressful situations or give up in the face of difficulties. They were more trustworthy and dependable. They were more likely to accept additional responsibilities and take the lead on new endeavors. Academically, they were far superior: more articulate speakers, better writers, and stronger critical thinkers. They displayed greater levels of concentration, discipline in homework, and eagerness to learn. They had a whopping 210-point advantage on the traditional math and verbal form of the SAT.[12]

The marshmallow test demonstrates the importance of impulse control. Without it, few achieve excellence, and no one reaches their potential. The book of Proverbs reminds us that "a person without self-control is like a city with broken-down walls" (Proverbs 25:28, NLT).

Let's look at two aspects of impulse control that will be vital to our teens: resisting sinful pleasures and regulating legitimate pleasures.

Resisting Sinful Pleasures

Being future-oriented—and delaying gratification—is as crucial for our teens' spiritual life as it is anywhere else. The Bible routinely calls us to say no to sinful activities, even though they offer short-term happiness. Ecclesiastes 11:9 commends the pursuit of happiness but reminds us of our accountability to God:

> Young people, it's wonderful to be young! Enjoy every minute of it. Do everything you want to do; take it all in. But remember that you must give an account to God for everything you do. (NLT)

The fact that we must give an account is meant to act as a set of guardrails, protecting us from activities that dishonor God and that, whether we realize it or not, would ultimately harm us.

Here's the problem: many teens believe that having fun and obeying God are mutually exclusive. This distortion has led to the view that people should "live it up" while they're young because they can get serious about religion when they're old. Sadly, this way of thinking is pervasive. So it's up to us to teach our teens that God invented pleasure. He wants us to be deeply happy. But he also knows that the pathway to this deep happiness requires self-denial. This is true because as sinners, our appetites aren't always aligned with what's best for us.

This principle is at the heart of the Christian life. As we learn to trust God, we're able to say no to the passing pleasures of sin because we know (by faith in God's promises) that the path of obedience to God yields the greatest blessings, both in this life and in eternity.[13] And while that path sometimes requires delaying gratification, God always provides the strength we need (see 1 Corinthians 10:13).

Encourage your teens to remember that the self-denial to which we're called is never an end in itself. It's always a means for us to experience a *greater* measure of happiness. We want our teens to cultivate self-control so that they can channel their energies in ways that ultimately maximize enjoyment, putting off short-term, sinful, and deceitful pleasures so that they can experience long-lasting, pure, authentic delights.

Sinful pleasures wreak havoc in our relationship with God, leaving us empty. They lead to heartache and frustration. They ruin relationships, hurting others and leaving us corrupted. At the end of the day, they're *deceitful* pleasures— they don't keep their promises—and they lead to our missing out on God's best. Being controlled by our urges may come easily, but it doesn't lead to happiness or freedom. It leads to misery and slavery.

When we're warning our teens about temptations to

sin—and we should—we need to be careful about prohibitions without explanations. Those can be fine with children, who ought to obey because God gave us authority for their good, whether or not they understand the ins and outs. But remember, teens are young adults. If we want them to act like adults, we need to treat them that way. And that means appealing to their consciences and intellects because 1) their reasoning skills exceed that of children, 2) they'll be out on their own in a few years, and 3) they can probably go behind our backs even now. Total control is an illusion at best.

When we give prohibitions, we need to acknowledge that the behavior we're prohibiting *would*, in many cases, bring immediate pleasure. It helps to genuinely acknowledge the reality and power of temptations—but then point our teens to a better way. Yes, remind them that just because something feels good doesn't make it right. And yes, remind them that the pleasure offered is deceptive—sin leads, in the end, to frustration and pain, because it's living out of sync with how God made us. But those are both negative motivations.

Ultimately, our teens need positive motivations as well. "Those who hunger and thirst for righteousness . . . *shall be satisfied*" (Matthew 5:6, emphasis added). "The pure in heart . . . *shall see God*" (Matthew 5:8, emphasis added). This pattern holds throughout the Beatitudes and elsewhere in Scripture (such as Ephesians 6:2-3: "Honor your father and mother . . . that it *may go well with you* and that you *may live long in the land*," emphasis added). There is nothing wrong and everything right with appealing to your teens' self-interest

Q: *I want my child to grow up into the high expectations I have of her, but how do I avoid being a "tiger mom"?*

A: In *Battle Hymn of the Tiger Mother* (New York: Penguin, 2011), Amy Chua articulates several good points. Many parents prioritize giving their children what they *want* over giving them what they *need*. High expectations tend to drive high performance. Doing something well makes it fun, but to get there requires perseverance.

Still, the tiger mom goes too far. It is idolatrous to raise our children to believe that accomplishments are the chief aim in life. Faithfulness to Christ is a greater and broader goal than a perfect GPA, performing in Carnegie Hall, or getting into an Ivy League college. Bible reading, prayer, service, missions work—these things don't seem to register in the narrow value system of the "tiger mother."

So how do we set high expectations but avoid being tiger parents? By exhorting our teens to develop their talents from within the context of Christian discipleship. We hone our skills and pursue excellence not to impress others but out of love for God and to more effectively serve others. We resist the idolatrous tendency to define ourselves by our accomplishments. We labor to put God's greatness on display, not to make a name for ourselves. And we do so from the firm foundation of having *already* received God's favor because of the finished work of Jesus Christ on the cross.

in warning them of the dangers of sin and encouraging them of the many benefits that come with living in a God-pleasing manner. Failing to do so is a good way to come across as a fuddy-duddy and a killjoy.

Bottom line: don't expect your teens to fight temptations with mere prohibitions. It's not enough to just say no to a sinful pleasure. We also must say yes, with God's help, to a greater, God-honoring pleasure—and one that is longer lasting because it *is* in sync with how God made us. If our teens are to "remember [their] Creator in the days of [their] youth" (Ecclesiastes 12:1), they must know that nothing can be more satisfying than a God-mastered life, from childhood to death and every day in between.

Regulating Legitimate Pleasures

Sinful pleasures are never permissible. Legitimate pleasures, on the other hand, can be enjoyed, but not in a manner that enslaves us. Teen life, unfortunately, is sometimes characterized by the domination of pastimes such as video games, social media, texting, shopping, and watching movies. And just as teens need to learn that work and responsibility are gifts of God (see conversation 1), they must also learn that recreation, entertainment, and amusement are undeserved blessings to be received in moderation and with thanksgiving.

The apostle Paul writes, "'All things are lawful for me,' but not all things are helpful" (1 Corinthians 6:12). Just because we *can* do something doesn't mean we *should*. A teenager who receives a last-minute invitation to join his friends at a basketball game but has a prior work obligation has to make a tough sacrifice. The basketball game would be fun, and totally appropriate on another occasion, but a prior responsibility cannot be ignored. Of course, if a creative solution can be found (maybe he gets someone to sub for him), more power to him. My point is that recreation should be *intentional*—a choice, not an impulse. Teens sometimes speak about recreation as if they'll die if they don't participate.

There may even be certain legitimate activities that your teens find so addictive they're better off avoiding them altogether, or at least setting up firm boundaries. Confession: I know I'm not capable of playing a video game for 20 minutes. It would not happen. I would play it for three hours and then dream about it until I figured out how to win. That's why I gave up video games many years ago. It's not a pleasure I can keep under control. That's a bit embarrassing to admit, but I'd rather be faithful than made a fool by my lack of self-mastery.

For many teens, cell phone usage, and particularly texting, has become an addiction. Their cell phones are always on and always with them. Many even sleep with them on. I don't regard cell phones as sinful, but when the average teen sends or receives about 2,200 text messages per month, you have to wonder if something else might be going on.[14] Physicians and psychologists agree that all that texting is leading to anxiety, distraction in school, falling grades, and even repetitive stress injury and sleep deprivation.[15]

One reason teens sleep with their phones on is so that they don't miss "important" texts—texts that keep them in the know. They also don't want to appear unresponsive to their friends, so they simply "must" reply promptly to incoming messages. I think this is part of the anxiety factor. They're being controlled by what they perceive others expect from them, which is a terrible basis for decision making and an unstable source of self-esteem. As a college professor, I can tell you that all that texting is not making students more ready for the rigors of higher education. It shortens their attention spans and makes them less comfortable with silence, which makes it harder for them to study.

If this is an issue in your house, you may want to think about a "no cell phone until your homework is done" rule. Come to think of it, you may want to extend that to certain family times and church services. We don't want to be overly controlling, but it's right to help our teens form habits and safeguards that will benefit them when they've left our homes.

Teach your teens that recreation, amusement, and socializing are gifts from God. We all need time to smile, laugh, and play. The role of recreation is to refresh and empower us to return to our labors with new energy, having been invigorated by activities we find restorative. When properly pursued, recreation energizes us for our work rather than distracts us from it. Failure to keep recreation from becoming all-consuming is probably the number one reason students flunk out of college. So if you can help your teens develop a balanced, biblical appreciation of work and play, your efforts will be every bit as vital as any SAT or ACT prep course.

ADULTS PERSEVERE IN COMMITMENTS

Brandon makes the soccer team, but he isn't getting much playing time. So he quits. Alyssa agrees to babysit on a Friday night but cancels at the last minute when her best friend wins tickets to a concert. Tyler takes a summer job delivering newspapers. A couple of weeks in he decides it's too hard to get up early, so assuming (incorrectly) that he can easily find a better job, he quits.

Words like *commitment*, *obligation*, and *responsibility* have bad connotations in our day. We prefer words like *flexible*, *refundable*, and *nonbinding*. We like keeping our options open. When things become unpleasant, we look for an exit strategy. Very few people today stay in a tough place simply because they gave their word. It's harder to teach our teens the value of perseverance in a world with so little permanence.

I heard a staggering statistic a few years ago on CBS News. At the height of the housing crisis, 20 percent of all foreclosures were intentional.[16] These were people who could pay their monthly mortgage payment, in some cases easily. They weren't under financial duress. They simply decided it was not in their interest to keep paying an expensive mortgage when they could get a better deal with a new purchase. So they bought a larger home for less money and then walked away from their underwater property, leaving their bank, neighbors, and communities high and dry. It was perfectly legal, as far as I can tell. But I think it's fair to say that a previous generation of Americans would have found such

Two Lessons for Teens on Perseverance

Persevering means showing up on good days and bad, when we feel like it and when we don't. And what college, employer, friend, or prospective spouse wants anything less? Here are two related lessons we need to impart to our teens:

1. Perseverance over the long haul is the only way to achieve a level of mastery in anything. But the route will, at times, be difficult and painful.

2. Perseverance has public consequences, because others are counting on you to follow through on your commitments. If you quit going to orchestra practice because the snow melts and you'd rather be playing outside, you won't just fail to develop your musical talent. You'll be letting down the conductor and all your fellow musicians. Moreover, you'll be strengthening a reflex that, if not vigorously opposed, can lead to you someday walking out on other, more serious commitments.

behavior unimaginable, too shameful to even contemplate. (And as you know, the bill ultimately got dumped on the rest of us and our children.)

So how do we teach our teens the value of commitment? By reminding them of the benefits of following through in their pursuits and not just bouncing from one thing to another. Teens can move a mile a minute. Their interests and passions can be intense. We should encourage them to channel this energy into work by taking on extracurricular commitments—the kind that enable them to explore interests, develop talents, and practice faithfulness. Think sports teams, musical groups, theatrical organizations, academic clubs, community service, art projects, piano or voice lessons, political volunteer work, short-term missions, church-related service, and more. When they get involved, encourage them not to dawdle too long at the periphery but to actually *join* a group or make some commitment. It doesn't have to be for a lifetime, but once they join, don't let them quit before a natural end date (such as at the season's completion or after a major performance) and for a good reason. Quitting when things get tough can become a hard habit to break later in life. After all, quitting is easy—anyone can do it. Persevering—doing what you said you'd do—takes discipline, courage, and integrity.

The actual activity isn't what matters (provided it's not immoral). Whatever it is, it's an opportunity for teens to learn more about themselves, to improve their skills, to develop a work ethic, to make a difference in the lives of others, and to learn what it means to have others depend on them. It's a chance for them to learn the value of faithfulness. If they become the kind of young adults who are always jumping from one thing to the next, they'll never make a substantial contribution in anything. They'll fail to maximize their God-given talents.

Traditionally, education experts have emphasized the role of IQ and standardized test scores in future academic success (the latter still play a crucial role in college admissions). We've been led to believe that those who succeed are those with the most God-given mental power. And I'd agree that natural talent is a key ingredient. But researchers are catching on to the importance of character qualities like perseverance, curiosity, self-control, conscientiousness, and optimism. These traits now appear to be more determinative of lasting success than IQ.[17] That's definitely what I've seen as a college professor. I'll take a student who had a 2.8 high school GPA but has since grown up and become hardworking and motivated over a lazy, flaky student with a 3.6 high school GPA. I've seen plenty of the former go on to success and some of the latter take a turn for the worse.

Bottom line: while talent still matters (see conversation 9), exceptional skills are born of hard work and smart work, consistent effort applied in the best possible ways. And such skills give rise to lasting success. I pray that will be a reality for your sons and daughters, whatever path they end up taking.

....

Do you see a man skillful in his work? He will stand before
kings; he will not stand before obscure men.

—PROVERBS 22:29

....

Let's shift now to the public consequences of quitting. If
we accept a job—any job—our bosses, coworkers, employees, and customers are depending on us. If we join a sports
team, that team is counting on us. Keeping commitments
teaches our teens the value of integrity, and the natural by-
product of integrity is a good reputation. The Bible places a
high value on having a good name (see Proverbs 22:1; Ecclesiastes 7:1), because it usually is based on our true character, whether virtuous or otherwise (see 1 Timothy 5:24-25).
Teach your teens that public victories are often born from
strong character. And when you hear in the news of great
men and women whose reputations are shattered, seemingly
in an instant, remind them that no fall of that magnitude
occurs overnight. It is the fruit of a thousand smaller, private
missteps and indiscretions.

Finally, help your teens see the connection between keeping their word and empathy. You want them to have a revul-
sion to the idea of leaving others to pick up the pieces when
they fall short. Psalm 15 illustrates the blameless life, in part,
as "swear[ing] to [our] own hurt and . . . not chang[ing]."
This means keeping our promises and not seeking to get out
of them, even when it's costly for us. Better that it be costly
for us than costly for others.

Our teens are entering a narcissistic young-adult culture, and we need to teach them to swim upstream. Narcissists lack empathy. They're not as attuned to how failing to keep their commitments impacts other people. But being a flaky commitment breaker will not help anyone be successful. Nor will a lack of consideration for others. In fact, these qualities will limit their ability to benefit from college or any other form of training. And it will make them less effective—and ultimately less happy—in their adult lives. Regularly encourage your teens to be faithful today in the smallest of commitments so that they can someday succeed in the greatest of endeavors.

All this character stuff is fine and good, but if you're a Christian, then you know what I know: good works that don't flow from a vital faith in Jesus Christ make someone a moralist at best and a Pharisee at worst. We're not trying to raise mere adulthood-embracing, self-controlled, "good" teens. Ultimately, we desire for our teens to live out of the overflow of a personal walk with Jesus Christ whereby he is empowering them, moment by moment, to put sin (including self-righteousness) to death and to live a new life by the power of the Holy Spirit (see Ephesians 4:20-24; Colossians 3:5-10). For unless *their* righteousness exceeds that of the Pharisees, they will by no means enter the kingdom of God (see Matthew 5:20). The best way for our teens to accept the big vision of adulthood we've been talking about is for them to internalize the Christian faith. And that's what we'll tackle in the next chapter.

What If I Blew It?

Some of you are reading this and thinking, *That's why we started training our kids to be future-oriented well before the teen years!* Praise God! But for the rest of you, be encouraged. It's not too late to start. You can still make a difference in the lives of your teens. If necessary, take steps to win back their trust or repair any damage to your relationship. The old refrain is still true: "They won't care what you know until they know that you care." Once you've earned some moral authority, start imparting these future-orientation principles to them, being careful to convey that it's their best interests you have in mind.

SUMMARY

- Teens live up (or down) to our expectations for them.
- Teens need a positive vision for the teen years as a season of preparation for adulthood.
- Teens must learn that successful people consistently do things they don't—at that particular moment—want to do.
- Teens must dominate their responsibilities or be

dominated by them. And their recreation must rejuvenate them for work rather than distract them from work.

- A future-orientation enables teens to delay gratification, avoiding sinful pleasures and regulating legitimate pleasures.
- A future-orientation enables teens to persevere in their commitments, faithfully keeping their word. This honors God, shows respect for others, and contributes to their own personal development and maturity.

CONVERSATION STARTERS

1. Ask your teens to list character traits that come to mind when they hear the word *teenager*. Use that as a springboard for talking about a biblical perspective on the teen years. (Consider using the examples of David, Daniel, and Joseph given in this chapter.)

2. Tell your teens how you've done battle with the desire for instant gratification. What safeguards have you implemented? Which struggles remain? Ask them where they struggle. What safeguards might be effective for them?

3. Discuss the value of persevering with commitments. Use something they enjoy as an example. What has persevering in that activity made possible for them? What have they learned along the way? What might perseverance in this activity lead to in the future?

4. Though not discussed much in the chapter, there is

a time and a way to quit a job or a club in order to free up time for something else. How should your teens make transitions in ways that protect their reputation and don't leave others in the lurch? Give examples from your life.

PART 2
FAITH

CONVERSATION 3
Raising Teens Who Internalize Their Faith

MY COLLEGE FRIEND Andrew was the kind of teen every Christian parent hopes to raise. He was courteous and respectful, attended classes, did his homework, and was honest. When .Andrew arrived as a freshman at Alfred University, he sought out a Christian church and attended every Sunday morning. He even called his mom every Sunday afternoon to tell her how his week had gone. (That was a big deal before cell phones.)

Late in his sophomore year, Andrew began to skip church every now and again. He got really into his major (computer programming—the Internet was just becoming mainstream). He expressed a variety of reservations about Jesus and the Bible. Over time his faith fizzled out, and he drifted away. By graduation, he had completely severed his ties to Christianity and the church.

The most frequent question I get from parents who know about my book *Thriving at College* is "Will my child's faith be strong enough to withstand the tests of college?" If we're honest, what happened to Andrew is what we all fear could happen to our children.

Internalizing the faith is the number one concern for Christian parents, and rightly so. It's the most important thing *any* teen can do—college bound or otherwise. We're talking about our children's eternal salvation here. Moreover, an internalized faith naturally becomes the foundation for a life of integrity and character, including the assumption of responsibility and having a future-orientation, as we discussed in the previous chapters. Likewise, it's the motivation for financial and academic stewardship (to be covered in future chapters), as teens come to understand that God's call on their lives encompasses every aspect of their activities.

We'll approach the faith aspects of college preparation over two chapters. In this chapter, we'll look at what's happening inside our teens: their doubts, convictions, and struggles to own the Christian faith for themselves. The teen years are a time to help our kids come to own *what* they believe, *why* they believe it, and *how* to live in the light of it. We need to help our teens embrace the biblical God, the biblical Jesus, and a biblical worldview—and to be passionately and permanently transformed by these ultimate realities. But don't worry—it won't require that you have an advanced theological degree. It involves teaching, but it's mainly modeling. We'll paint a picture in this chapter of what it can look like.

In the next chapter, we'll explore how our teens, as Christians, should relate to and interact with those around them. It's not uncommon for teens today to assume that the Bible can be true for them but not necessarily for others. That's because they've absorbed our culture's new definition of tolerance: the acceptance of differing (even mutually exclusive) views as being equally valid for different people (with no view being *absolutely* true or binding on all). Ultimately, we want our teens to be salt and light, winsomely engaging others, not with arrogant condescension but with brokenhearted, humble boldness, pointing them to Jesus Christ.

When we hear stories of teens like Andrew who go to college and leave their faith, we naturally want to know two things: *Why* do they leave the faith? And what sorts of things can we, as parents, do to prevent it from happening?

WHY DO THEY LEAVE?

In 1 John 2:19 we read: "They went out from us, but they were not of us; for if they had been of us, they would have continued with us. But they went out, that it might become plain that they all are not of us." We see two things in this verse. One, that true Christians persevere over the long haul. And two, that those who go "out from us" prove themselves to never have been Christians ("not of us"). The sad truth is that some who are raised in Christian homes leave those homes for college or elsewhere in an unconverted state. They were never born again or made alive unto God (see John 3:3-6, Ephesians 2:1-5), even though they may have looked like Christians while in our homes due to supportive circumstances.

Being raised in a Christian home is a significant advantage. First Corinthians 7:14 reads, "For the unbelieving husband is made holy because of his wife, and the unbelieving wife is made holy because of her husband. Otherwise your children would be unclean, but as it is, they are holy." Just before this verse, Paul teaches about the importance of a Christian husband or wife remaining married to a non-Christian spouse (assuming the spouse consents). What is meant by "the unbelieving (spouse) is made holy"? Paul isn't saying that the non-Christian spouse is saved by this association (verse 16 of this chapter makes that clear). Paul is saying that the non-Christian spouse (and children) come under the regular influence of a Christian and are therefore more likely to be saved in the course of time by virtue of this relationship. The Greek word interpreted as "holy" literally means "set apart." There's a sense in which the children of Christians (particularly if both parents are saved) are "set apart" from other non-Christians in the world, who don't have the blessings of being raised in a Christian home. We know that God saves people through their hearing the gospel message (see Romans 10:14). So regularly attending a church where the gospel is preached, seeing their parents sincerely pursue a Christian lifestyle throughout the week—not as a formality, but out of genuine love for God—these are huge advantages.

We should be encouraged. Being raised in an explicitly Christian home *often* has the effect of bringing a person into a saving relationship with Jesus Christ. An August 2013 Focus on the Family study found that among those who had a very strong Christian faith as children and came from a home where a vibrant faith was taught and practiced, almost nine out of ten (89 percent) remained practicing Christians into adulthood.[1] And the Barna Group has reported that two out of three born-again Christians (64 percent) made a commitment to Christ before their 18th birthday.[2]

The fact is that there are concrete, tangible steps we as parents can take to plant the seed of faith deep inside the hearts of our teens before they leave our homes. We should teach them that they're sinners before a holy God, deserving of judgment, and that Jesus willingly bore God's judgment in the place of everyone who would ever trust in him, love him, and obey him. And we should model to them how a Christian aims above all else to please God in everything. While it's ultimately God's work to draw people to himself (see John 6:29, 44), he calls us to be fellow workers with him in the process (see 2 Corinthians 5:20). As parents, we have a uniquely influential role in the lives of our children, even in the sometimes difficult teen years.

THE ROLE OF PARENTS

God expects parents to be the primary influencers in the spiritual lives of their children. In Proverbs 22:6 we read, "Train

Q: *One of our children wants to go to their own church, rather than tag along with us. Any advice?*

A: It's not ideal. Deeper relational bonds are formed—both within the family, and between that family and others—when a family attends church together. Church involvement shouldn't be like a food court, where everyone orders whatever they want. A consumer mind-set encourages churchgoers to stay on the fringes instead of committing. But joining a church should be as much about *giving* as it is about *getting*.

That said, parents should choose a church home with full consideration of their children's spiritual needs. Church involvement is an important component of bringing up children "in the discipline and instruction of the Lord" (Ephesians 6:4). If your teens aren't feeling engaged at church, that should be discussed. Legitimate issues should be brought to the attention of church leaders. In an extreme case, perhaps the entire family needs to find a more suitable church home. Then again, teens may need help brainstorming ways to get more connected (including ways they can serve).

Some families are involved at churches that don't have midweek youth activities. If their children wish to connect with other Christian teens, and if a neighboring church's youth group is biblically oriented, I would not see that as problematic. However, if their reason to go elsewhere is shallow or superficial, that's another story. Such teens need help understanding the purpose of a youth group in strengthening young adults in the faith.

up a child in the way he should go; even when he is old he will not depart from it." And Deuteronomy 6:4-7 reads:

> Hear, O Israel: The LORD our God, the LORD is one. You shall love the LORD your God with all your heart and with all your soul and with all your might. And these words that I command you today shall be on your heart. *You shall teach them diligently to your children*, and shall talk of them when you sit in your house, and when you walk by the way, and when you lie down, and when you rise. (Emphasis added)

We parents should be about the business of passing the baton of faith to our children, in one way or another, on a 24-7 basis. The New Testament admonishes fathers to not "provoke [their] children to anger, but [to] bring them up in the discipline and instruction of the Lord" (Ephesians 6:4). The apostle Paul said of his disciple Timothy that "from childhood you have been acquainted with the sacred writings, which are able to make you wise for salvation through faith in Christ Jesus" (2 Timothy 3:15). We read earlier in this letter that this instruction was imparted by his mother Eunice and grandmother Lois (see 2 Timothy 1:5).

The manner in which we seek to influence our children depends on their age and capacity. In their early years, we provide abundant structure (bedtimes, rules on dessert, and so on) but are content with a less than sophisticated understanding of the biblical message. For example, many of us teach our children to memorize Bible verses long before they can comprehend what the words mean. This is a sensible strategy—it builds their mental library, which they (like Timothy) can draw upon in later years.

The early years, exhausting as they are, generally come with an important benefit, courtesy of God's wise design: children are hardwired to seek their parents' praise. Yes, children can be deceitful and sometimes manipulative. They're born sinners, just like us. But their natural desire for praise, their overwhelming dependence on their parents, and their lack of independently accessible relationships makes them really want to please *us*. This causes them to do many right things, even if their motives aren't always right and even though their hearts still need the supernatural change that only the Holy Spirit can effect.

Three things happen in the teen years that can lead to conflict. First, our children's natural desire to receive praise from us diffuses into a more general desire to be liked and respected. They still want our praise, but they also want affirmation from their peers, sometimes more than from us. They want to be known, in *their* world, as having it together, as being competent, smart, attractive, and desirable. Second, their intellectual capacity grows, so they're no longer content to do what we say just because we say so. They want to know why. Moreover, they want to decide whether they should do this or that. In short, they are coming to know themselves as independent from us, and they're trying to figure out who *they* are and what *they* believe and what *they* want to live for. This is normal and healthy, but it's scary for us parents, because we fear they might reject what we hold dear—the very things we've raised them to cherish.

So what's the third thing, you ask? As our kids enter the teen years, their interaction with society and culture broadens. They start to form their own opinions—about music, movies, friendships, and more. They develop an interest in the opposite sex. We sometimes sense a new distance from them—it seems harder to connect than it used to be. We don't seem to understand them as easily. The reality is that we were in the habit of relating to them in one way (as children), and now we have to relate to them in another way (as young adults). To complicate matters, this transition often comes when we're in our prime working years. Maybe we've recently been promoted or our bosses need us to travel more. We're feeling squeezed at work and unsure of our place at home in the lives of our changing kids.

On Sundays, we're happy to be at church as a family, though maybe our kids start wanting to sit with their friends instead of with their parents. At least they're at church, we tell ourselves. The youth pastor starts welcoming them to midweek events, and we're delighted if they want to go. Over time, it's easier to check out of making deep connections with them. We tell ourselves, consciously or unconsciously, that everything is fine, the youth pastor or other youth leaders are investing in their lives. And unlike us, they're actually *good* at relating to our teens. After all, it's their job.

So we justify staying silent on spiritual issues and not

Within our youth group, we have a student ministry team. This group is made up of juniors and seniors in high school, all of whom have committed to using their God-given gifts to minister to their peers. They serve the ministry by welcoming new attendees, doing the menial setup and teardown tasks, and helping to plan events. Over the years, we've been struck by the makeup of this group, as it is a commentary on the importance of family. While there are some outliers, by and large these leaders of our youth group come from stable homes where at least one parent has purposely invested in their spiritual lives. These same students seem to fare the best in their transition to college as they have been well prepared for the challenges that await them. They are grounded in their faith, able to make decisions wisely, and quickly get plugged into ministries on campus. It's hard to overstate the importance of parents in shaping the character, conviction, and long-term stability of the next generation of Christians.

Dan

giving our kids the active modeling they need—and in many cases truly desire. As valuable as relationships with other Christian adults can be for them, there's something fundamental about the child-parent relationship that cannot be replaced. You may feel less qualified, less articulate, or less theologically sophisticated than the youth pastor, but God has given you a unique duty, and he can empower you to discharge it beautifully. Your teens look up to you, for better or worse. As in other areas of life, they are learning from you how an adult man or woman relates to God. So even if your teens are in a great youth group, don't check out of their lives. Remember that they are looking at you the other six and a half days of the week. Take advantage of the chance to show them how, day-in-and-day-out, you try to live out an authentic faith in the real world of a very busy life.

MODELING A TRANSFORMING FAITH

Sociologist Christian Smith has written several books about the spiritual lives of young adults. His studies have found that parental involvement is absolutely crucial to the internalization of teens' faith.[3] It makes sense. Teens aren't dumb. If we invest in their spiritual lives, they'll see faith as important. And if we don't, if we act as if faith doesn't matter or that it can be taken for granted, they'll do the same. So what are some practical ways parents can model a transforming faith for their teens?

Consider What You Model

First of all, it's not a question of *whether* we're modeling; it's *what* we're modeling. Our teens are constantly listening to our lives. And the evidence is in: we get what we are. How we relate to God is how our teens will relate to God.

Smith's research has found that the majority of churched teens held to a system of beliefs that could be summarized by the moniker "Moralistic Therapeutic Deism" (MTD). The creed of MTD, Smith writes, goes like this:

1. A God exists who created and orders the world and watches over human life on earth.
2. God wants people to be good, nice, and fair to each other, as taught in the Bible and by most world religions.
3. The central goal of life is to be happy and to feel good about oneself.
4. God does not need to be particularly involved in one's life except when he is needed to resolve a problem.
5. Good people go to heaven when they die.

If this is what teens believe, where did they pick it up? The unflattering truth is that it probably came from us, their parents. MTD, in a nutshell, treats God as our cosmic butler. He exists to serve our needs, to help us have happier marriages, be more successful at work, get wealthier, and retire comfortably.

We need to take a hard look at what we're modeling. Are we at the center of life, or is God? Do we approach God only when we're in a jam, hoping he'll bail us out? Or do our teens see us making sacrifices, sometimes even choosing the hard road, because it's the right thing to do? In our weakness, do our children see us seeking and depending on God's strength? Do we prioritize comfort and professional success, or conformity to the image of Christ and the glory of God? When we're enjoying a beautiful day at the beach or a nice vacation, do we act like we're entitled to these good things, or do we receive them with thanksgiving, as undeserved gifts to be enjoyed for the sake of the Giver? Do these gifts increase our worship or turn our hearts inward? Do we seek to win our neighbors and coworkers for Jesus, or do we merely go along to get along, content that nobody is making fun of us? Are we open about our ongoing struggle with sin and our desperate need for fresh applications of God's grace, purchased for us by the sacrificial death of Christ? In all these things, the scary truth is that our teens are watching and picking up our habits and inclinations.

If we want our teens to catch the Christian faith from us, we have to show them how Jesus Christ has caught us. We need to invite them into our lives and into our conversations at home and at church so they see how we live out our faith, through good times and bad. Our teens need to see that MTD cannot fill the God-shaped vacuum in their hearts. MTD is too small in scope and too weak in substance to sustain them when hardships come (as they always do). And it's simply not consistent with reality: God is about much more than our personal comfort or professional success. In fact, excessive wealth, accomplishment, and luxury can be spiritually hazardous, and God sometimes keeps them from us for our good.

Stay in the Game

Don't check out. Keep pursuing a deeper relationship with your teens.

Be interested in how their day went and in the details of their lives. Be interested in what your teens are interested in, for their sake. If your teens want to talk about the latest teen movie, maybe you should see it together and then talk about it at a coffee shop. You don't have to pretend you're one of their peers to pull this off. The key is that you love them enough to enter their world. It won't go unnoticed. And it gives you a chance to influence the way they interpret the underlying worldviews conveyed in media such as movies and music.

Seek to identify with your teens. Since you were a teen once, you can fill them in on how you dealt with the common struggles of that life stage, as well as the lessons you learned along the way. But patterns of sin and temptation are remarkably similar, even at different stages of life. Their desire to be liked by the "in" crowd is not unlike our desire to put on a good show for the "important" people at work or church. Their temptation to cheat on a test is not unlike our temptation to take credit for someone else's contribution. Their wanting to talk back to their parents is not unlike our wanting to tell an irritating coworker how we *really* feel. The desire to be loved and admired, the fear of failure, the tendency to bristle under authority—these are human experiences. Practice seeing your teens as fellow sinners in need of grace, more similar to you than different beneath the Cross.

> *Practice seeing your teens as fellow sinners in need of grace, more similar to you than different beneath the Cross.*

At the dinner table, in the car, and when you're out and about, talk about how your faith impacts how you manage your priorities at work, in the home, and everywhere else. Tell your teens how you go about fighting sin and, with God's help, growing in holiness. Apologize when appropriate—this models the kind of openness you want them to feel toward you and shows them you're trusting in Jesus, not your performance.

Likewise, treating your teens with love and acceptance, especially when they've fallen short, is a great way to imitate our heavenly Father. This doesn't mean we can't discipline. But there's a world of difference between "If you don't get your chores done, you can forget about using the car this weekend!" and "Because we love you, we want you to learn responsibility. That's why we've assigned you some of the work in this house." The former motivates from fear and anger; the latter, from love and acceptance. Our teens need to see that we have their best interests in mind.

Pray for your teens, and ask them in what ways they need prayer. Follow up with them on those things in the course of natural conversation. Assure them of your love for them, regardless of what struggles they may be going through. Make sure you give them enough space to bring up faith matters on their own. And don't expect it to always happen at times that are convenient for you.

Pray *with* them after difficult conversations and at other times. This builds intimacy, diffuses anger, and models humility. If your kids see that you think it's normal to go to God in prayer, they are more likely to do the same when they're on their own. Moreover, your prayers become a model for their prayers.

Have Family Devotions

I know this is hard; my wife and I have young children with short attention spans. Your teens may roll their eyes. But setting aside a regular time to read the Bible and pray together or to explore a topic from a Christian perspective is a great way to show your children that Christianity has relevance beyond Sunday morning. Different families do this different ways, and I'm not prescribing one "right" way. The point is that your teens benefit tremendously by seeing *you* attempt to engage them with Christian teaching, particularly at the level of their worldview. You want them to leave your home deeply convinced that Christianity makes sense, and that it makes sense of the world around them. It is something big and strong, something they can build their lives on.

Fathers, your role in this process is vital. Anecdotal evidence suggests you're more likely than Mom to detach from your teens. But for better or worse, fathers have a

Suggested Topics for Family Devotions

With any of these, you could read and discuss relevant Scripture passages along with a Christian book.

- Money
- Speech
- Humility
- Sexuality
- Integrity
- Wisdom
- The truthfulness of Christianity

An alternative approach would be to set aside time on Saturday evening (or Sunday lunch) to read the passage your pastor will be preaching (or just preached) and to discuss it. These conversations may give you ideas for future topical discussions/studies.

disproportionate impact on the preservation of faith in the lives of their children.[4] If Dad sends the message, spoken or unspoken, that the Bible is for women and children, or that Christianity can be confined to two hours a week on a Sunday morning, there's a much higher chance his kids (male *and* female) will disengage from Christianity and the church when they're older. But if Dad takes the faith seriously and seeks to integrate it into the family's home life, there's a much higher chance his sons and daughters will do the same when they've established their own households.

I came to faith in Christ early in my high school years, but since my father was not a Christian, faith wasn't a regular conversation topic in my home (which was a wonderful place in many other respects). I had Christian friends, though, and I occasionally found myself engaging my friends' fathers in lengthy conversations about a range of topics that, for whatever reason, I didn't feel I could broach at home. It was as if I'd been holding back a stream of thoughts, questions, and emotions, and in the presence of the right person, they came gushing out.

Your teens' interests may seem trivial or shallow at times. I know mine often were. But be assured that somewhere in the background they are trying to process what they will build their lives around. And they really do want help. They'll go to someone they trust, to someone they think has wisdom and will really hear them. Even if they aren't always interested in talking, they're not tuning you out nearly as much as it may sometimes feel.

WELCOMING QUESTIONS ABOUT THE FAITH

Part of teens' journey to adulthood is determining their belief system, their worldview, what they will build their lives upon. This won't look the same for every teen, but it's not uncommon for them to "kick the tires" of the Christian faith—to see if it's legit, if it can handle the tough questions. And we should welcome such inquiry. Our faith is rooted in historical events, and its teachings are consistent with the real world. Christianity is intellectually credible and experientially satisfying, and it can withstand as much honest inquiry as our teens can muster.

Christianity is intellectually credible and experientially satisfying, and it can withstand as much honest inquiry as our teens can muster.

Studies have shown that those who felt they could express their doubts while in high school often go on to experience stronger faith and greater spiritual maturity in college.[5] So welcome your teens' concerns and difficulties—these are signs that they're wrestling with the faith for themselves, an essential step in coming to own it. And isn't it better for them to first wrestle with these questions at home, with you, than in a freshmen philosophy class with an atheist professor? You can even turn their questions into research projects that you pursue together.

This isn't an apologetics book, and I can't possibly anticipate every possible question your teen may ask. We already covered the "I can't have any fun if I obey the Bible" idea in the last chapter, when we talked about future-orientation. So let's address two common areas of intellectual difficulty. Even if your teens aren't expressing doubts about their faith, it's helpful for them to know that Christianity can withstand scrutiny. False belief systems will be less alluring to them if you've first exposed and debunked them.

Anti-science: Is Christianity at Odds with Science?

It's not uncommon for intelligent teens who enjoy science to think there's inherent tension between science and faith. The myth that science is incompatible with the Christian faith has been purported by skeptics for years and continues to be promoted at elite secular universities in our day. Fortunately, it's a house of cards that crumbles upon inspection.

Science is about the discovery of the laws and patterns that, in God's wisdom, govern behavior within his created order. Science seeks to explain how the world works. God is a God of order; therefore, we have scientific laws and patterns of highly repeatable behavior in nature. And since God made us in his image as rational, creative, intelligent, and resourceful creatures, he intends for us to discover scientific laws and to harness them into the creation of products, goods, and services by which we can love our neighbors, improve their lives, and treat illness, alleviate suffering, and lift up the destitute.

God loves when his children study the universe and learn more about it. It's part of the mandate he gave our first parents (see Genesis 1:28). Science doesn't argue that there's no God; on the contrary, the presence of order in the universe, of repeatability in chemical reactions, of universal constants that show up in mathematical equations that precisely describe the motion of objects large and small—all these things scream that there is an intelligent, eternal Creator (see Psalm 19:1-6; Romans 1:20). And that's the very reason we *can* study science.

We need to distinguish between *science* and *scientism*. *Science* seeks to understand how the material world works, to make inferences and deductions, and to (where possible) encapsulate mathematical predictions in the form of equations. *Scientism* is the false assumption that all discernible truth is scientifically verifiable. Ever heard the phrase "Unless I see it, I won't believe it"? The claim is that the only "truths" out there are those that can be empirically verified: if the senses cannot test it, we can't know it.

The natural response is "Can we empirically verify the claim that all true knowledge can be empirically verified?" No, we

> Science seeks to understand how the material world works, to make inferences and deductions, and to (where possible) encapsulate mathematical predictions in the form of equations. Scientism is the false assumption that all discernible truth is scientifically verifiable.

can't, which makes the claim self-refuting. Moreover, what are we to make of human morality, responsibility, and dignity? These can't be verified by our senses either. Are they also illusory? Even those who hold to scientism (like many atheistic university professors) don't normally live in a manner

The Role of Apologetics

If you've ever tried to make a reasonable defense for Christianity, you've probably noticed that responses are quite varied. On one end of the spectrum, apologetics can help committed Christians gain a greater depth of assurance. On the other end of the spectrum, there are scoffers who just want to dispute anything we might say. Jesus withdrew from conversations with people asking for a sign (see Matthew 12:38-42) or by what authority he taught (see Luke 20:1-8).

Some who saw Jesus raise Lazarus from the dead put their trust in Jesus (see John 11:45), but others conspired to kill Jesus (see John 11:53). Both groups considered the same evidence, but their responses could not have been more different. I've known non-Christian teens and adults who were helped in their journey to Christ by apologetics. But here's what they've later acknowledged: information and logical arguments are helpful in making Christianity understandable and credible and in dismantling false worldviews, but ultimately an act of the will (and the work of God in someone's heart) is involved. We cannot browbeat anyone into the Kingdom of God. It's right to clearly and winsomely defend the faith and to reason with non-Christians (see Acts 26:24-29), but ultimately they must willingly surrender to Jesus Christ. And for this we can only pray.

that's consistent with the necessary inferences of their system. If they did, it would lead them to the cynicism of atheists like Bertrand Russell, who once said, "There is darkness without and when I die there will be darkness within. There is no splendor, no vastness, anywhere; only triviality for a moment, and then nothing."[6] I've worked with people who say stuff like that, but their hearts know better. They seek to live consistently with a moral code that they genuinely see as binding on all humanity. They simply cannot erase God's image from their being. Instead, their lives are marked with tension between their theoretical belief and their actual practice.

Christianity, by contrast, is consistent with the real world, our ability to make genuine progress in understanding it, our sense of justice, and our intuition that life must have meaning. As C. S. Lewis said, "I believe in Christianity as I believe that the sun has risen: not only because I see it, but because by it I see everything else."[7] The more we expose and encourage our teens to love and pursue the real deal (science), the more they'll be able to detect and stay clear of the counterfeit (scientism).

But let's go beyond whether our teens ultimately pursue science. The wonderful reality is that it's not just science that's compatible with faith. Rationality itself—logic, reason, and intelligence—are also compatible with faith. God doesn't expect us to check our brains at the doorway of discipleship. He does not bypass our intellect, which is part of his image and intrinsically good (though marred by sin). He gave us a book to read, study, memorize, meditate on, and live out.

Recommended Reading on Science and Faith

- Stephen C. Meyer, *Signature in the Cell* (New York: HarperOne, 2010)
- C. John Collins, *Science and Faith* (Wheaton, IL: Crossway, 2003)
- Stephen C. Meyer, *Darwin's Doubt* (New York: HarperOne, 2013)
- Vern Poythress, *Redeeming Science* (Wheaton, IL: Crossway, 2006)
- Nancy Pearcey, *Total Truth* (Wheaton, IL: Crossway, 2004)

And he gave us an orderly universe to study and explore. The faith he calls us to is rooted in historical events (see 1 Corinthians 15:1-8). It's not faith versus reason. It's faith *based on* reason: because Jesus rose from the dead, everything he said about himself is true (see Romans 1:4). And we, like his first disciples, can build our lives upon it.[8]

The Bible: Inerrant and Accurate?

Christians are people of the Book. Our faith depends on historical events that have been recorded for us in the Bible, along with authoritative teachings that flow from the events of the gospel. If our teens are to internalize the faith, they need to both know the Bible and regard it for what it truly is—the inerrant and infallible Word of God.

Unfortunately, David Kinnaman, president of the Barna Group, offers this unflattering assessment:

> Young people are skeptical about the reliability of the original biblical manuscripts; they tend to read the Bible through a lens of pluralism; their changing media behaviors and vanishing attention spans make a physical medium of Scripture less viable; and they seem less likely than previous generations to believe the Scriptures have a claim on human obedience.[9]

And regarding their knowledge of the Bible?

> The vast majority of churchgoing teenagers said they understand the teachings of the Bible "very well." But when we asked specific questions about the basic content of these teachings, most teens in the study performed quite poorly.[10]

It seems that teens from Christian homes don't know and respect the Bible the way they should. This leaves them in a vulnerable position once they get out on their own. As parents, we can change that.

For one, we can familiarize them with the Bible's story

Tip

A Barna Group Youth Poll conducted in 2009 found that 52 percent of teens aspire to science-related careers, but only 1 percent of church youth workers said they had addressed issues of science in the past year.[11] We need to close this gap by finding mentors in the church who can help our teens see that science is wonderful to study and can enhance, rather than destroy, a relationship with Jesus Christ.[12]

and with its major teachings, starting from our children's earliest years. But we also need to deal honestly with our teens about whatever doubts they may have about the Bible. Encourage them to get their concerns in the open—if not with you at least with their youth pastor or with someone who can intelligently respond from a Christian perspective. For example, here's a common one: "To err is human," so isn't the Bible flawed? After all, it was written by humans, so how can it truly be without error?

The answer is that God wrote the Bible via human personalities. It's not self-refuting to claim that humans could write the Bible, yet in such a way that they flawlessly recorded the very words of God. Jesus referred to every section of the Bible during his earthly ministry, and he treated the writings as sacred and authoritative. If they weren't, that would impugn his integrity.

But isn't the Bible full of contradictions? No. Different

passages sometimes unpack different aspects of the same event or doctrine, but there is no actual contradiction. For example, Paul talks about our right standing with God as coming by faith (see Romans 4:4-5), whereas James stresses that such faith, if it's legitimate, invariably leads to a changed life (see James 2:14-26). On historical matters, archaeological findings and other writings have only strengthened the case for the Bible's reliability.[13]

If you were to test the Old and New Testament writings the way a historian would test any old book, you'd find thousands of ancient manuscripts, dated closely to the time of the actual events, whose texts overwhelmingly agree with one another and which have been translated with care into

Examples of Worldview Resources

- *The Truth Project* (www.thetruthproject.org)
- The *TrueU* series (products of Focus on the Family)
- Worldview Academy Leadership Camps (www.worldview.org)
- Stand to Reason (www.str.org)
- Summit Ministries (www.summit.org)

modern languages. We can trust that what we have today is an accurate reflection of what the original authors intended.

There are dozens of biblical worldview camps, courses, and curricula out there that can reinforce your teens' faith. You don't have to be an expert theologian, philosopher, or apologist. If you're willing to help your teens find answers, God will lead you to resources you can explore together or to other believers (such as pastors) who can explain things in ways that perhaps you cannot.

"Kicking the tires" is a normal part of the process for many teens—take it in stride. God has placed us in our children's lives for their eternal good. Ask God to make you a blessing, and then work at drawing out your teens on spiritual matters. Be intentional and consistent, but try not to be pushy. If they're not yet interested in talking, you can at least let them know you'll be there for them and that doubts won't freak you out.

While a positive relationship with parents is vital, studies show that teens also benefit from having a *multitude* of friendships with Christian adults. They can develop such relationships through their local churches. A good church home is also a place where teens can develop a solid understanding of the Bible and a conviction that it truly is God's Word. Pastors and youth leaders can wonderfully complement what you're doing in the home. Since many Christian teens participate in youth groups, let's look at what makes for a great youth group experience.

A GREAT YOUTH GROUP EXPERIENCE

Let's start with the bad news: not all youth group activity has a positive impact on teen assimilation of faith. Jim Rayburn, the founder of Young Life, had a saying: "It's a sin to bore a kid with the gospel." He makes a valid point—we should present the Good News of salvation in an attractive manner. Unfortunately, many youth ministries have gone beyond presenting the gospel attractively to merely being attractors. They've adopted a recreation-oriented model that majors on outlandish competitions, pizza dinners, and video game nights and minors on gospel presentation, Bible study, and discipleship. Get 'em to church, they figure, with things they can relate to. Then sneak in a little bit of Bible and hope they don't object.

Jesus went about things differently. When large crowds followed him, he warned them of the cost of discipleship (see Luke 14:25-27). The truth is that the Christian life is hard and may include ridicule and the loss of friendships. It will involve saying no to things that seem appealing and trusting that God knows best and will ultimately "withhold no good thing" from us (Psalm 84:11, NLT).

It's not uncommon for adults who leave the church in their twenties to have fond memories of their youth group days. The problem is that once they get to college, there are more interesting things to do than play laser tag and eat pizza with a bunch of church-raised teens. The sad truth is that ministries that focus on good times, while giving short shrift to Bible teaching and discipleship, rarely nurture lifelong followers of Christ. Jesus warned us in the Parable of the Sower (see Mark 4) that mile-wide and inch-deep "faith" tends not to last.

I'm not against youth ministry; my time in youth group was a positive experience, and I had lots of fun, too. There's nothing wrong with teens having a great time at church and building precious memories. But the fun and games should be secondary, not foundational. Cake and ice cream are great for dessert, but they make a lousy main course. What teens *need* from youth ministry are solid Bible doctrine, a chance to ask questions and express skepticism without being ridiculed, and intergenerational mentoring on the outworking of Christian life.

The funny thing is that even though the recreational model of youth ministry is somewhat common, surveys show that young Christians are looking for meaning, not entertainment, at church. They want to be instructed with sermons that relate the Bible to their lives. They want guidance on what it means to live an authentic Christian life. They prefer depth to cultural relevance.[14]

The great thing is that youth groups can have all this *and* intergenerational mentoring in the best scenarios. That combination is one of the distinct advantages of youth ministries (and church involvement in general). The more examples of godly men and women your children have—the more men and women who are willing to befriend them, engage them, nurture their faith, and then follow their lives into the college years—the better.

SUMMARY

- Parents have enormous influence in the spiritual lives of their children. Stay involved in their lives as they move through the critical teen years. Be involved in a good church where your teens will regularly hear the gospel message in a variety of settings.
- Model a dynamic faith, and talk with your teens about it. Give them space to process any questions or doubts, and help them find solid answers.
- Science is not inconsistent with the Christian faith; on the contrary, meaningful scientific inquiry makes the most sense within the context of the Christian faith.
- Christianity is rooted in historical events, and the Bible is completely trustworthy.
- If youth groups provide strong teaching, intergenerational mentoring, and a place to ask questions and find answers, they can be helpful to the formation and growth of a vibrant faith in teens' lives.

CONVERSATION STARTERS

1. Think about how your teens' faith is developing. Are they going through the motions, doing the right things just because you're watching, or does it seem to be something they're internalizing? Then talk to your teens. What is their assessment of their faith? What can you do together to strengthen their faith?
2. Ask your teens to describe what their friends think

the Christian message is. Ask them what they think about the elements they mention. Lovingly correct any traces of "moralistic therapeutic deism."

3. Ask your teens what doubts they've heard others express about Christianity. What effect did those doubts have on their faith? Talk to your teens about how you've dealt with any doubts in your life, or how you've responded to doubts in the lives of others.

4. Though this wasn't in the chapter, your teens may be interested to know that even the biblical writers didn't always have it all together. Some of the Psalms record bold, raw prayers expressing anger, fear, and disillusionment. Remarkably, these powerful feelings can draw us closer to God rather than away from him. Tell your teens about a time in your life when a powerful emotion drove you closer to or farther from God, and what you learned in the process.

CONVERSATION 4

Raising Teens Characterized by Conviction and Tolerance

IN THE LAST chapter we talked about the tangible steps we as parents can take to nurture the faith of our teens. We discussed two common intellectual challenges: the suspicion that science and faith are at odds and the idea that the Bible is a less-than-perfect guide. This chapter addresses another big issue. For some, it's an overt deterrent to faith. For others, it's a major obstacle to communicating their faith. I'm talking about the exclusivity of the Christian message and the teachings of the Bible on a few hot-button contemporary issues.

Growing up, I was a big fan of C. S. Lewis and Josh McDowell. I became a Christian when I was about 14, but soon afterward I entered a period of wrestling with how I could *know* that Christianity was true. In school I was more of a math and science guy than anything else, and the notion of objective religious truth immediately made sense to me. Just as the rules of math, physics, and chemistry did not depend on my knowing them or believing them, so the reality of God and of Jesus Christ's life, death, and resurrection were true regardless of what I believed. I placed religion alongside math and science in the world of objectivity. So I loved books like *Mere Christianity, More Than a Carpenter, Evidence That Demands a Verdict*, and *The New Testament Documents: Are They Reliable?*

I was grateful for the abundance of archaeological support for the historical accounts in the Bible. I was amazed by the number of Old Testament prophecies fulfilled in the life of Christ and by the strong attestation of the New Testament accounts, not only of Jesus' ministry but also of the acts of the apostles as they established first-century churches in a wide variety of cities. I found it highly improbable that Jesus' disciples invented the doctrine of the Resurrection or had experienced a series of mass hallucinations. After all, their belief in the bodily resurrection of Jesus not only became the foundation of the Christian message, but it cost them their lives, too. People don't die for a lie when they know it's a lie.

AN EXCLUSIVE FAITH IN AN INCLUSIVE WORLD

But many of today's teens look at these kinds of arguments and say, "Yeah, this Jesus stuff works for some people, but it's not for everyone. We all have to find something to believe in. We wouldn't want to say Jesus is the *only* way to

God. That'd be intolerant."[1] Your teens might not *say* those words, but even if Jesus "works for them," chances are they've either *thought* them or have friends who operate from this perspective.

A former generation sought spiritual truth the way I did as a teen—with the assumption that such truth was objective and universal. Jesus either rose from the dead, or he didn't. The Bible is both accurate and trustworthy, or it isn't. But today's generation doesn't believe in universal, objective truth, at least not in the realm of religion.[2] It's an age of personal "truths," not universal "Truth." It's also about whatever "works." Jesus is fine, but so is yoga, self-help literature, or hiking in the mountains—whatever gives you a spiritual connection, an inner peace and happiness, or a deeper sense of purpose in life.

Don't get me wrong: "Christian" teens who take this view don't throw Jesus out the window. They just park him on the sidelines. They shift religion away from the realm of historically rooted fact into the realm of personal preference. The statement "I'm a Christian" is in the category of "I like basketball." If someone went around insisting that *everyone* like basketball, you'd think the person was loony. Liking basketball is a mere preference. But that's exactly how loony an exclusive Christian message seems to those acclimated to the dominant perspective of our day, particularly young adults at secular universities. To them, religion *cannot* be anything more than personal preference.

We need to help our teens deal with the new status quo on

several levels, because we're training them to enter a world that's very different from the one we grew up in. First, what does it mean to claim that something ethical or religious is "true" or "right"—does it mean "true for me, but not necessarily for everyone"? Or can ethical and religious truths have universal implications? Can they be grounded in objective reality? Second, what does it mean to be *tolerant*? Does it mean being kind and gracious to those with whom we strongly disagree while supporting their right to believe and speak differently, or does it mean letting go of any firm convictions whatsoever? Is the mere affirmation of a universal truth a manifestation of intolerance? For many today, tolerance involves thinking that everyone's beliefs are equally true—which leaves no room for universal convictions. (It's also impossible to live by.)

Yet the Bible calls us to be unflinching in our Christian beliefs, to hold them as universally binding on all humanity, *and* to be gracious toward those who don't agree. Popular pastor and author Rick Warren says it well:

> Our culture has accepted two huge lies: The first
> is if you disagree with someone's lifestyle you must
> fear them or hate them. The second is that to love
> someone means you agree with everything they
> believe or do. Both are nonsense. You don't have to
> compromise convictions to be compassionate.[3]

Our teens need to have both firm conviction and genuine tolerance (in the true sense of the word) if they're to avoid spineless compromise and overt arrogance. Because there are two kinds of mistakes teens can make here. They can accept the world's sentimental view of tolerance and never share the Good News of Jesus with anyone (or water it down so completely that it becomes trivial). That's tolerance without conviction—a commitment to "niceness" but not truth. On the opposite extreme, some teens become argumentative and rude, insisting that all their friends immediately come to Jesus, while looking down in contempt on those who don't. Many new converts, out of genuine zeal for their embryonic faith, make this mistake. A pastor friend of mine told a story of how, as a teen, he once punched a kid in the face while talking about Jesus. That is conviction without tolerance!

So how can we help? We must remind the convictionless teen that the biblical authors (and Christ himself) declared there was

> We must seek to win people rather than arguments.

only one way to God: receiving by faith the substitutionary sacrifice of Jesus, God's Son, on the cross (see John 14:6; Acts 4:12; 1 Timothy 2:5). It's not humility to be more open minded; it's an arrogant rejection of Jesus' explicit message. And we must remind intolerant teens that God's grace is the only thing that causes them to differ from their unbelieving peers (see 1 Corinthians 4:7). Since only God opens blind eyes, we must aim at embodying the goodness and mercy of Jesus to others while asking God to do in their hearts what we are powerless to do ourselves (for example, see John 6:22-65, particularly verses 29, 37-40, 44, and 65). We must seek to win *people* rather than *arguments*. The reality is that our behavior dramatically impacts our persuasiveness, for better or worse (see Proverbs 16:21; 2 Timothy 2:24-26).

TOLERANCE: WHAT IS IT?

We know what conviction is: firmness, strong belief, resolve. But what's tolerance? In *Merriam-Webster's 11th Collegiate Dictionary*, the first definition of tolerance we find is a "capacity to endure pain or hardship," as in, "George had developed a high tolerance to pain."

The second definition is "sympathy or indulgence for beliefs or practices differing from or conflicting with one's own." This one fits our context. A tolerant person is one who has *sympathy* for, or *allows*, or *tolerates* others whose beliefs and practices *conflict* with his own. Note the word *conflict*. You cannot *tolerate* someone you agree with; we generally enjoy people we agree with. There must be conflict for there to be tolerance.

> You cannot tolerate someone you agree with; we generally enjoy people we agree with. There must be conflict for there to be tolerance.

That's the historic definition of *tolerance*, and there is ample biblical support for it. It's something we should practice and develop in the lives of our teens. We're to strive to be at peace with all people (see Romans 12:18). We're to speak graciously "toward outsiders" (i.e., non-Christians; Colossians 4:5-6). In Babylon, Daniel and his friends did not tell the king to change his diet or lifestyle, but they respectfully sought permission to follow their Jewish convictions (see Daniel 1:8-16). In 1 Corinthians 5, where the apostle Paul tells the believers to disassociate from a brother living in unrepentant sin, he clarifies that such instruction does not apply to immoral people "of this world" (i.e., non-Christians) because that would require us to "go out of the world" (verse 10).

And on the contrary, we're to be in the world—rubbing shoulders with non-Christians. Though not *of* the world, Jesus clearly sends us *into* it (see John 17:14-18). We're to be countercultural, swimming against the current, influencing the world for good. In love, we're to be gracious toward non-Christians with the hope that God might save them, in part through our example and our speech (see 2 Timothy 2:24-26). God himself is tolerant, graciously showering humanity with undeserved kindness (see Romans 2:4) while mercifully delaying the return of Christ to give people time to repent (see 2 Peter 3:9). That said, biblical tolerance does not preclude challenging others with the truth (see Acts 26:25-29).

In your hearts honor Christ the Lord as holy, always being prepared to make a defense to anyone who asks you for a reason for the hope that is in you; yet do it with gentleness and respect, having a good conscience, so that, when you are slandered, those who revile your good behavior in Christ may be put to shame.

—1 PETER 3:15-16

THE NEW DEFINITION OF TOLERANCE

But there's been a shift in our day to a new understanding of tolerance, one that goes well beyond the old definition. It's no longer enough to allow someone to have a different perspective on an issue and to stand up for their right to speak and promote their views. We are now expected to accept diverging and conflicting views as also being true—or at least as true as our own perspective. Rather than merely allowing space in public discourse for vigorous yet amicable disagreement, we must now affirm that all beliefs, all truth claims, are equally valid. Truth, in this view, is subjective (depends on the subject or person) and relative (depends on the situation).

I once saw a funny bumper sticker that read, "Militant Agnostic: I don't know, and neither do you!" And I've had good friends who thought that way: Since you can't prove anything about Jesus, Muhammad, or Buddha in a laboratory, why discuss it? Let's all just get along.

This isn't the Christian perspective, of course, but the new concept of tolerance goes even further. It's not based on the idea that we should have a friendly debate over which religious path is right because open-minded inquiry is the best way to find out, nor is it even based on the idea that we should all be gracious to each other because religious truth is indiscernible. It's this: *since* everyone's perspective is equally true, it's unreasonable to suggest that anyone's religious views are less valid than anyone else's. We must be tolerant because all paths are equally right.[4]

Sure sounds nice, doesn't it? After all, we wouldn't want

to offend anyone by telling them they're wrong. But there's a bitter aftertaste. What this new tolerance is really saying is that all religious paths are equally right . . . *unless* a path claims to be exclusive, objective, and universally binding on all humanity. That perspective would be narrow-minded and intolerant. This pushes religious claims into the realm of personal preferences. Saying, "I'm a Christian" means "Jesus works for me." And that's all it can mean. We're not allowed to claim what the Bible says: that Jesus is the only Son of God and the only way to heaven and that he demands obedience from everyone. *That* Jesus is not to be tolerated. Nor are those who follow him.

Jesus promised that his followers would experience rejection in this life: "If the world hates you, know that it has hated me before it hated you. If you were of the world, the world would love you as its own; but because you are not of the world, but I chose you out of the world, therefore the world hates you" (John 15:18-19). Elsewhere we read, "Everyone who wants to live a godly life in Christ Jesus will suffer persecution" (2 Timothy 3:12, NLT). In these moments we can rejoice that we are counted "worthy to suffer dishonor for the name" (Acts 5:41). In fact, not returning evil for evil is part of how we glorify God and show Jesus to the world.

We need to be honest with our teens. There's a natural conflict between the people of God and those who currently live in rebellion toward him. Jesus hasn't (yet) brought full and final peace to the earth; he's brought a sword of separation, sometimes even within families (see Matthew 10:34-39). Put simply, our teens need to grow thick skin. Even if they speak politely and behave winsomely, some people will reject them on account of their Christian convictions—and it has always been this way. If Christianity continues to lose influence in the wider culture, it may get worse. Some around the world continue to make the ultimate sacrifice for their identification with Jesus Christ.

Given the ugly face of rejection, many of our teens will be tempted to keep their Christian faith in a neat, Sunday-morning compartment. The problem with such compartmentalization is that Christianity, rightly understood, does not permit it.

CHRISTIANITY CLAIMS TO BE TOTAL TRUTH

Christianity is about a personal relationship with God through his Son, Jesus Christ. But it's also a worldview—a mental map, a set of assumptions and beliefs that make sense of our experiences. It tells us why we're here (God made us in his image), what went wrong (we disobeyed God, bringing evil to the world and subjecting the creation to futility and suffering, see Romans 8:20), and why we can have hope (Jesus died in the place of sinners, to redeem those who trust in him, bringing them back into fellowship with God).

Our believing in Christianity doesn't make it true. But if it *is* true, it should work in the real world. It ought to cohere with and explain reality. Christianity is consistent with the universal human intuition that life has meaning and purpose, that humans have dignity and should be treated with respect.[5] These hardwired sentiments are the direct result of being made in the image and likeness of God.

Even the reality of brokenness and evil makes more sense from the Christian perspective, because a righteous, personal God is what legitimizes our own sense of morality, not to mention our indignation toward obvious injustice. Certain behavior is good and right because it's consistent with God's character. Though evil may at times appear to have the upper hand, God will eventually establish true and lasting justice. Even now God triumphs over genuine evil by using it to bring about ultimately good outcomes (see, for example, Genesis 50:20).

But Christianity does claim universal applicability—Jesus isn't Lord only if you make him Lord. He's Lord whether we live in submission to or rebellion against him. So let's help our teens tackle the "that's just true for you" objection. The answer to this is that such relativism is incompatible with the historical events that comprise the basis of Christianity, mainly the perfect life and the death, burial, and resurrection of Jesus Christ (1 Corinthians 15:3-4). Jesus either never lived, he's dead, or he rose from the dead. Our preferences can't impact what happened.

Moreover, we're rescued from our sins, and made into new creations, and adopted into God's family as sons and daughters, only if Jesus died in our place and rose from the dead. Christianity cannot be reduced to a series of moral platitudes about how to live a good life. It's about acknowledging our inability to live a good life and recognizing that

Jesus is the only truly good person who ever lived. When Jesus died on the cross, the real sins of real people were really paid for. And by believing in Jesus, we become God's children (John 1:12), and we receive power to walk in newness of life (Romans 6:4). The gospel—the Good News, the central teaching of Christianity—is about something that happened outside of us, in history, that has ongoing implications for every person on the planet.

But when people say, "That's just true for you," what they probably mean is "Jesus works for you . . . but not for me. I find Christianity unappealing, restrictive, repressive, and narrow." Our teens' response should be, "Okay, what do you believe? Does it make better sense of reality than Christianity? Can you live in a manner that's consistent with your worldview, or do you find yourself in constant tension?"

Christianity is a worldview in competition with other worldviews in the marketplace of ideas. I'm convinced that helping our teens engage their peers winsomely—to hold firmly to Christian convictions while displaying love and grace toward those who don't yet follow Christ—requires that we help them expose non-Christians to points of tension (or inconsistencies) in their worldviews. This requires careful, compassionate listening, motivated by a deep concern for those who are stuck in worldviews that don't make sense and cannot satisfy. It can't be about adding a notch on their belts. Any boldness or intensity needs to be tempered with self-control and patience. This approach also keeps the focus objective, on belief systems, rather than making people the enemy.

A few years ago I went to see the movie *Avatar* with a number of high school students. In discussing the movie with them afterward, I discovered they had really enjoyed it and were blown away by the story and the special effects. To my surprise, they had completely failed to notice any of the pantheistic elements of the film: they had been watching the movie for entertainment and as such had not filtered any of what they saw through a critical lens, much less a biblical one. At that point, we decided we needed to help students interact with media on a deeper level, helping them to see that every song and every movie is influenced by a particular worldview, and that it isn't necessarily built on the same values as the Scriptures.

As we began to have discussions at this level, we found that the Bible came alive in new ways. In a subsequent discussion of *Avatar*, we examined the biblical Creation narrative in a fresh way, noting that God was separate from his creation, not part of it, but also that the longing for a perfect utopia so vividly expressed in the movie has been the longing of every human heart since Adam and Eve were banished from the Garden. Rather than being a danger to the faith of our students, we've found that thoughtful and guided interaction with the culture in which they live can actually help them better understand and own what they believe.

George (youth pastor)

HELPING CHRISTIAN TEENS UNDERSTAND AND ENGAGE NON-CHRISTIANS

What are the main worldviews in competition with Christianity on college campuses? Let's come at this by describing three kinds of people your teens will encounter in their college years: the success-oriented, the ideals-oriented, and the pleasure-oriented. Granted, these categories aren't mutually exclusive; not every student will neatly fall into one of them. But these portraits will help you understand the kinds of people with whom your teens will need to practice true tolerance while holding fast to their convictions. Their challenge will be to show these students that Christianity provides a more satisfying, robust framework upon which to build a life.

The Success-Oriented

These students are motivated by good grades, career opportunities, networking, and padding their résumés. They're climbing the ladder and aiming for greatness, narrowly defined in financial and professional terms, idols they probably picked up from their parents. Even if they were raised in a religious tradition, they operate as if there is no God, no spiritual world, and no afterlife. Making the grades and setting themselves up to achieve status in their profession, earn a lot of money, and garner the respect of their peers—these are the things that make life meaningful for them. But eventually they will wonder, *Is this really all there is?*—because the truth is they were made for much more, and they won't be satisfied until they're delivered from their small, fragmented world-view. As Augustine of Hippo put it, "You [God] have made us for yourself, and our heart is restless until it rests in you."[6]

The Bible says that God has revealed himself to everyone through the natural world, but that we suppress this knowledge (see Romans 1:19-20). The truth is that success-oriented adults will experience stabs of transcendent joy, and not just in moments of professional or financial triumph. Falling in love, seeing their child enter the world, gazing upon the splendor of the Grand Canyon—these kinds of moments can yield a profound sense of peace and happiness. They will feel as if they've received a gift and will want to thank someone. But whom will they thank?

Christianity confirms our intuition that our lives must have meaning while not negating our experience of suffering and brokenness.

If they ascribe to the moralistic therapeutic deism described in the last chapter, perhaps that's not a problem. They assume it's God's job to make things go well for them. But what will they do when injustice, disappointment, and pain visit them and they're forced to grapple with how little control they actually have? A loved one is the victim of a horrific crime, and the perpetrator escapes. A parent learns they have cancer and, in spite of all medical efforts, dies shortly thereafter. A sudden turn in the economy or a corporate merger costs them the job upon which they based their identity. Suffering has a way of prompting us to revisit the purpose of our lives, to seek an anchor for our soul in something more stable than our circumstances—something nonmaterial, something greater than ourselves, which in our heart of hearts, we know must exist. Deism doesn't work because the God of the universe isn't our genie in a bottle.

To whom will the success-oriented cry out? Christianity confirms our intuition (denied by atheism) that our lives have meaning while not negating our experience of suffering and brokenness. God will not always save us from suffering, but his grace can sustain and even strengthen us through suffering. Better yet, God has promised a future world that will somehow be greater for having once been broken. Our teens can help their success-oriented friends see the futility of finding their identity in accomplishments and point them to the God who made them for himself.

The Ideals-Oriented

These college students truly want to make a difference in the world through a life of service and the promotion of social justice. This perspective is gaining popularity in our day, which in many ways is a good thing. It's right to want to live for something greater than ourselves. It's what we were made to do.

Students in this category regard the various world religions as teaching basically the same things—live a life of good deeds, treat others with respect, care for the poor, and so on. Some of these students are themselves personally religious, but it's something they hold as true "for them" and not necessarily for others. As far as God goes (if there is one), there's no "right" way to reach him. If we're sincere, we'll be received with open arms by whoever or whatever awaits us upon death.

Orienting a life around doing good in the world is nobler than living for financial and professional success. A commitment to great causes—like ending human trafficking, or eradicating extreme poverty, or addressing environmental hazards—can be deeply energizing. As God's image-bearers, we all have an innate attraction toward moral goodness, beauty, and justice.

Here's the problem: What is the basis of morality for such students? What makes justice just? Is there any transcendent, transcultural foundation for this sense of what ought to be? Most people in this group would acknowledge that no, there really isn't. Morality is relative and culturally specific. One group can't impose standards on others without being hegemonic. Our concepts of truth (like our religious beliefs) come from our families and our cultures. This postmodern understanding of human limitation, of our inability to see the whole picture, tends to be accepted without question.

But what if an entire culture decides that one group is inferior and unfit to live? Who are we to say that Hitler, Mao, or Stalin was wrong? After all, as popular political leaders, they were simply advancing the morality of their particular culture—they were trying to make the world a better place. The only way to say they were objectively wrong is to reference a transcendent, external, and absolute moral standard.

And the only credible source for such a standard is a deeply moral, personal God—the very concept we find in the Bible. Ideals-oriented students inevitably experience tension between the "justness" of their celebrated causes and the lack of foundation for their moral impulses. It's a tension worth graciously pointing out.

And there is a catch here. Accepting God as the foundation for objective morality requires that we also accept his verdict against immorality—all immorality, including our own. As Aleksandr Solzhenitsyn said, "The line dividing good and evil cuts through the heart of every human being."[7] Even those with the best, most noble intentions have fallen far short of God's moral standards.

Yet even here there's good news. The same God who provides the basis for morality has also provided a remedy for our immorality. He has made a way for the guilty to be made clean.

In the last section I described the paradox of success-oriented students. I said they would someday want to thank someone other than themselves and cry out for help to someone far greater. It's the same with guilt. What do you do with it? James Sire, in his classic book *The Universe Next Door*, describes the problem like this:

> In a universe where God is dead, people are not
> guilty of violating a moral law; they are only guilty
> of guilt, and that is very serious, for nothing can
> be done about it. If one had sinned, there might be

atonement. If one had broken a law, the lawmaker might forgive the criminal. But if one is only guilty of guilt, there is no way to solve the very personal problem.[8]

In other words, guilt is universal because moral awareness is inescapable. God made us that way. For Christians, our guilty consciences draw us back to the Cross, where we're reminded that our Savior paid for our sins—past, present, and future. But for those without an objective category for sin, guilt becomes a personal problem to be ignored, suppressed, or psychologically explained away. None of those options is deeply satisfying.

> The same God who provides the basis for morality has also provided a remedy for our immorality. He has made a way for the guilty to be made clean.

The Pleasure-Oriented

If the success-oriented lack deeper meaning in life and the ideals-oriented lack a basis for morality, at least the pleasure-oriented are always ready for a good time. Or so it seems. At college your teens will meet lots of partiers—those seeking to maximize enjoyment at every turn.

The stereotype of the carefree college student doesn't come from nowhere. When I went to Alfred University, the unwritten rule was that weekends started on Wednesday. The music would kick off around 8:00 p.m. and continue until at least midnight. The lifestyle is associated with a significant amount of alcohol and sexual experimentation (more so now than in my day).

The appeal of the party lifestyle is multifaceted. First, it offers a sense of belonging. Alcohol and loud music loosen inhibitions, enable relaxation, and give people an immediate, surface-level sense of community. This is especially attractive for incoming freshmen at large, secular universities, but also on smaller campuses in "college towns" (like the one where I did my undergraduate work). Alcohol has served as a social lubricant since time immemorial. Second, the bodily sensations are themselves enjoyable, not to mention addictive. Third, the party lifestyle, for some, is a celebration of freedom from the "strictness" of Mom and Dad. It feels like a step of independence. Finally, there's an aspect of immediate gratification—intense pleasure, now. And if there's pain later? Drown it out with more intense pleasure. Rinse and repeat.

Pleasure-oriented partiers don't think of themselves as holding a worldview. But the truth is they do. It's called hedonism, and it can be particularly alluring for Christian teens. It plays on our natural curiosity—*I wonder what it's like.* . . . Then there's the dimension of peer pressure, particularly if the party scene is big at that college and if the teen hasn't yet had a chance to establish closer friendships.

But let's say your teens' convictions are firm and they're not being drawn toward the party lifestyle. Partiers can seem like difficult people to engage. But the truth is that beyond the facade, this type of college student is often desperately empty and lonely. I have a friend who came to Christ his freshman year at a large university. One weekend he went to a fraternity party, got drunk to fit in, and ended up vomiting for hours. The next weekend he accepted an invitation to an InterVarsity retreat, where he enjoyed real conversations with people who were genuinely interested in him. The rest is history. Countless others have had similar experiences.

Christians can offer partiers genuine community, because the Christian message is one of grace and acceptance. God knows what we're really like, and he loves us anyway—loves us enough to have died in our place, taking our penalty upon himself. He calls us to live in submission to him, but "[his] yoke is easy, and [his] burden is light" (Matthew 11:30), because his acceptance of us isn't based on our performance; it's the basis of our performance. We want to follow the one who loved us.

CHRISTIAN TOLERANCE: TWO TEST CASES

Raising teens to hold Christian convictions and practice genuine tolerance gets uniquely tested in areas where the Bible is considerably out of step with the prevailing culture. In fact, the Bible can seem so "backward" in these areas that our teens may be tempted to completely capitulate to the culture. But if they do, they'll undermine the basis of their faith, because they'll be walking away from the authority and relevance of the Bible.

The key is to help our teens respond to catch-22 conversation starters. For example, "I heard you're a Christian. So you must think homosexuality is wrong. But isn't it obvious that God makes some people that way?" It's clear that homosexuality is acceptable to a growing number of young American adults. Among Christians, there is increasing discomfort with the topic, precisely because of these catch-22 questions.

We fall into the trap if we immediately go after the behavior, citing Scriptures that condemn same-sex relations. It's far better to start with worldview (big picture) and Creation: God made everyone in his image, but as a human race, we're fallen. Therefore, we have a variety of disordered appetites—wanting good things but wanting them too much or wanting things we shouldn't want at all. When we become Christians, we're united to Christ. He takes all our sin and shame and shares with us his righteousness and blessing. Though this happens in an instant (justification), it gets worked out over a lifetime (sanctification). None of us has fully arrived.

Can genuine Christians experience same-sex desires? They can. But our behavior should flow from our identity. Having been united with Christ, we're to submit our entire lives, including our sexuality, to Christ's lordship. We're not to see our identity as rooted in our physical desires, be they heterosexual, homosexual, or bisexual. People who do that are forming their identity around something other than God and his ways for us. They're putting themselves at the center and making their appetites the standard. The Bible calls this idolatry.

Here's another one: "Why are Christians so judgmental toward those who disagree with them? Doesn't the Bible say

Q: *Does conviction mean we* always *speak up?*

A: Classroom discussions at secular universities (and even public high schools) can be fairly one-sided. Does holding Christian convictions require that we *always* make a public defense for our faith?

I suggest that teens assess every situation independently. We're always trying to balance conviction and tolerance. A classroom discussion is only as fair as the professor allows it to be. I've seen some non-Christian professors who encourage open-minded discussions and others who were so blatantly one-sided that the most knowledgeable, respectful Christian had no way to meaningfully participate. Even Jesus walked away from some conversations (see Luke 20:1-8).

One way to engage in potentially hostile conversations is to ask questions. Questions have a way of disarming people, because everyone wants to pontificate (especially professors). Greg Koukl of Stand to Reason notes that it's helpful to conceive and ask questions that are meant to expose the other person to an inconsistency or weakness in their position.

And if your teens don't yet know enough about an issue to identify weaknesses, they can at least ask open-ended questions like "What do you mean by that?" Or, "How did you come to that conclusion?" They can listen for underlying assumptions or emotions being substituted in the place of reasons. For example, consider some atheists' statement that they "just can't stand the thought of a God knowing everything about me." The reply could be "Is that a *reason* or a *preference* for unbelief?"

not to judge others?" Mark Mittelberg does a great job of tackling this objection in his excellent book *The Questions Christians Hope No One Will Ask.*[9] As with the previous question, we need to help our teens clear the debris before jumping in. First, we can acknowledge (with sadness) that Christians are sometimes mean-spirited, judgmental, and hypocritical. But such behavior doesn't invalidate our faith. After all, the Bible accounts for both flawed and false Christians. In short, every Christian is flawed: our lives don't always match what we believe. We walk the road of repentance and with God's help get better. True, the Bible also says that some people who take the name "Christian" are actually frauds—they don't care one bit about their lifestyle matching their alleged beliefs. Still, fake Christians don't make Christianity fake.

Second, when the Bible says not to judge (see Matthew 7:1), it means we're not to have a condemning, overly critical attitude. We shouldn't rush to negative conclusions or be quick to nitpick others. It doesn't mean we're not to practice discernment (as Matthew illustrates in verse 6).

Third, some measure of judgment (the exercise of discernment) is inescapable—even for those who don't want to be judged. When people say, "Don't judge," what are *they* doing? They're judging. We can broaden this. Any normal person who thinks about anything thinks they're right about that thing. If you convinced them they were wrong, they'd change their mind. And once again they'd think they were right. Merely having a viewpoint and thinking we're correct is by no means unique to Christians.

Fourth, when our teens hear the "don't judge others" line, they should consider whether it stems from a relativist view of truth. In other words, "don't judge others, because whatever you think is only true for you." But does this perspective work in practice? If I were about to eat a piece of cake that was actually poisonous, and you knew it was poisonous, wouldn't it be the most loving thing in the world to tell me? If I objected, insisting that you not judge me, or that the cake was poisonous for you but not for me, wouldn't you think I was crazy? After all, if a piece of cake is poisonous, it's poisonous whether I believe so or not.

One last thing. Those who use the "don't judge others" line sometimes think that confidence leads to (or equals) arrogance. While some confident people are arrogant, the two don't necessarily go together. As Christians, we can be both confident *and* humble, because our confidence is in God, not ourselves. *God* gives us our reasoning skills, and *God* reveals to us objective truth in his Word. We merely submit to his rule. It would be arrogant to live under our own set of arbitrary standards.

SUMMARY

- Helping our teens own their faith before leaving home is only half the battle. The other half is training them to balance firm conviction on the essential aspects of the Christian faith with true tolerance and genuine respect toward those who differ.
- Jesus promised a measure of rejection even if we

do everything right in our engagement with non-Christians (see John 15:18-19). But our speech and behavior should not *add* offense to the inherent offense of Jesus himself.

• The Christian worldview accurately and satisfyingly explains the world around us. It tells us why we're here (Creation), what went wrong (the Fall), and why we can have hope (Redemption). It gives us a foundation for human dignity, morality, and significance. It makes sense of evil and suffering and equips us to persevere in the midst of life's hardships.

• Our teens can help their non-Christian friends see that orienting their lives around anything except God and his ways for us ultimately cannot satisfy. Those who idolize success will find that it can't sustain them in hard times. Those who live to do good in the world lack a transcendent, transcultural foundation for morality and justice apart from the personal and transcendent God of the Scriptures. And those who live for pleasure and parties will ultimately hunger for a deeper acceptance, one that only God can give.

CONVERSATION STARTERS

1. Ask your teens if their friends at school or in the neighborhood talk about things being true "for them." What do they mean by that? Can Christianity be true for some but not for others? Why or why not?

2. Ask your teens how their friends define the word *tolerance*. How would they themselves define it? Is it possible to be tolerant and still think others are wrong about something?

3. Describe for your teens the last time someone said something that really offended you, and ask them to do the same. Talk about whether the offense came from what was said, the way it was said, or the behavior of the person saying it (or some combination). Ask your teens if they can see why it might be offensive for someone to hear that Jesus is the *only* way to God. Talk about how such a message should be delivered to avoid exacerbating any offense.

4. What are the perspectives (or worldviews) out there that your teens see as the main "competitors" to Christianity? Ask your teens to describe them in their own words.

5. Ask your teens if there are any issues that come up in conversations with their friends that make them embarrassed to be Christians. Are there questions they hope nobody ever asks them? Why?

PART 3
RELATIONSHIPS

CONVERSATION 5
Helping Teens Pursue Quality Friendships

NICHOLAS HAD GREAT memories of his high school youth group. He had been a regular at the weekly meetings, the retreats, and the game nights. He had played countless hours of basketball, Ping-Pong, and foosball with Danny, Chris, and Mike. And Nicholas's parents couldn't have been happier with the youth pastor and the fact that their son had made it through high school without any significant moral lapse.

After graduation, Nicholas traveled a couple of hours away to attend a large state school. With his infectious sense of humor, the fraternity party invitations came quickly, as did a whole new crop of friends from his dorm and the Greek system. Nicholas's weekends started looking different than they had in high school. It's not like he was becoming a drug addict, but Nicholas found himself violating his conscience and then ignoring it. He had meant to join one of the campus ministries, but he didn't know anyone who'd be there. And given his late bedtimes, he ended up missing church the first couple of Sundays; after that, sleeping in and Sunday brunch became a habit.

In late October he went home for his university's mid-semester break. Mike and Chris also drove back from their colleges so they could all be together. The three enjoyed seeing even more of their old friends at church on Sunday morning, and they all went to lunch together. Driving back to school that night, Nicholas reflected on the weekend. He wondered why he didn't have friends like Mike and Chris at college. It occurred to him that for 18 years, he had never given much thought to making friends. It had always just "happened." But looking back on the last two months, Nicholas wasn't sure that was working for him anymore.

RELATIONSHIPS INFLUENCE TRAJECTORIES

Part of being created in the image of the Triune God is that we were made for community. Everybody wants to be deeply loved, known, understood, and accepted by others. We also crave affirmation and respect—recognition of our talents, abilities, and accomplishments. The goal of this chapter and the next is to equip you to be a positive influence on your teens' relationship habits—the way they form friendships, especially close ones. This will be a crucial area of their lives when they head off to college, and it's certainly important even now. This chapter is about same-sex friendships, and the next is about opposite-sex friendships (and the minefields associated with sexuality).

My wife and I approached our teens' friends (and potential friends) with a three-category system: some we encouraged (the really good ones), others we tolerated (the ones we saw as so-so), and a few we outright discouraged (the ones we saw as unhealthy and possibly dangerous). Our daughter recently said this was a helpful approach because it made her think more (*Why are my parents strongly discouraging this friendship?*) and take ownership for her decisions, rather than facing a blanket "thou shalt not" (which would have made the relationship more desirable—like forbidden fruit). Looking back, she valued having to take ownership for working within tthe relational guidelines we set.

Michael

Think back for a moment to your high school and college friendships. Many of us would say they had a dramatic impact, for better or worse, on how we turned out. Proverbs 13:20 reads, "Whoever walks with the wise becomes wise, but the companion of fools will suffer harm." I've yet to meet an exception to this rule. Psalm 1:1 talks about the blessings that come to those who do not "walk in step with the wicked or stand in the way that sinners take or sit in the company of mockers" (NIV).

Why are friendships so influential? Because they affect our values (what we believe) and our character (what we do) in profound ways—and we're most vulnerable to this in our young adult years, when the clay is still wet and our habits are still being formed. As we consider our teens, every parent I know is mindful that "bad company corrupts good character" (1 Corinthians 15:33, NIV). So how do we protect our teens while gradually letting go?

TEENS NEED HELP WITH AWARENESS

Many teens don't recognize how powerful an impact their peers, and particularly their close friends, have upon them. Like Nicholas, they go off to college and form friendships without discernment. They go with the flow, naturally gravitating toward those who are fun to be with or who have similar interests. They're not as attuned to the *character* of their friends. In the worst cases, students drift from their relationship with Jesus as they spend time almost exclusively with people who don't hold to a Christian worldview and its corresponding standards.

There's a place for true tolerance, of course, as we discussed in the last chapter. And there's a place for relational evangelism—for Christian teens modeling a biblical lifestyle and worldview, speaking grace and truth into the lives of their non-Christian friends. We are commanded to be salt and light (see Matthew 5:13-16)—but that presupposes our having the godliness, maturity, and resilience to *be* salt and light.

For that to happen for our teens, it's vital that they cultivate strong friendships with people who share their Christian convictions. I'm talking about people who can help them fight temptation, who pick them up when they're down, who encourage them to stay on the ancient, God-pleasing paths (see Jeremiah 6:16), and who help them keep the faith (see 2 Timothy 4:7). The apostle Paul had Barnabas and Titus. Even Jesus, who never sinned, had his 12 disciples, and among them, his three closest friends (Peter, James, and John). David had Jonathan, Saul's son, even before he became king. In Babylonian captivity, Daniel had Hananiah, Mishael, and Azariah. Ecclesiastes 4:9-12 says it this way:

> Two are better than one, because they have a good
> reward for their toil. For if they fall, one will lift up
> his fellow. But woe to him who is alone when he
> falls and has not another to lift him up! Again, if
> two lie together, they keep warm, but how can one

keep warm alone? And though a man might prevail against one who is alone, two will withstand him—a threefold cord is not quickly broken.

The point is that we all need friendships that make us stronger, more resilient in the face of adversity, more focused on the things that matter, more determined to put sin and foolishness away and to grow in personal holiness, and more consistent in our efforts to live a life of impact in Jesus' name. But I've found that if we're not mindful of how important this is—for all of us, not just teens—we'll end up going with the flow, having relationships based only on convenience or shared interests, and missing out on the vitality that "iron sharpening iron" relationships uniquely afford.

Our teens need to value these kinds of relationships *before* they go to college. Right now many of them are like Nicholas—coasting along on autopilot. They've got Christian parents, a church, and in many cases a network of church-based relationships, all of which are easy to take for granted. But at college they won't enjoy these supportive circumstances. If they don't value Christian relationships, there's a good chance they won't have any. Notice that Nicholas didn't join one of the campus ministries because "he didn't know anyone who'd be there." He hadn't made meeting Christians and befriending them a priority.

Worse, a lack of interest in Christian relationships can sometimes be evidence of a surface-level "faith" that won't last when the trials come (see Mark 4:1-9). Several church-raised

Q: *My son is going to a large public university next fall. How can he find fellow Christians to befriend?*

A: It's important to identify good Christian communities near campus at the college-selection stage. What does he gain by attending a well-reputed university, only to have his soul shrivel?

Evaluate potential churches online. Ask your pastors and friends for recommendations. With campus ministries, identify the leaders, speak with them, and find out what's actually happening. Online resources aren't always up to date.

Encourage him to make finding a strong group of Christian friends as quickly as possible a top priority, which means regularly attending church, taking time to meet people and make connections, and doing the same with a campus ministry. Being intentional from day one is crucial.

He has to be emotionally resilient if friendships don't form as quickly as he hoped. Loneliness is a common experience early in a freshman's first semester, and it can lead students to do things they never thought they'd do—things they later regret. Keeping busy with good things (school, sports, hobbies, and so on) can serve as an antidote for loneliness as new friendships are being formed. Phone calls home are good too—but not if they're overdone.

Finally, I'd encourage him to pray for God's leading as he seeks Christian community on campus and a new church home. God loves to bless such requests.

teens I grew up with who wandered away from their Christian relationships ended up wandering away from the faith. It makes sense; the more like-minded we are with someone, the closer we can naturally be. If the only people with whom our teens feel a deep connection don't share the faith in Christ that they *say* is important to them, it's less likely that such "faith" *is* important to them. As time passes and difficulties or new interests arise, such teens eventually move on.

It's a sobering thought, but the truth is that there really is a lot at stake in the close friendships our teens forge—in high school and especially at college.

AWARENESS PROMOTES INTENTIONALITY

The good news is that if we help our teens become aware of the significant influence that friends exert, they'll often become more intentional about who they spend time with, in what contexts, and to what extent. Even if they're already investing in Christian friendships, we want them doing so *intentionally*, rather than accidentally, so that it becomes a habit that carries over into college. We can also take the initiative to help structure the kinds of opportunities in which our teens will be more likely to establish friendships with strong, growing Christians.

In previous chapters we talked about the importance of staying involved in our teens' lives, being ready to discuss spiritual struggles, and modeling the outworking of our own faith commitment. An important aspect of this is being "quick to listen [and] slow to speak" (James 1:19, NIV). We normally think of this verse in the context of resisting anger, but it can apply equally to our tendency, particularly as parents, to preach to our teens rather than listen to them. There's a time to speak, no doubt, but it helps to first know where they're coming from. For that, we have to slow down and draw them out with open-ended questions.

Fortunately, getting teens to talk about friendships is probably easier than getting them to talk about faith. The joys and struggles of their friendships tend to bubble out naturally once they get going. We just need to have our antennae up and ask the right kinds of follow-up questions. As we listen and better understand where our teens are coming from, we can gently start to give them some principles to think about.

Our Teens Will Become like Who They Spend the Most Time With

This first principle, fully digested, may be all it takes to get them moving in the right direction. What I wish every Christ-following teen knew is that if their closest friends don't have a biblical worldview and the values and priorities that flow from that worldview, these friends are more likely to be a hindrance than a help to them. That might sound harsh, but years' worth of data show that it's inescapably true. Too many young Christians are careless in this regard. They end up drifting toward a lone-ranger model, where they're sincerely *hoping* to grow as a Christian but they're all alone in the fight. And that's both foolish and ineffective.

So what can we do, as parents, other than dialogue regularly with our sons and daughters about the state of their friendships? Recognizing that friendships tend to be forged in the crucible of shared experience, we can take creative steps to increase the likelihood that our teens will befriend strong Christian peers and mentors. That's what Joseph's dad did for him.

If your teens' closest friends don't have a biblical worldview and the values and priorities that flow from that worldview, these friends are more likely to be a hindrance than a help to them.

Joseph was an introverted and moody young freshman. His parents had just started attending a new church, and Joseph didn't really know anyone yet. Truth be told, he wasn't much of a people person. So it's no surprise that when he learned about his new church's Wednesday night youth group, he wasn't particularly interested. Joseph's dad had a few talks with him about how he might like the youth group, how it'd be a good way to meet people, and so on, but Joseph was unmoved. In the end, Dad required that Joseph attend.

Many of us would have stopped there, concluding we had done our duty. But Joseph's dad went further: he sought out an adult leader in the high school group as well as several of the older teens. He asked them to look for ways to include Joseph in conversations and activities. The adult leader began to spend time with Joseph both at the Wednesday night meetings and on other occasions, slowly earning his trust and drawing him out of his shell. Three years later, when

Joseph was a senior, he was on the group's leadership team and played piano in the worship band.

Here's the lesson: we cannot *create* friendships for our teens—only they can form true relational bonds through the interactions they initiate or to which they respond. But that doesn't mean we can't encourage opportunities for our teens to establish positive, long-lasting relationships.

The truth is that sometimes we need to step in and help our teens be intentional, even when they don't want or know how to be. Their outcome in life is at stake. None of us can sustain our faith for too long in the absence of Christian fellowship. Joseph's father helped him at what was probably a vulnerable time.

A related approach might be to open your home as often as possible for your teens to have friends over—both Christians and non-Christians. And look for ways to include them in family events. You may have to get creative, but shared time will give you a chance to get to know your teens' friends. This will inform your prayers and your private conversations with your teens about their friendship choices. (And as a bonus, the likelihood of behavioral problems goes *way* down if things are happening in your house when you're around.)

Faithfulness Is Rare and Desirable

It's interesting to see how much ink is spilled in the book of Proverbs on the value of faithfulness in friends. In Proverbs 18:24 we learn that "one who has unreliable friends soon comes to ruin, but there is a friend who sticks closer than a brother" (NIV). I can't think of a clearer statement on the importance of choosing friends wisely. And Proverbs 17:17 explains that "a friend loves at all times, and a brother is born for adversity." In both verses, faithfulness is held out as a litmus test for the quality of a friendship. Negatively, we learn that "a poor man is deserted by his friend" (Proverbs 19:4), while the rich have no shortage of fair-weather friends, each eager to get something in return (see Proverbs 14:20; 19:6). The conclusion we can draw is that faithful friends are rare and highly desirable. They're worth going out of our way to pursue.

We talked about the importance of having a future-orientation in conversation 2. It has application here, too. We should encourage our teens to consider the long-term potential of their friendships. Some of your teens' relationships are by nature short-term. Their connection is tenuous, rooted purely in shared circumstances (such as being lab partners in biology). They'll part ways eventually—and that's okay. It's not necessarily a reflection on either person's character. I would put fair-weather friends in a different category. These are often the partiers, the ones who entice your teens to join in the good times but won't be there for them in the bad. That *is* a reflection on their character. You can spot this kind a mile away by their shallow, superficial interest in your teens.

My point is that our teens should not allow either type of friend (short-term or fair-weather) to monopolize too much of their relationship time. If that happens, it will infringe on their ability to form long-term, substantive, "iron-sharpening-iron" friendships of the kind previously described.

Technology and Friendship

Social media and cell phones have made it easier than ever for teens to stay in touch with each other, even after they graduate high school and start attending different colleges. One drawback, however, is that it's easy to be a mile wide and an inch deep in relationships: a teen can have a thousand Facebook "friends," few of whom know how they're actually doing. The truth is that real friendships take work, work takes time, and nobody gets more than 24 hours in a day. Therefore, while some of us have a greater relational capacity than others (for example, extroverts vs. introverts), we all face natural limits with regard to maintaining friendships.

There also seems to be a biblical priority with regard to cultivating friendships in geographic proximity (Proverbs 27:10: "Better is a neighbor who is near than a brother who is far away"), which argues for college students being invested where they are rather than continuously keeping in touch with their old friends who are now elsewhere. The loneliest college freshmen are often the ones spending the most time on Facebook.

Only a Few Friendships Last

Teens haven't lived long enough to know this, but we have. High school and college go by quickly, and in the end, there are really only a few people we'll be able to keep in touch with in a regular, significant way (not counting social media). Think back to your high school and college days. How many of those friendships could you call upon if you lost your job, were diagnosed with cancer, or were going through some difficult season and just wanted someone to talk to? If you're like most of us, it's probably only a few people.

If teens don't invest in their Christian friendships now, apart from depriving themselves of these friends' positive influence, will they really be able to grab the phone and call them five years from now when they need help? It's only the friendships we invest in now that have any chance of being there for us later. So encourage your teens to look around and think about it. Who might be a good investment, not just today, but for the long haul? Once they identify a few people like that, they should take the time to strengthen those friendships now, before they spread out for college.

CHARACTER QUALITIES TEENS SHOULD SEEK (AND DEVELOP)

We've said that teens will become like those they spend time with and that they should prioritize faithfulness and relationships with good long-term potential. What other character qualities should they be looking for in friends and seeking to develop in their own lives?

Truthful

Proverbs 27:6 tells us, "Faithful are the wounds of a friend, but deceitful are the kisses of an enemy" (NASB). Elsewhere we read, "A man who flatters his neighbor spreads a net for his feet" (Proverbs 29:5). A friend speaks the truth that will help us in the long run, even if it causes us pain today. An enemy tells us what we want to hear now, even if our remaining ignorant of the truth causes us more pain later. Imagine a doctor who is too chicken to say you have cancer. That's just the kind of cowardice our teens need to avoid in close friendships.

The best friends are those who have a higher agenda than continuously needing our affirmation. Needy people easily become flattering people—they're more interested in themselves and in what we think of them than in actually serving us with the truth. Teach your teens to look for earnest, truth-telling friends, whose counsel is reliable in good times and bad, who aren't afraid to say what needs to be said, even if it stings.

Encouraging

The above notwithstanding, you wouldn't want your teens forming close friendships with those who regularly left them discouraged. Even if a painful truth must be shared, it should be done in love, with the goal of building up, not tearing down. Proverbs 18:21 tells us, "Death and life are in the power of the tongue." The apostle Paul wanted to see the Romans so that they could be "mutually encouraged by each other's faith" (Romans 1:11-12). Thankfully, this quality is relatively easy to detect. Teens generally know encouragers because they leave their presence looking forward to the next time they'll be together. These kinds of people are relational magnets.

Challenging

Proverbs 27:17's "Iron sharpens iron . . ." reminds us that good friends make us stronger for the inevitable hardships and adversities of life. Their encouragement has the effect not of leaving us where we are but of helping us rise to the next level. Our teens should stay clear of the kind of empty encouragement that allows them to wallow in excuse-making rather than follow missionary William Carey's admonition to "expect great things from God and attempt great things for God."

For teens, older friends can do this marvelously—even people just one or two years older. And there's no reason teens cannot seek relationships with much older people of the same gender (coaches, youth ministry leaders, teachers, choir directors, and so on). Teens won't be able to spend as much one-on-one time with a coach as they would with a classmate, but the interactions can still be highly impactful.

I'm talking about a mentoring relationship, but it doesn't

have to be formal, with regular meeting times and the like. Teens benefit tremendously from informal mentoring friendships, assuming they have the maturity and wisdom to appropriately maintain them. Parents, it's worth taking the initiative to expose your teens to these kinds of opportunities. The other benefit is that with a modicum of effort on your teens' part, these relationships can often be sustained during the college years (when they're home on breaks), because unlike your teens' peers, their potential mentors are probably not leaving town.

Responsible

Because assuming responsibility is such an important aspect of embracing the mantle of adulthood (see conversation 2), we need to help our teens be drawn to disciplined, conscientious, responsible friends. Teens with slacker friends will think it's normal to be a slacker. Lazy, undisciplined, excuse-making, commitment-breaking friends will not have a helpful impact on your child. Colleges don't ask merely for GPAs and test scores but also for lists of activities and leadership roles precisely because they want to know how applicants shoulder their various duties and what kinds of endeavors they successfully undertake. The latter often tell them more about students than their test scores. Brilliant but lazy students bomb out of college more frequently than hardworking students with average ACT or SAT scores.

The ability of a 16- or 17-year-old to manage a schedule and stay on top of a wide variety of duties says a lot about

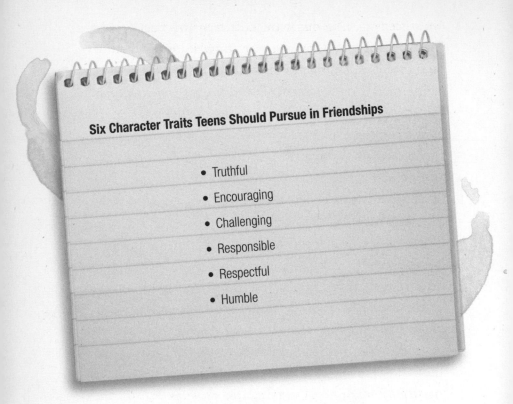

Six Character Traits Teens Should Pursue in Friendships

- Truthful
- Encouraging
- Challenging
- Responsible
- Respectful
- Humble

them. You've probably heard the old phrase "If you want something done, give it to a busy person." No matter how much they already have on their plates, busy people often know how to handle one more thing. The assumption here is that the busy person is fruitful and dependable—busy with useful activities. Every teen today *claims* to be busy, but it's sometimes a silly kind of busy—a kind that doesn't have much in the way of productivity to show for it. Encourage your teens to hang out with other teens who believe in getting their chores done, keeping up with their schoolwork, and excelling in extracurricular activities as a means of honoring God, helping others, and developing their potential. Too much idle time is often a teen's worst enemy. Your teens will not rise above their close friends in this area. It's critical.

Respectful

Though teens are not often known for their etiquette, respectful teens are certainly possible. Look for the way teens speak to those around them, particularly those in authority. Look for the way they listen. Look for tact, discretion, self-control, and a genuine interest in others.

Respectful teens don't expect to exchange text messages at 2:00 a.m., nor do they pressure others to violate their consciences. They don't leave an earbud stuck in when others are around or senselessly stare at their cell phones in the middle of conversations. And they're able to speak complete sentences of coherent English.

Look for respecting relational boundaries, which is particularly important in friendships where there are unequal levels of interest. Suppose Ashley really would enjoy spending more time with Jessica, but Jessica rarely wants to get together with Ashley. Ashley is frustrated: *Why is Jessica always so busy?* And Jessica is annoyed: *Why does Ashley bug me so much?*

We should help our teens understand that the person who wants the relationship less has more power. The challenge for Jessica is to be gracious (rather than rude) and to be principled (rather than manipulated by guilt). Jessica should not feel obligated to spend time with Ashley every time she calls. She must learn how to politely say no (a skill that will come in handy with unwanted suitors).

Ashley's challenge is more difficult. Proverbs 25:17 reads, "Let your foot be seldom in your neighbor's house, lest he have his fill of you and hate you." Ashley needs to understand that even if Jessica likes her, Ashley may be driving her away. She needs to give Jessica space and the chance to reciprocate. A friendship cannot move faster than the pace of the less interested party. If Ashley is always calling Jessica, she needs to stop and give Jessica a chance to call her.

A friendship cannot move faster than the pace of the less interested party.

True friendships can never be forced. All we can do is seek to serve the other person, to present a part of ourselves that would encourage, help, or attract them. If we're constantly striving to *get* instead of *give*, we'll wind up disappointed.

Humble

Self-obsession may be the defining characteristic of the young adult culture our teens are entering. From TV protagonists, to popular musicians, to star athletes, being "real" has come to mean self-promotion, insensitivity, and vulgarity. Many young adults have become accustomed to a new level of crassness in communication, perhaps exacerbated by social media, which make everyone the manager of their own "brand." From leaving obnoxious comments on blogs to regularly broadcasting pictures and videos of themselves, teens everywhere are learning to seek social validation from the applause of others. It's as if we're all the next American Idol.

This culture teaches our teens to emote, gossip, brag, flaunt, spew venom, shock with profanity, and insist upon their wishes—all of which feed the ego. We lavish praise on charismatic extroverts who command the admiration of a wide following, apart from whether their character and private lives are worthy of admiration. Even when extroverted young adults become powerful, articulate communicators, they often employ such skills in the service of self rather than the edification of others. In short, humility is rare.

Teach your teens to fight self-absorption and to distance themselves from those gripped by arrogance, even if they're popular. As pastor Tim Keller has explained, true humility is not thinking less of ourselves but thinking of ourselves less. It's being free to not connect every conversation and event back to ourselves. We can model this for our teens by inviting them to our social gatherings, where they (hopefully) will see positive examples of others-oriented adults. In fact, if teens simply learn to ask good questions and listen, they'll be well on their way to thinking less about themselves and becoming more humble people (and more interesting conversationalists).[1]

Summing up, we need to help our teens understand that they will invariably develop the character traits of those with whom they spend the most time. If they want to become faithful, truthful, encouraging, appropriately challenging, responsible, respectful, and humble men and women, they should pursue others who are on that same journey. But there's another danger they need to overcome if they're going to make wise, deliberate relational decisions. And it can be especially pernicious in our day. I'm referring to the lure of the crowd—peer pressure.

THE ALLURE OF PEER PRESSURE

Peer pressure is the stress people experience to do or say certain things in order to be liked, accepted, admired, or respected. The stress can be *actual*—"Oh, come on, taste a few sips of whiskey! Everyone else is having some!"—or perceived, as in the case where a teenage girl believes her friends will think she's mad at them if she doesn't respond to a text message right away. Whether it's actual or perceived, the experience of pressure is just as real.

Peer pressure can be alluring. A dare to drive 80 miles an hour down the freeway or to try marijuana—these kinds of invitations can be intrinsically desirable from a thrill-seeking perspective. But there's also a relational angle. The temptation is to come do it *with the rest of us*. Even the girl who feels the need to respond instantly to her friends' texts is feeling this; she doesn't want to miss out on the acceptance and inclusion of her circle of friends, whenever such inclusion might be offered. So peer pressure can be a strangely honoring experience—especially to the extent that it's coming from people teens admire and from whom they desire affirmation.

Here's the upshot: the more I need you to like me, the

greater the power you'll have over me. Your son will feel more pressure (perceived or actual) if it's coming from a group of teens that includes the cute girl he has a crush on. He'll feel less pressure if it's coming from a nondescript bunch of younger teens (which is why juniors rarely feel peer pressure from freshmen—they don't admire or look up to them).

Being sympathetic listeners is essential to staying in our teens' relational lives. If we do, we'll win their trust and gain moral authority (see conversation 1). We'll be better listeners if we recognize that teens are particularly susceptible to peer pressure, for at least the following reasons.

Their Reputation Is Continuously in Flux

Many teens are regarded as "moody"—they're flying high one day, in the depths of despair the next. Sure, hormones may be doing a number on them. But teens are also bombarded with feedback from those around them (actual and perceived), which varies by the day and affects their level of confidence during the pivotal years when they're transitioning from childhood into adulthood. It could be anything: last night's exchanges on Facebook, unflattering comments shared in their presence over lunch, not being invited to an event to which others were invited, how well or poorly they're doing on a sports team, or whether their friends are outperforming them academically. The vicissitudes of teen life are many and complex. We need to anticipate that our teens will experience these ups and downs and then be there to share their joys and sorrows.

Because teens are coming to know themselves as young adults, separating from their parents, and establishing their own identities, you'll sometimes see them want to try things. Your son might want to grow his hair long. Your daughter might want to color her hair or get a henna tattoo. Every household will decide where to draw the lines—just understand that these interests are often nothing more than passing fads to see how it feels or how others react. It may have nothing to do with peer pressure or overt rebellion. Evaluate each case individually. I suggest taking the long view and picking your battles wisely. Recognize that overreacting can cost you more than you might gain.

It *Is* a Big Deal—For Them

A teen's perception of time's passing is different from ours. Any chunk of time (a year, a month) seems longer to someone who hasn't lived as long. While our children seem to grow up so quickly, for them it feels like a drawn-out process. One result is that things that seem minor to us can have *huge* significance for them. A disagreement with a friend can make your teens feel like their life is over. We know that "this too shall pass"—but they don't yet know that, because they haven't lived long enough to see these things pass. We're tempted to chide our teens for being overdramatic, and there may be truth to such claims, but if we're going to be sympathetic listeners, we need to resist making them feel invalidated.

What Is Cyberbullying?

A word must be said on the rise of "cyberbullying"—the practice of one teen intimidating, taunting, humiliating, threatening, or harassing another teen via the Internet, interactive and digital technologies, or mobile phones. In extreme cases some teens (particularly females) have even committed suicide after being the victims of cyberbullying. Sadly, cyberbullying has become so common that school districts have initiated campaigns to stop it, both at the middle school and high school levels. Some are advocating that children less than 10 years old receive online etiquette instruction.

What drives this kind of viciousness? Part of the problem is that it's easy to type out the most vile insults on a keyboard (or cell phone) when we don't have to look at the other person—particularly if we can do so with total anonymity. Sometimes it's premeditated; other times it's an impetuous reaction. Sometimes the cyberbullies are a teen's "friends" who later act as if it was all a joke.

Our teens need parental involvement in both their actual lives and their virtual lives. If they aren't ready to live on their own, why would we allow them to create a secret parallel life online? Stay connected with what your teens are doing with their cell phones, Facebook profiles, and the like. Their safety and emotional well-being may depend on it.

I had a friend growing up whose dad used to tell him that his life wasn't a piece of cake, it was the whole cake. I'm sure his dad's motives were good. He wanted to boost his son's confidence, to get him to say, "This is no sweat; I can handle it." And sure, compared to his dad's, my friend's struggles were minor. But your teens don't yet have fortysomething years of life experience to draw upon. So don't minimize their trials, but don't solve their problems for them either. The former will make them feel weak; the latter will ensure they stay weak. Instead, come alongside them and strengthen them for the challenges they must face—the challenges that will develop them into resilient men and women.

INORDINATE DESIRES STRENGTHEN PEER PRESSURE

We've spelled out a few reasons why peer pressure can be particularly strong among teens. Now let's explore what's really happening in peer pressure at a foundational level and why it can cause such a powerful downward spiral. There's nothing wrong with wanting others to love and affirm us—that's perfectly normal, as is the pain that accompanies rejection. The problems start when our legitimate desires for love and affirmation rise to the level of ultimate "needs," as sometimes happens for our teens (or for anyone, really).

For one, it makes people more likely to violate their consciences. If Lauren desperately fears the rejection of her girlfriends, and they're all planning to sneak into an R-rated movie, it will be tougher for her to say no. What's happening? Her intense fear of rejection and her overwhelming desire for her friends' acceptance are effectively putting her on a performance treadmill. Lauren feels obliged to keep acting in certain ways lest she lose the approval of her friends. Moreover, to keep their approval, she hides things from them (like her convictions about sneaking into movies). But those acts of hiding leave her feeling isolated and lonely—deprived, ironically, of the love and acceptance she desperately wanted.

It gets worse. Not only does Lauren's hiding and need for approval make her less able to experience friendship from others, it makes her less able to give friendship to others. Because when Lauren's desire for love and acceptance becomes the center of her life, it makes *her* the center of her life.[2]

Don't minimize your teens' trials, but don't solve their problems for them either. The former will make them feel weak; the latter will ensure they stay weak.

So that's the dragon that must be slain—and it's a lifelong battle. Who among us never feels this tension? Wanting praise and affirmation more than we should, distorting our priorities in order to get them—these are things with which we all struggle. So how can we help weaken the power of peer pressure in the lives of our teens?

Peer pressure feeds on inordinate desires—healthy desires for love and acceptance that become all-consuming cravings. Decrease the cravings, and you deflate peer pressure. So how do we do that? By helping our teens find their identity in who they are in Jesus Christ, as blood-bought children of God. By helping them focus on God and pleasing him rather than always thinking about themselves and how others are reacting to them. We can do this by helping our teens own their faith and grow in their relationship with Jesus.

But we can also weaken peer pressure by building strong relational bonds with our teens while modeling the character of God the Father to them. As teens sense that their parents love them unconditionally and are coaching them into adulthood, and as the parent-child relationship grows and strengthens, teens feel less need to win and maintain the affection of their peers. As a result they become more discriminating in their choice of friendships and in what they're willing to do with peers.

Our children's first conception of what God is like will come from us (particularly dads). If we model righteousness and goodness, along with love, warmth, and acceptance, our teens will learn that God is like that. If we push them away when they fall short, they'll conclude that God's acceptance of them is performance based, and they'll find it unnatural to be secure in his love.

I still remember from my high school days how this principle played out, family by family. Those friends of mine who came from loving, secure homes—where their parents had not only raised them to love and know Jesus but had showered love and acceptance on them—were usually the most immune to the passing fancies of the "in" crowd.

But if their parents had not modeled the fatherhood of God, if they didn't have a strong relationship with their parents based on Mom and Dad's love and acceptance, they were more susceptible to the whims of peer pressure. This principle is crucial in the area of sexual purity, the subject of our next chapter.

SUMMARY

- Many teens don't consider the moral influence of prospective friends, yet our teens' friendships affect their values and character, for better or worse.
- Faithful friends are particularly crucial because they're more likely to be there for our teens in the tough times and because those friendships are more likely to stand the test of time.
- Our teens should seek out friends who are truthful, encouraging, challenging, responsible, respectful, and humble. And they should seek (with God's help) to develop these attributes in their own lives.
- Peer pressure can be intense for our teens, because they're transitioning from childhood to adulthood. Their reputation and sense of self-worth are constantly in flux, creating occasional (if not frequent) insecurity. We must be understanding and sympathetic listeners, even as we seek to speak truth into their lives.
- We must weaken peer pressure by helping our teens find their identity in Christ as blood-bought children of God and by modeling the character, grace, and unconditional love of God the Father.

CONVERSATION STARTERS

1. Examine your own adult friendships and the interactions of those friends with your children. Ask your teens how they feel about your family's friends.

2. Share with your teens how your high school and college friends made a difference in your life—in how you turned out, for good or for bad. Tell them if there's anything with regard to friendships that you'd do differently if you could do it over again.

3. Ask your teens to identify their top five friends and why they like them so much. Look for opportunities to talk about the character qualities mentioned in this chapter (faithful, truthful, encouraging, challenging, responsible, respectful, and humble).

4. Read some of the passages cited in this chapter with your teen—Psalm 1:1; Proverbs 13:20; 27:17; Ecclesiastes 4:9-12; 1 Corinthians 15:33. See if they're able and willing to talk about the impact that their close friends have upon them. Do their friends encourage their faith in Christ or make it harder? Do they motivate them in their schoolwork or distract them? Do they help one another move beyond childish ways, or do they reinforce immaturity in one another? Discuss.

5. Ask your teens if there's ever been a time when their friends have been a negative influence or encouraged them to compromise their standards. Assure your

teens that you aren't looking to get anyone in trouble but that you want to be there for them, to support and help them, because a sullied conscience is often God's warning. Ask them if there's anything in their lives that you should know about. (You may not get anything profound, but saying this once in a while helps maintain open lines of communication. The goal is for them to feel it's safe to talk to you if and when something challenging does come up.)

CONVERSATION 6
Helping Teens Pursue Purity

FOR MOST TEENS, going away to college will be the first time they live for an extended time in close proximity to a large number of available and attractive members of the opposite sex. On the one hand, college can be a great opportunity for them to meet quality, godly men and women, maybe even someone with whom they can spend the rest of their lives. Perhaps that's what happened for you. On the other hand, it can be a minefield of temptation, a place where romantic and even sexual bonds can be readily and carelessly forged. Such bonds often prove difficult to sever and can spin teens' lives in a decidedly negative direction.

A book on *Preparing Your Teens for College* would be

woefully incomplete without a discussion of how to prepare teens for the opportunities and potential pitfalls of opposite-sex relationships in college. As with same-sex friendships, if our teens develop the right habits while in our homes, they're much more likely to practice them at college, where the dangers are greater and the stakes higher. So how do we get them ready? By being their friends and guides through the confusing experience of puberty and all that comes with it.

STAYING PURE IS GETTING HARDER

My parents were wonderful and involved in many ways, but I don't recall having "the talk." Maybe that was your experience too. If so, please don't let the same thing happen with your kids. I guarantee you that the culture around us has made purity much more challenging. There's raunchy prime-time television, sexual content in popular music lyrics and even PG-13 movies, and online pornography available 24-7 on Internet-connected devices, including cell phones. Teens today have more privacy and anonymity, as well as an ability to contact more people in more ways, than ever before in history. Many are texting each other flirtatious messages accompanied by sexually explicit images (a trend known as *sexting*). And video games have come a long way since *Pac-Man*, *Donkey Kong*, and *Super Mario Brothers*. In 2004, researchers found that half of teen-rated games had sexual overtones (suggesting the games were misclassified).[1] In September 2013, *Grand Theft Auto V*, a game featuring graphic sex and torture, exceeded one billion dollars in worldwide sales in its first three days on the market.[2] For girls, there are Bratz dolls and product lines of immodest clothing designed to teach them to show off their bodies from a disturbingly early age.

Here's a more subtle influence. Once upon a time, the divorce rate was low, and teens grew up with their biological mothers and fathers, who were married to each other. Not that all was idyllic, but people generally grew up with positive views of marriage, and the societal expectation was that sex and marriage went together. The '60s and '70s shook up these associations, and people raised in that era are now shaping the culture through media channels, in higher education, and as parents. As I write, an estimated 15 million children (one in three) live without a father, and another five million live without a mother.[3] For women under 30, the *majority* of births now occur outside marriage.[4] When a child today is raised by a single mother, there's a really good chance that the mother is not divorced but has simply never married.[5]

The sad truth is that, on average, children who grow up in such homes have greater developmental and psychological problems, including a higher incidence of teen pregnancy.[6] They grow up more likely to cohabit than marry.[7]

If you're a single parent, please understand that I don't mean to heap any extra sorrow upon you. You've got an amazingly difficult task, and we—the church—should be doing all we can to support you. The trends I cite here are for the general population. Any explicitly Christian child-raising efforts on your part *will* make a huge difference in the outcome of your child.

Young adults today are not as marriage oriented as they used to be. They *want* to marry—someday. But more of them are reasoning, "I need to finish college, of course, and then I need to pay off my loans. I may need to go to grad school. It'll be a while before I can settle down and marry." Older Christian teens are increasingly taking this perspective as well, with fewer of them expecting or even *hoping* to meet their spouse in college than in previous years. They see marriage as far off in the distance. Until then, true love waits, they've been told. Unfortunately, with the onset of puberty occurring earlier and marriage coming later, sex often won't. You probably know that sexual activity before marriage is now the norm among young adults, including college students. The sad truth is that far too many Christians are participating.[8]

Wait . . . why am I even talking about *marriage*? They haven't even gone to college yet! Here's why: the teen years involve coming to know ourselves as sexual beings, with desires for physical and emotional intimacy. And unless teens learn to associate their natural desires for intimacy with God's gift of marriage, they're likely to express their sexuality outside marriage. Think about it. Does our culture associate sexuality with marriage? Emphatically not. Those of us seeking to raise our teens to esteem purity and self-control in their college years have less societal support than in previous generations. We must step up our game if we're going to train our teens to swim against the cultural tide, to think differently—to think biblically—about sex and marriage, namely, that God designed them to go together, both for our good and for his glory.

> *Unless teens learn to associate their natural desires for intimacy with God's gift of marriage, they're likely to express their sexuality outside marriage.*

Let's look at how we can best serve our teens, because it may look different from how our parents guided us.

ONE AWKWARD MONOLOGUE, OR AN ONGOING DIALOGUE?

Perhaps you recall the awkward moment when your mother or father told you about "the birds and the bees." There's a stereotypical expectation out there that parents are supposed to give their teens or preteens a one-time explanation of all that comes with puberty. Perhaps it's right around the corner, or it has just arrived, and we're sweating bullets just like they are, only for different reasons. It's a conversation many parents don't know how to start, and one that both participants are often eager to end. Some of you may be putting it off right now.

But the metamorphosis of puberty requires much more than a one-time information dump—though even that, done well, is probably better than nothing. What I have in mind by "the conversation" (as opposed to "the talk") is the first of a series of dialogues about the changes in their bodies *and* their minds (their new thoughts, feelings, desires, and

Helping Our Teens Overcome Pornography

The need to talk with our teens about their sexuality is heightened by the fact that the average age of first Internet exposure to pornography is 11. While early exposure tends to be accidental, as teens age, most find that their new sexual interests prompt them to seek illicit material online or from peers. The Internet can be a cesspool of unspeakable filth waiting to drown our children. We dare not be naive about this.

Christian teens may be particularly reluctant to acknowledge this attraction or to admit any missteps with their parents. A sense of shame, a desire not to disappoint, or a fear of consequences holds them back. So it's imperative that we initiate the conversation with them, ideally before temptations come their way. Our teens must know that although the immediate thrill of indulgence is real, the scarring and addictive effects are even more real. Porn radically distorts our understanding of intimacy. It turns us inward, robbing us of the capacity to love.

Here are a few resources that might equip you to engage your teens about lust, pornography, and how to get free and stay free:

1. Heath Lambert, *Finally Free: Fighting for Purity with the Power of Grace* (Grand Rapids, MI: Zondervan, 2013).

2. Joshua Harris, *Sex Is Not the Problem (Lust Is): Sexual Purity in a Lust-Saturated World* (Sisters, OR: Multnomah, 2005).

3. Randy Alcorn, *The Purity Principle: God's Safeguards for Life's Dangerous Trails* (Sisters, OR: Multnomah, 2005).

temptations). The truth is that many teens really want to be having these conversations with their parents. And done correctly, they can profoundly strengthen the father-son, mother-daughter relationship, serving as a vital means of preparing your children for their future marriages. Moms, your daughters need to know that what may seem like innocent flirtation can lead to much more. Likewise, your sons need to be aware of what signals they're sending. Dads, your daughters need the security that comes from a strong relationship with you, and your sons need guidance in controlling their newly discovered yet powerful impulses.

It may take some work to get them talking, of course. I once read a man's story of how he went to have an initial conversation on this subject with his son. They went to Burger King, and he picked a booth in a private section of the restaurant so they wouldn't be overheard. He began with an open-ended question and received silence by way of reply. He asked another question. Again, silence. Finally he asked, "Okay, what do you already know?" Dad started drawing sketches on a napkin and began using anatomical, gritty language to show his own knowledge, wooing his son into a mini-battle of the minds. His son finally recognized that Dad meant business and really knew what he was talking about. An open dialogue finally ensued.

Breaking the ice on this sensitive subject can be a frightening proposition, but here's the truth: if we don't talk to our teens, others will—friends, TV shows, popular music, and the Internet. And we won't always like what those other sources have to say. Much of it will be morally perverse, and some of it may be scientifically false. So we might as well get out in front of this thing before other voices fill the gap. If you don't know all the facts or can't answer all the questions, find answers from medically reliable sources.[9]

But let me encourage you. The biblical message on this subject is ultimately quite straightforward—difficult to practice at times, but refreshingly clear: our sexuality is a wonderful gift of God. It was made to initiate and sustain a comprehensive union between a man and a woman, a union that is meant to reflect the spiritual union God wants to have with his people. Therefore, it must be enjoyed only within the lifelong bond of marriage. Anything else is a misuse of God's gift and a distortion of the message sex was intended to convey.

As with everything else, it's important that we also listen to our teens, taking seriously their questions and concerns. And as illustrated above, you may find that your kids have already heard more about this topic than you and I had 20 or 30 years ago. But they still need us. We've lived well past adolescence; they haven't. We're a reliable source of information; their friends and the Internet aren't. We need not fear this issue. God invented human sexuality, and he knows how it works best. God is not a killjoy, out to rob us of bodily pleasures. No, his commands are designed to *maximize* our joy while protecting us from needless pain.

But since this is a book on preparing your teens for college, many of you may have long since started "the conversation."

Perhaps your children are planning to move out within the year. What must we impart before they leave our homes?

A BIBLICAL UNDERSTANDING OF SEX

Our teens need to have a biblical understanding of sex in order to navigate the challenges that await them in college. For starters, let's define the term, not on an anatomical level but at a foundational level. Here's how pastor and author Tim Keller puts it:

> Sex is perhaps the most powerful God-created way to help you give your entire self to another human being. Sex is God's appointed way for two people to reciprocally say to one another, "I belong completely, permanently, and exclusively to you."[10]

And that's true. But Keller (and the Bible) would go a step further. Sex is a physical picture of a spiritual reality: God wants to dwell among and deeply know his people. God invented sex not just to propagate the human race and to give us enjoyment but to be a picture of the salvation story—Jesus Christ laying down his life for us (his bride) to bring us back to God (see Ephesians 5:25-27; 1 Peter 3:18). Gerald Hiestand and Jay Thomas say it well:

> God created sex to serve as a living portrait of the life-changing spiritual union that believers have with God through Christ. . . . God created the physical

oneness of sex to serve as a visible image, or type, of the spiritual union that exists between Christ and the church.[11]

At stake in our sexuality is nothing less than our representation of Jesus Christ's relationship with those who follow him.

Maybe you're saying, "This all sounds great for an adult Sunday school class, but is it really *practical* to explain this to our teens?" While I wouldn't expect the same level of interest from a 12- or 13-year-old as from a 17- or 18-year-old, I do believe teens need a big-picture perspective on what sexual intimacy represents if they're going to win the battle for purity in college and throughout their adult lives. And a biblical understanding of sex is the best antidote to the culture's sexual lies. Our culture believes that sex is all about *me*. *My* desires. *My* satisfaction. It's about using others, not serving them. But the Bible tells us that sex is all about God and his glorious work in bringing us into relationship with him. In the context of marriage, sex is about giving ourselves to serve our spouse (see 1 Corinthians 7:3-5).

A BIBLICAL MOTIVATION FOR PURITY

A biblical understanding of sex leads to a biblical *motivation* for abstaining until marriage. I fear that sometimes we motivate teens to sexual purity in small, even worldly ways, rather than in big, biblical ways. I have friends who grew up in Bible-believing churches that faithfully preached chastity, but the rationale was "Hey, you wouldn't want to get pregnant, or get someone pregnant, or contract a sexually transmitted disease (STD). And watch out for those condoms! They're not as effective as your health teacher says they are."

The problem is it's assumed that teens know that sex before marriage is a sin and little to no explanation is given as to *why* it's a sin. Of course, we should want our teens to avoid out-of-wedlock pregnancies and STDs, but neither of these is an explicitly Christian goal. You don't have to believe the Bible to want to avoid those things. Moreover, this argument doesn't confront the cultural lie that sex is all about self.

Flee from sexual immorality. Every other sin a person commits is outside the body, but the sexually immoral person sins against his own body. Or do you not know that your body is a temple of the Holy Spirit within you, whom you have from God? You are not your own, for you were bought with a price. So glorify God in your body.

—I CORINTHIANS 6:18-20

If our teens know something about how human sexuality is meant to represent the permanent, spiritual union between Jesus Christ and his bride, it gives meaning and motivation to the prohibition on sex outside of marriage. Sexual intimacy in any context besides marriage dishonors God by telling a lie about how Jesus Christ relates to his people. And it massively disrupts our relationship with God (see 1 Corinthians 6:12-20). In contrast, the fear of the Lord teaches us to hate all evil (see Proverbs 8:13), to abstain from sexual immorality (see 1 Thessalonians 4:3-7), and to be holy because God is holy (see 1 Peter 1:13-16).

Once our teens understand what sex is, what it represents, and why it must be reserved for marriage, they'll be better able to understand that there is a whole range of behaviors that are sexual in nature and that therefore must all be reserved for marriage. I fear it's too easy for those with small, worldly motives for "staying pure" to cut corners, focusing on how close they can get to the edge without falling off. For example, ministry leaders in Christian college settings will confirm that a significant number of professing Christian students (like their non-Christian counterparts) do not consider oral sex to be sex. Why not? Because it doesn't fit their overly narrow definition of "sex."

But if they had a more comprehensive understanding— one rooted in the perspective summarized above—they would see that of course oral sex is sex. It's the giving of oneself to another person in an incredibly intimate way. Likewise, a lot of other physical acts would fall into this category.

Which leads us to the age-old question Christian teens and singles ask: How far is too far before marriage?

AN OBJECTIVE STANDARD FOR PURITY

Growing up, many of us were taught that since dating didn't happen in biblical times, it's up to us to determine the physical limits of our premarital relationships. We should be careful, we were told, because one thing could lead to another, and things could quickly get out of hand. But what few dared to answer was this: Even if we exercise self-control, what things (if any), besides intercourse, are automatically off the table?

Thankfully, God has not been silent on this sensitive subject. Consider two key passages:

> For this is the will of God, your sanctification:
> that you abstain from sexual immorality; that
> each one of you know how to control his own
> body in holiness and honor, not in the passion
> of lust like the Gentiles who do not know God.
> (1 Thessalonians 4:3-5)

> I wish that all were as I myself am. But each has
> his own gift from God, one of one kind and one of
> another. To the unmarried and the widows I say that
> it is good for them to remain single as I am. But if
> they cannot exercise self-control, they should marry.
> For it is better to marry than to burn with passion.
> (1 Corinthians 7:7-9)

The first passage teaches that we're to abstain from sexual immorality by controlling our bodies. The second teaches that those who cannot exercise such self-control ought to get a girlfriend or boyfriend. Wait—it says they ought to *marry*. The implication is that *all* sexual activity belongs only in marriage (see also 1 Corinthians 6:18-20).

"But what constitutes sexual activity?" our teens will ask. If it's too intimate to do now with your sister or brother, it's sexual. If it's too intimate to do 10 years from now with this person if he or she is married to someone else, it's sexual. Why? Because the Bible doesn't distinguish between a biological family member and a person who isn't your spouse. What's improper with one is improper with the other. In fact, 1 Timothy 5:2 connects the two groups: "Treat older women as you would your mother, and treat younger women with all purity as you would your own sisters" (NLT). Everything sexual belongs to your spouse.

Everything sexual belongs to your spouse.

But your teen might ask, "Isn't that legalism?" We should anticipate this response. Many Christian teens will recognize that "getting physical" with someone they don't really know is pure lust and clearly wrong. If they struggle at this point, remind them of 1 Corinthians 6:12-20, the forgiveness available in Christ, and that their past behavior need not determine their future. For others, the clear line of purity gets fuzzy when they develop a mutual attraction. Maybe they agree to be "exclusive," to be boyfriend and girlfriend. They begin to see this other person as "special"—more than a friend but less than a spouse. So things get a bit physical (i.e., sexual), but they tell themselves, *It's not like we're having sex, Things aren't getting out of hand,* and *We know when we need to stop.* And they tell others, "Don't judge us—you don't understand." (As if we never lived through those years.)

Teach your teens what's wrong with this logic before

they're in the throes of temptation and every ounce of their being wants to believe they have the right to decide "how far is too far." The idea that Christians are allowed to set their own sexual standards, as long as they accomplish the goal of avoiding intercourse, is dangerous and misleading.

It's dangerous because it often fails—we step too close to the fire and get burned. But it's also misleading. Let's say a teen thinks he can make out with his girlfriend for a few minutes because they're able to stop and go no further. *We're controlling ourselves*, he thinks. But that's the wrong mind-set. What he should ask is whether the activity is sexual in nature. If it is, it's inappropriate (i.e., sinful)—*even if it doesn't lead to anything further*. Sexual acts are not just wrong because of what they might lead to; they are wrong in and of themselves when they occur outside marital relationships. Because everything sexual belongs to your spouse.[12]

This is not legalism. It liberates our teens from being captive to their own subjective standards, which can be profoundly flawed, especially in the heat of the moment. And we can really help them as parents, because if you're married, I'd imagine that the boundaries of propriety toward other women or men are pretty clear for you. If our teens are to relate to young men and women "in all purity" (1 Timothy 5:2), they need to have this same clarity.

THE BIBLICAL RESOURCE FOR PURITY

As was mentioned earlier, the fear of the Lord teaches us (and our teens) to hate all evil (see Proverbs 8:13), to abstain from sexual immorality (see 1 Thessalonians 4:3-7), and to be holy because God is holy (see 1 Peter 1:13-16). In training our teens, it's important that we also emphasize that this is not a fight they can win in their own strength. The Holy Spirit empowers our pursuit of holiness (see Romans 8:13), prompts us to repent when we fall short, and picks us up again (see 1 John 1:9). The Holy Spirit also assures us of God's unwavering acceptance of us on the basis of Christ's perfect obedience, not our faulty record (see Romans 8:15-16). The forgiving and transforming grace of God must be the foundation of our (and their) lifelong quest for all that's consistent with sexual purity.

THE IMPORTANCE OF BOUNDARIES, WISDOM, AND BIBLICAL PRINCIPLES

I know what I've outlined above doesn't address all the scenarios parents of teens have to consider. Is it okay for 16-year-old Jimmy to take Amanda to dinner and a movie alone? Or should they do things only in larger groups? What's a reasonable curfew for teens in mixed company? What about going to school dances, like the prom? And what about emotional intimacy—how much time can Jimmy and Amanda spend together? Should their parents monitor their texts?

An objective standard for sexual purity helps, but there are countless situations for which we must apply biblical wisdom as prayerfully and wisely as we can. And each family has the right to establish guidelines based on their convictions and their knowledge of the strengths and weaknesses of their own teens.

Q: *How do we navigate technologies that provide anonymity and new ways for our teens to encounter sexually charged material?*

A: Introduce expectations and accountability with any use of electronics. Your teens should understand that sexually illicit material is *all over* the Internet. Even reputable news sites now feature racy images or suggestive links to make money. Teach your teens to guard their eyes, minds, and hearts when on the web. It helps to start them out with Internet use only in public places, like in the living room, not in a bedroom. Internet filters—such as Bsecure Online, Covenant Eyes, or Safe Eyes—are also helpful.

Accountability is crucial. Encourage your teens to talk to you if they've viewed illicit material, whether intentionally or not. Be careful not to react in anger. Point them to the grace, forgiveness, and power of the Cross.

A second aspect of accountability deals with their correspondence. Teens may consider any monitoring of their social media or text messages an unwelcome intrusion, but they need to understand that it's really a loving protection from genuine danger. You are training them to be out on their own someday. Until then, you are the "system administrator" in your home, and as such, you have the right to check into anything suspicious. Even better, model a healthy distrust for secrecy by sharing access to *your* social media and e-mail accounts with your spouse and explaining to your teens why this is a helpful safeguard.

Think of it this way. Knowing that all sexual activity belongs in marriage tells our teens what they certainly may *not* do. They may not treat a date as a quasi-spouse. What they *may* do—that's a matter of wisdom, wisdom they should gain in your presence during high school and then apply in your absence at college or elsewhere. Fleeing temptation means knowing how we are tempted. Failing to prepare often means preparing to fail. We must help our teens internalize principles of healthy, respectful, and pure interactions with the opposite sex before they leave home.

Let me unpack five principles for your consideration.

Marriage Is a Worthwhile Pursuit

I know—the thought of your teens being married may scare you (or seem too hard to believe). But for most of them, that's what the future holds. The only question is whether their path to the altar will be filled with many or few regrets, and how you train them will have a lot to do with that. For one, the happiness and health of *your* marriage will be among the top factors in encouraging your teens to pursue or avoid a marriage of their own.

Here's how I see it: since sexual activity belongs only in marriage, and since teens have strong desires for the opposite sex (especially at college, where they're living close to so many of them), we should shoot straight with them, commit to pray for them and their future spouse, and walk with them as they make decisions, all the way to the altar.

I'm not suggesting teens immediately marry the first girl

or guy who attracts them. They do need to enter adulthood, be ready to accept the financial implications, and have some idea of what they're getting themselves into (to the extent any of us does). Singleness into the adult years may be strategic for some. But I fear our culture, even in many churches, has swung the pendulum to the other extreme. We don't teach teens to associate their desire for the opposite sex with marriage or to associate marriage with adulthood. We tell them to stay pure, but we don't celebrate the goodness of marriage or hold out marriage as a good and noble goal, not just for sex, but for companionship and for having someone to sharpen us on a deeply personal level, helping us grow in holiness.

Instead, we teach them to value academic success, the pursuit of a high-paying career, and the flexibility that comes with singleness. They have their whole lives before them, we say. What's the rush? If we're honest, many of us are afraid they'll make a big mistake if they marry young, that they just won't be ready. That fear is sometimes well founded, but the answer is to train them, not just hope a few more years will make them better. Many can attest that those extra years can also be a time of wandering, intense sexual temptation, and occasional failure, causing them to carry unwelcome baggage into their marriage.[13]

Consider that the average age of marriage today is about 27 for women and 29 for men (far higher than figures in previous generations).[14] It's no easy feat to stay a virgin for *that* long, over multiple years of peak sexual interest and fertility

When I got pregnant at 21, my parents were shocked. Though I was raised in a Christian home, my parents were not intentional in their training with regard to purity. They assumed I would not have sex until I was married because I was a "good girl." They figured there was no need to discuss the "uncomfortable" topic of sexuality because I was avoiding other "bad things" like drugs and alcohol.

I was not, however, avoiding the wrong crowd. I *thought* I was obeying God's guidelines because I (technically) maintained my virginity—while enjoying everything shy of intercourse. Other than a once-a-year generic anti-sex talk in youth group, I received no biblical input.

At college I had a traumatic sexual encounter against my will—an event I could have avoided had I been more prudent about the company I kept. But the following years of promiscuity were of my own free will. I was living at home. I would sit across from my parents at dinner, screaming inside, *Say something! I need a way out of this, but I just can't do it alone!*

And then I got pregnant. With God's help, I have walked a road of repentance ever since. But only recently have I come to see the beautiful picture of purity that God has designed for our good: everything sexual belongs in marriage. My husband and I are anxious to share this picture with our two young daughters.

Jessica

in a culture where most non-Christians are sexually active, where many view (or read) pornographic material, and where some view one-night stands as the sexual equivalent of going out for a hamburger. The Puritans said that marriage provided companionship, procreation, and protection (from sexual immorality). Help your teens understand that the Puritans got this one right—chances are marriage has been all three of those things in your life.

Dating Should Be Associated with the Prospect of Marriage

Whenever it is that you decide your teens are ready to go out alone, teach them to have the prospect of marriage in the back of their minds. This means several things. One, the girl or guy they're with will probably be someone's wife or husband someday. They ought not do anything with this person that would make them ashamed to attend their wedding and shake hands with their spouse.

Two, there's no need to date someone who wouldn't make a good mate. That means all non-Christians are out—period. No discussion. To marry a non-Christian is to shoot your walk with Christ in both feet—for life (see 2 Corinthians 6:14-18). To date one is to invite heartache, sexual temptation, and all kinds of moral compromise. Even if their prospective date *is* a Christian, look at where they're going in life and help your teen exercise discernment. But approach this with biblical values, not worldly standards. Getting good grades and aspiring to medical school don't necessarily mean a young man is godly or would make a good husband. And be especially mindful of perpetually adolescent males in the making and young women who are overly insecure, indiscreet, or sexually aggressive.

Three, if your teens need to wait to marry, they should pace themselves accordingly, knowing that the more time they spend with someone, the faster the relationship will go. When a pair of college freshmen hit it off and start spending *lots* of time together, it's very easy for things to go too far too fast. That said, once your teens find someone who is a great fit, they should not assume a need to keep "shopping around" or to put off marriage indefinitely.

Sons Should Be Men and Daughters Should Be Women

Male-female differences are more than anatomical. Our sons need to refuse passivity, embrace responsibility, and understand that God created them to be protectors and initiators in their relationships with women. And they don't need a girlfriend to practice on. They can organize or host group activities, look out for the physical safety of women (including their sisters), and be diligent about extending courtesies to the young ladies in their lives.

Guys should learn to take risks when they have a romantic interest in a woman. Dads, teach your sons that if someone's going to get rejected, it needs to be them. They shouldn't fish for information, hoping the girl will declare her interest first. That's weak and cowardly (and the sharper women can detect it anyway). On the other extreme, some young women use sex appeal as a weapon of power over men—they aim to seduce and conquer. Talk with your sons about how important it is to flee dangerous situations. Be blunt about how much is at stake.

Girls should avoid moving guy-girl relationships forward. Though many girls at college do, and they regularly "catch their man," they spend the next few months (and possibly years) wondering why the men they caught are passive and immature and never initiate with them. It's because they've learned they don't have to. Guys value what they're required to pursue, what takes effort to secure. Aggressive women end up with passive guys whose passivity continually bugs them.

Dads, protect your daughters from losers at college who masquerade as men. They're all over the campus, and they have enough good sense to notice your daughter. Consider interviewing the men who express interest in dating your daughter.[15] It's a great way to protect your daughter without being manipulating or controlling, and it builds into the lives of young men—men who may have been raised without a godly, masculine role model. And with technology, distance doesn't need to be a show stopper. Use Skype, FaceTime or some other tool that lets you look into the whites of their eyeballs. You can visit face-to-face when you come to campus, or (if their relationship is blossoming) invite him home for a weekend with your daughter. Stay involved.

And what is it that gives your daughter strength, firmness of conviction, and high standards in guys? Primarily it's what she sees in your life, Dad, and the quality of relationship she senses you have with your wife and with her. Women tend to marry men like their fathers, for better or worse.

Boundaries Must Be Set and Maintained

You don't prepare for a test while you're taking one. The time to set boundaries is in *advance* of when they'll be needed. Being alone with an attractive member of the opposite sex creates temptation. It's that simple—so don't be stupid. Better to be in public places; you can still have a nice conversation at Starbucks. There's no need to converse alone in the other person's dorm room. And better to converse in the day than late at night, when we get drowsy and have less self-control. Lots of sexual activity happens at college when a pair gets together alone late at night in one of their apartments "to study."

> *You don't prepare for a test while you're taking one. The time to set boundaries is in advance of when they'll be needed.*

Though we should train our daughters to be careful and to take responsibility for their own choices, our sons should learn to be particularly diligent about guarding the moral purity of their female friends at college. Teach them not to even ask women to join them in situations where there will be a heightened degree of temptation or the appearance of impropriety. This isn't legalism—it's basic courtesy and wisdom. "The prudent sees danger and hides himself, but the simple go on and suffer for it" (Proverbs 22:3).

Emotional Intimacy Leads to Physical Intimacy

One of the biggest lies in our culture is that sex is just a bodily, physical act—which implies that if we so choose, we can have sex with "no strings attached." But God did not make us into neat, discrete compartments. We are social-emotional-physical-spiritual beings made in God's image. Which means that what happens in our physical life messes with our emotional life, and vice versa. A sexual act between two people produces a real union, one that God designed to initiate and sustain a permanent, lifelong commitment. When we use it in any other way, we cheapen it and inevitably hurt each other.

Here's what teens need to know. If they get physical with someone, bonding chemicals are emitted (such as dopamine and oxytocin) that get them "hooked" to that person. They'll want to be with that person again in that same way. Withdrawal will be painful. Sexual activity creates real bonding. "No strings attached" is a destructive and cruel myth, particularly for women, whom research shows are increasingly prone to anxiety and depression the more sexual partners they have.[16]

There's also an opposite error, one that serious Christian teens—perhaps less prone to promiscuity—often commit. It's the myth of platonic friendships. If no-strings-attached sex is the myth that two people can have a "purely physical" relationship, the myth of platonic friendships says that two people can have a "purely emotional" relationship.

Simply put, a guy and girl who get together a lot and say they're "just friends" probably won't stay that way for very long. Either she'll fall for him, or he'll fall for her, or both. (Think of the various romantic comedies that play on this theme.) Maybe John and Rachel spending a lot of time in college ministry together and then falling for each other wouldn't be such a bad thing. The point is that teens need to understand that this phenomenon is real and not think that their "friendship" will somehow be the safe exception.

You see this sometimes in what becomes a missionary dating situation: David is a leader in the college ministry, and he's "helping" Abigail, a young lady who came from a broken home and is trying to get grounded in the Christian faith after breaking up with her non-Christian boyfriend of two years with whom she was sexually active. This is a disaster waiting to happen. Seasoned pastors and counselors know to be leery of such situations because they can lead to full-blown, long-term affairs, but young adult men are often too confident to know their vulnerability in this regard (and if they're unmarried, they lack the protection of accountability to a spouse). Teach your sons to understand the damsel-in-distress phenomenon and to cut it off at the pass. David needs to refer Abigail to a godly older woman at her church. Quickly.[17]

NOT EVERYONE IS DOING IT

Perhaps you're thinking, *Okay, those boundaries and principles make sense, but is college as bad as I've heard? Especially at secular schools, with all the rampant drunkenness and sexuality, is purity even possible?* Let's approach these questions from two angles: your teens' dangers can come from within (the sinful inclinations of their heart) or from without (a corrupt environment, enticing them in a manner for which they're not prepared). If you think a Christian college is somehow going to provide a perfect community, free of all temptation, you're in for a big surprise. That said, the reality even at secular universities is usually not as bad as what you hear. If motivated, your teen can find a great group of Christian friends on many secular university campuses.

Conversely, if they want to "walk on the wild side," they'll probably find others of that persuasion even at a Christian college. In fact, a good way to know if your teens are serious and intentional about finding Christian community at college is if they bring up the importance of finding such a community (at a church and on campus) when they get to college. (We'll discuss this further in conversation 10— there's a lot that can be done from home on the Internet and with a few phone calls.)

Maybe you've seen news reports of the "hook-up culture" on college campuses. In case you haven't heard, the "hook-up culture" is about going out in a group, drinking lots of alcohol, and then having sex with someone who interests you at the moment (with no prior relationship per se and no clear expectation of any future relationship). Though some of this goes on at high schools, we're told that hooking up now dominates the college scene to the extent that dating has become passé.

I'm happy to report to you that while "hook-ups" do

occur at colleges, their frequency is sometimes overblown by the media. Hook-ups are more common at elite, private secular universities, particularly in the Northeast.[18] Don't get me wrong. *Most* non-Christian college students in "committed" relationships become sexually active within a matter of several months. Your teens must anticipate this reality and be prepared to buck the trend, especially if they attend a secular school. And of course, these relationships aren't really "committed." They feel like mini-marriages because of the sex, but that just makes the break-up all the more painful. That said, if these people didn't have girlfriends or boyfriends (and many don't), they wouldn't just be throwing themselves at anyone. Although the sex-crazed party animal is presented as the face of campus life by Hollywood and its affiliates (who stand to gain financially), the happy reality is that not all college students recreate via inebriation and casual sex.

Unfortunately, the image of the sex-crazed party animal has been so successfully advanced that college students themselves overestimate the amount of sexual activity occurring. For example, in one large study of college freshmen, around 30 percent of men and women said they'd had at least four sexual partners in their lifetime. But get this: the men in the study estimated that the same was true of 53 percent of other freshmen males, while women estimated that the same was true of 45 percent of other freshmen women. You see what happened? They predicted their peers were more promiscuous than was actually the case.

How about going the other way, predicting abstinence?

Students *under*estimate it. About one in four college men and women (25 percent) are still virgins and intend to remain so until marriage. But college men guessed that this was true of only 13 percent of other college men, while college women guessed this was true of only 19 percent of other college women.[19]

Students have been duped into believing the "everyone is doing it" lie—which itself begets promiscuity. In reality, if your son or daughter attends a secular university, they won't be alone in their pursuit of purity. They will have to reject the Hollywood stereotype and be intentional about finding a community that reinforces their convictions regarding chastity, dignity, respect, and honor. But if they do, purity is not only attainable; by God's grace it can be expected.

SUMMARY

- Sexual purity is particularly challenging in our day due to the cultural acceptance of promiscuity, widespread lewdness in popular media, and constant accessibility of illicit material (combined with the total anonymity afforded by the Internet).
- We should impart to our teens a biblical understanding of sex, a biblical motivation for purity, an objective standard for purity, and a reminder of the biblical resource for purity. But we must also provide a grace-saturated environment in our homes. If our teens fail, we want them to run into our arms (and the arms of Jesus), not fall deeper into a sinful lifestyle.

- We should help our teens connect their desires for physical and emotional intimacy with the goodness and goal of marriage, even if it's years away. And we should help them establish wise boundaries and safeguards that promote purity and protect them from avoidable temptation.
- We need to teach our sons to reject passivity. Although they're unmarried, their interactions with women should be a shadow of how Christ calls husbands to treat their wives: namely, laying down their lives in servant leadership (see Ephesians 5:22-33). And we must help our daughters maintain high standards, requiring that a man first earn her respect before she views him with romantic affection.

CONVERSATION STARTERS

Because of the sensitivity of these topics, you might want to initiate these kinds of conversations between father and son or mother and daughter, to the extent that's possible for you. (If it's not possible, you might consider enlisting the help of another trusted adult of the same sex as your teens—perhaps a church leader, uncle, aunt, or grandparent.) Consider tailoring the questions and the depth of your interaction to the age and maturity of your children. Lastly, as your children leave for college, you might consider asking them to read chapter 4 in my book *Thriving at College*, where I speak directly to the teens, covering a number of topics related to dating and romance that I did not address here.

1. Discuss the idea that sex belongs only in marriage. What do your teens think? Other than sex outside of marriage, is there anything else that should be avoided?

2. Ask your teens: What kinds of behaviors with girls or guys do you think might later bring you or them shame? Have you thought about creating boundaries to protect yourself from making regrettable decisions?

3. How have the Internet, movies, or other media impacted the way your teens view dating, romance, and sex? What's a proper biblical response? Temptations to pornography are extremely common among high school guys. Dads, get it out in the open, and help your son slay this dragon. Without going into needless detail, be vulnerable about how you may have failed in this area, how God has grown you, and how you daily fight for sexual purity at the heart/thought-life level. Girls' attitudes toward dating and sexuality are influenced by media too. Whether they're watching romance movies with their friends, reading erotic material, or viewing pornography (yes, it happens), Moms, look for ways to address this topic with your daughters.

4. Ask your teens: Have you ever considered that your desire for a girlfriend/boyfriend is ultimately a God-given desire for a wife/husband? What qualities are you looking for in a spouse? What kind of man/

woman are you seeking to become for a future mate? Talk about how intimacy and companionship are maximized by the security and commitment of marriage.

**PART 4
FINANCES**

CONVERSATION 7
Teaching Your Teens Financial Responsibility

ELIZABETH WENT AWAY to a great college, but it was a bit pricey. Her parents had saved diligently but could only pick up half the tuition and living costs over four years. Not a problem, she figured. She'd take out a loan and get a part-time job.

Elizabeth quickly found a job at a department store. While at work one day, she flipped through a credit card flyer. It sounded like she qualified and that having a card would be a great way to improve her credit score. Two weeks later a shiny plastic card with her name on it arrived in the mail. A few of her friends had also gotten them.

The food at the dining hall soon got old, so Elizabeth and

her friends started hitting the local restaurants. It was nice to mingle with new people in more private settings. Then they started taking getaway trips on the weekends. There was always something fun to do.

Her first credit card bill came in the mail: $629.87. A bit higher than she'd expected, and more than what she had earned that month. But her grandpa had given her $500 as a high school graduation gift, so she just dipped into that. To pay the next month's statement, she used all that was left of Grandpa's money. When the third month's statement was issued, she paid what she could and rolled the rest over to the next month. By then it was time to buy books for the spring semester, which jacked up her credit card statement even higher.

The balance continued to grow. By April Elizabeth had racked up just over $1,000 of credit card debt. It didn't help that there was a 13-percent interest rate (which she didn't remember reading about). She'd been planning to work as a camp counselor that summer, but the pay was pitifully low. Elizabeth realized that the debt would just keep growing if she didn't pay it off. Confused, she called her parents.

Which required telling them what had happened.

BIG EYES, SMALL WALLETS

Elizabeth's story is all too familiar for college-aged young adults. According to Sallie Mae, only about one in three (35 percent) college students had a credit card in 2012. But two-thirds of card owners carry a balance instead of paying their bill in full on a monthly basis. The average outstanding credit card balance among freshmen: $642.[1]

We shouldn't be surprised. Spending more than we have has become a way of life for many of us. Among Americans between the ages of 35 and 54, almost half (45 percent) held credit card debt as of 2011—to say nothing of those among us who purchased homes we ultimately couldn't afford.[2] It's easy for our eyes to grow larger than our wallets.

Maybe you've successfully avoided these hazards. If so, good for you. But most precollege teens have yet to learn, by experience, that diligence leads to riches (see Proverbs 10:4), that we should work hard and not be dependent on others (see 2 Thessalonians 3:6-12), and that the borrower is the slave of the lender (see Proverbs 22:7). These are lessons that either we can teach them the easy way or life can teach them the hard way.

I tell Daniel's powerful story in *Thriving at College.* Daniel was a college student whose parents bailed him out of a $10,000 credit card debt. Years later he got into over $40,000 of debt—and this time had to pay it all off himself. He wrote, "I wish my parents wouldn't have bailed me out the first time, because then I probably would have learned my lesson earlier and at a smaller cost."

While protecting our children from serious, life-altering mistakes, we must give them increasing levels of financial responsibility as they grow up. If their leash is so short that minor failure today is impossible, the likelihood of massive failure in the future increases. Require that your teens take ownership of their relatively small financial actions, and unlike Daniel's parents, let them reap the consequences for any missteps. Painful lessons in the school of hard knocks are long remembered, but only if the pain is allowed to do its work.

Like Elizabeth, most students don't really understand the consequences of not paying their credit card balance in full every month. The phrase "compound interest" makes their eyes glaze over. And most don't read the fine print regarding late payment fees and the like. We can and must address these issues by teaching them the basics before they go to college: things like how to balance a checkbook, the difference between a debit card and a credit card, and how compounding interest works. But head knowledge in these areas is less than half the battle. The real issues are matters of the heart and will: *wants* that masquerade as *needs* and a lack of self-discipline to live within their means. And behind these two shortcomings lies an underdeveloped concept of stewardship.

> *Require that your teens take ownership of their relatively small financial actions, and let them reap the consequences for any missteps. Painful lessons in the school of hard knocks are long remembered, but only if the pain is allowed to do its work.*

AN UNDERSTANDING OF STEWARDSHIP

I realize the word *stewardship* may sound like a cliché to some of you and that others may not have heard the word in quite some time. So let me define it and then explain why it's so foundational. A steward is "someone entrusted with another's wealth or property and charged with the responsibility of managing it in the owner's best interest."[3] We are stewards entrusted with God's wealth. Psalm 24:1 reads, "The earth is the LORD's, and everything in it. The world and all its people belong to him" (NLT). Right up there with "remember[ing] [their] Creator in the days of [their] youth" (Ecclesiastes 12:1), our teens must understand that God owns everything—all the money in the world and everything it can buy—and that he alone gives anyone the power to gain wealth (see Deuteronomy 8:18). The worldly goods we possess today, as well as those that our abilities allow us to secure tomorrow, have been entrusted to us by God. Our duty is to faithfully manage them in a way that promotes his interests (see 1 Corinthians 4:2).

For many of our teens, going to college will be a wise investment, an opportunity to develop a well-trained mind and cultivate their talents into well-honed skills. With these skills they can glorify God throughout their lives as teachers, engineers, lawyers, accountants, and so on. In *any* employment, they should understand that helping others flourish should be their primary goal. Receiving remuneration is the by-product. Employers pay us not for showing up but for being *useful*.

Fight an entitlement mentality at every turn. Studies show that teens today are more materialistic and less likely to work hard than previous generations.[4] This is a problem on two levels. First, materialism is idolatry (making "stuff" God) and a failure to understand why God blesses us financially. He does it not so that we can live in ridiculous ease but so that we can promote the spread of the gospel in word and deed, showing that our citizenship is in heaven and our heart is set on eternal rewards (see Luke 12:33-34; 16:1-13, especially verse 9). Second, money comes from hard work. Yes, God is our Provider, but he generally provides for us through the means of our diligent labor, which prevents us from becoming a burden to others and allows us to contribute to the financial needs of our local churches (thereby supporting pastors, missionaries, and the needy—see, for example, 2 Corinthians 8–9; Ephesians 4:28; and 1 Timothy 5:17-18).

I tell you, use worldly wealth to gain friends for yourselves, so that when it is gone, you will be welcomed into eternal dwellings.

—LUKE 16:9, NIV

Your teens don't have much money yet. Now is the time for them to start thinking about money in a way that recognizes it all belongs to God, not us, and that we're to use it to advance his purposes. Only from this firm foundation can they learn to properly manage it. Let's explore some implications.

Don't Spend More than You Earn

This sounds simple enough, but many college-bound teens have never internalized the concept of spending less than they earn—in part because they may currently be spending what *you* earn.

James was raised in an upper-middle-class home. He stayed busy with sports, music, academic camps, and other expensive, résumé-boosting activities. In his limited free time, James's desires for video games, movies, skiing, and eating out were fulfilled by his generous parents.

But it's not just rich kids who haven't learned to manage their money. Consider Michael, who comes from a lower-middle-class home. His parents work hard to provide for their family. Michael is 17, works part-time in a restaurant, and puts his money in a bank account his parents helped him set up. Whenever he wants to buy anything of significance, his parents forbid it, telling him it'd be a frivolous waste.

Now consider Chris. Chris is also 17, and his parents give him a salary of $100 a month in exchange for lawn care, garbage duties, and a few other regular chores, from which he's to pay for anything above a basic phone plan and auto insurance (both of which his parents put on family plans). But Chris is naturally frugal and not interested in trendy clothes or eating out, so the money mainly sits in his dresser drawer.

What do James, Michael, and Chris have in common? None of them has gotten into any financial trouble. But none of them has learned to manage money. They've never had to make a connection between *their* earning, *their* spending, and *their* giving. We dare not conclude that any of the three has yet developed an internal compass with regard to financial restraint.

The best way to teach your teens to manage money is to

let them do it. Okay, so where do we start? With a budget. A budget tracks dollars—the ones coming in and the ones going out. And a budget *tells* every dollar where it should go. As many of us have learned by experience, if we don't tell our dollars where to go, there's no telling where they'll go. A budget allows us to plan rather than react. Even if not kept perfectly, a budget helps us do better for having made the effort.

Some of you are like Chris, naturally frugal, or you have teens who are that way. I never budgeted as a high school student because I didn't earn much and spent less. There simply wasn't much that I wanted to buy. Even in cases like this, I think teens can learn a lot by tracking their expenses for a month or two, then discussing their spending with Mom and Dad. They may not *need* a budget now, but they probably will in college, and they certainly will someday. So why not teach them the skill now?

Let's say that, within reason, you currently buy your teens' clothes, but you won't when they go to college. After discussing this with them, could you determine (from prior spending) what a reasonable clothes budget for them would be, then give them the money on a monthly or quarterly basis and have them spend it themselves? Ditto for school supplies, or other areas. If you're expecting them to assume additional financial responsibilities when they go to college, practicing now is the best way to see what might happen when they're gone. Best-case scenario, they'll get a taste of money management with larger figures, and the fact that frugality in one

I grew up being an early adopter of new technology without thinking through the implications. When I was a freshman in high school, I remember buying a minidisc right after they came out. It was so cool! But then the iPod was released, and it was better, and everybody was buying one. I went to sell my minidisc so I could (once again) purchase the latest thing, but I couldn't find an interested buyer. I soon realized I had thrown $300 down the drain.

The funny thing is that my parents suspected I was making an unwise impulse purchase. But they let me do it anyway. They figured I had worked for the money, had set aside a portion for saving (as they taught me), and had given God what was his. They let me learn via natural consequences in the school of hard knocks.

I had wanted to be the cool guy with the latest gadget—and it cost me, big time. My identity had been wrapped up in what I had and in what others thought of me. It wasn't right, let alone sustainable. Tough lesson, yes. Important lesson, absolutely. But to this day it has saved me from making purchases that would have been similarly foolish, and with larger sums of money.

Jason

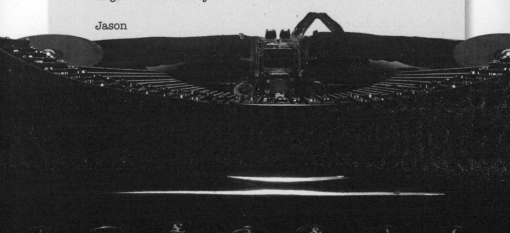

area leaves them more to spend in another. And worst case? They make a few frivolous purchases, suffer a few natural (but minor) consequences, and both you and they know better what to watch out for when they go to college. If your son insists on pocketing the clothes money and dressing like a slob, you can nudge him to the store or throw away his old clothes. Or if your daughter spends her quarterly clothes budget in the first three weeks, you can help her find a way to earn more money.

It's worth making sure your teens are in the habit of living within a reasonable budget and spending less than they earn *before* they go to college. Once they get there, they'll be hit with a tidal wave of new spending opportunities—for things you can't fully anticipate. Immediately before they go to college, when you have a better idea of what their necessary, regular expenses will be, you can help them come up with a rough budget. The point is to help them have a reasonable idea of what their expense categories will be, put in some target figures, and then look at how much money they'll need in the way of income on a monthly basis. Assuming your child will be a residential student on at least a partial meal plan, you might come up with something like this:

Food	$100
Clothes	$75
Toiletries/ Laundry	$25
Phone	$50
Entertainment	$50

Gas	$50
Miscellaneous	$50
Giving	$50
Saving	$50
TOTAL	$500

Depending on your teens, they may be willing to spend less on food or clothes, or they may need more for gas money (especially if they plan to drive home occasionally). In any event, the student in the above scenario would need to bring in $500 per month (either through gifts from family members or from a part-time job).[5]

If your teens hold part-time jobs, they might (like Elizabeth) qualify for a credit card. But I would discourage them from getting one. The idea that an 18- or 19-year-old college student needs to immediately establish a credit history to earn a higher FICO score is overblown, in my view. There are secured credit card options (in which a cash collateral deposit becomes the credit line), but these typically have annual fees and can end up being a bad deal. My take is that a debit card is the way to go, at least until they turn 21. It provides the convenience of a credit card without the risk.

Teens not only need precollege training in the area of budgeting, they need accountability once they get there. Once you've made a monthly college budget with your soon-to-be freshmen teens, I'd recommend asking them to agree to show you their expenses for the first few months of college to see if the budget you made is working or if there were any unforeseen gaps. This could easily be done by agreeing that you will log in to their bank account on occasion, just to see what's going on. Knowing that you'll be checking should prove to be a helpful deterrent from excess spending, and it will help them ease into their newfound freedom and independence. Once they prove themselves faithful, you can step back.

The message of spending less than you earn must be consciously ingrained in our teens, but it's not especially spiritual or countercultural. It's true that many Americans spend more than they earn, but you don't need to be a Christian or know anything about the Bible to understand that living within your means is a good idea. Giving to a church (and to other Christian causes), by contrast, *is* countercultural and therefore more difficult to learn.

Give God at Least 10 Percent, Off the Top

Many of you taught your kids about giving far earlier than their teen years, which is fantastic. In our house we're using the popular three-jar system: giving, saving, and spending. But if you've never explicitly talked to your teens about giving, you really need to. They're not likely to learn it elsewhere; giving money away defies common sense in today's young adult culture. We're training our kids to swim upstream in this area.

Giving flows from an understanding of stewardship. Since God owns everything, giving to God is nothing more than returning to him a portion of what he has entrusted to us.

This concept is introduced to us quite early in the Bible as the *tithe*, through the examples of Abraham with Melchizedek (see Genesis 14:17-20) and Jacob's vow (see Genesis 28:20-22). But it was formally encoded in the Mosaic law: "Every tithe of the land, whether of the seed of the land or of the fruit of the trees, is the LORD's; it is holy to the LORD" (Leviticus 27:30). The word *tithe* simply means "a tenth part."

Other passages go further, instructing us to give the tithe from the *top* of our earnings: "Honor the LORD with your wealth and with the *firstfruits* of all your produce" (Proverbs 3:9, emphasis added). We see this word *firstfruits* again in Deuteronomy 18:4: "The firstfruits of your grain, of your wine and of your oil, and the first fleece of your sheep, you shall give him." It's so important to keep God first in our lives that we're given commandments like this to remind us that any provision, any income, ultimately comes from God, our Provider (see Deuteronomy 8:18). Most of us no longer live in an agrarian society, but the fact remains that Christians who choose not to give off the top often have little to nothing left to give at the bottom. The statistics are grim: only one in eight self-professing born-again Christians actually tithes.[6]

> Giving flows from an understanding of stewardship. Since God owns everything, giving to God is nothing more than returning to him a portion of what he has entrusted to us.

The passages cited above make clear that giving should not be a perfunctory or begrudging afterthought but an immediate, overt recognition of our total dependence on

God. In fact, other passages show that the Israelites also gave voluntary (or freewill) offerings *above and beyond* the obligatory tithe (see, for example, Numbers 15:3; Deuteronomy 12:6, 17). These constituted "true giving" since the tithe was already considered God's by right—not providing it was considered robbery (see Malachi 3:8-10). The New Testament likewise encourages generous giving (see, for example, Luke 6:38; 2 Corinthians 8:1-15; 9:6-15).

Many teens who have observed their parents faithfully tithe or have even practiced tithing while growing up may struggle to maintain the habit when they go off to college. As with the avoidance of reckless spending, everything is simpler when they're living with you. You put a roof over their head, give them three meals a day, and provide unlimited snacks conveniently available in the pantry. In most cases, they have access to one or two cars, whose maintenance you oversee (and pay for).

Giving should not be a perfunctory or begrudging afterthought but an immediate, overt recognition of our total dependence on God.

Once your teens are in college, you're probably planning to have them pick up the tab in more areas. And as Elizabeth discovered in our opening illustration, college brings a whole new world of entertainment and recreational options combined with virtually unlimited freedom to pursue those options. It's easy to get carried away having a good time, lose track of spending, and forget entirely about giving. In other cases, students are scrambling to keep up with necessary expenses (like textbooks) and don't think they can afford to tithe. They find it difficult to trust that God will meet their true needs with the remaining 90 percent of their income. Before they get into these situations, we need to teach them that tremendous blessings flow toward those who live within their means and trust God with their finances.

Good stewardship may involve working more hours, starting at a community college, or moving in with a relative to lower their living expenses. It may mean saying no to expensive social outings and coming up with less expensive ways to enjoy time with friends. In fact, living strategically and keeping recreation in its place during the college years is important both financially and academically.

Tip

If you or a relative are planning to provide your teens with an allowance in college, give them 10 percent more and expect them to tithe from it. You *could* say, "This is all for you; we already tithed on it," but that deprives them of establishing the discipline of tithing for themselves. It's better for them to learn to give from their earliest days of receiving income, whether earned or gifted.

Live Strategically and Keep Recreation in Its Place

It's worth talking to your college-bound son or daughter about lifestyle expectations in their college years. They may be coming from homes in which they have their own large bedroom—and be on their way to small dorm rooms that they'll share with roommates. If there's still time, encourage them to participate in opportunities like mission trips and summer camps, where they can experience the joys and trials of communal living.

When you start visiting college campuses, you'll notice a few things have changed since you passed through. As you know, tuition has gone up a little bit. But that's not all. Traditional dorms are losing favor, and fancier dwellings are increasingly commonplace. From 1995 to 2004, just 17 percent of the 113 residence halls constructed on college campuses were traditional dorms.[7] Most residence halls are now apartment-style suites, equipped with spacious, lavishly furnished lobbies and well-lit study rooms, in some cases featuring gorgeous views and even fitness centers and rock-climbing walls. Not surprisingly, these kinds of buildings are more expensive to construct: the median cost per square foot for a new residence hall rose by 63 percent from just 2008 to 2012—an astounding increase if you consider the condition of the United States' economy during this period.[8] And when you visit university dining halls, you'll observe similar upgrades: large, newly furnished buildings equipped with multiple "venues," each serving different types of high-quality organic food, with the occasional sushi bar and Mongolian BBQ grill thrown in. Critics are calling the trend toward upscale living and dining arrangements an "amenities arms race."[9] But the demand for these kinds of perks is coming from prospective students—teens raised, on average, in larger, nicer homes than you probably had growing up. Universities are merely trying to compete for the current generation of residential students (who are known for being a bit discriminating).

So watch the price tag carefully, and consider the difference between necessities and amenities. Help your teens remember they're going to college, not a country club. The purpose is to get a rigorous, well-rounded education; to grow in character and wisdom; to make lifelong friends who strengthen them in the faith; to learn to winsomely and intelligently engage those who think differently; to become lifelong learners; and to responsibly join the adult world with well-developed, marketable skills by which they can serve others, earn a living, support a family, and give to their church, missions, and other worthy causes. They can do all this and have a great time without living like kings and queens.

So what about keeping expenses down at college? Older students can be incredibly ingenious when it comes to cutting costs—they're a great source of local information at whatever college your son or daughter ultimately selects. But here are a few general areas to consider:

- *Housing.* Residence halls may have different prices, depending on amenities. Community living is much cheaper than living alone, as nice as that may be. Train your teens now to tidy their belongings, and request roommates who also value order. No teen does this perfectly, but if they don't even *try*, they'll never come close. If money is really tight, the Department of Education estimates that living at home during college can save roughly $6,000 per year, a figure which will likely rise over time.[10]

- *Textbooks.* New textbooks are ridiculously expensive, but used copies and rental options are more reasonably priced. And then there are electronic copies, often the most affordable option, but many students (as of now) find that it's harder to read and learn from a book without being able to physically touch it.

- *Meal plans.* Look at the various packages, and estimate what you're actually paying per meal. Then think about what's reasonable. If your teens are not breakfast people, are they really going to eat three meals a day, every day, in the dining halls? Do their dorm rooms (or apartment suites) come with a microwave, refrigerator, or oven? A friend of mine learned to cook some basic meals when he went to college. Together with his friends they had a dinner club, where they took turns cooking for the group.

- *Transportation.* A bicycle or skateboard is often more practical than a car, and without a car, your teens won't need to purchase parking permits or waste time looking for parking spots (a challenge on many campuses). If they're going to college a few hours away, might there be anyone they can carpool with for break times and occasional weekend visits?

Q: *How can I help my son understand how much college really costs?*

A: Semester tuition may seem incomprehensibly large. Break it down: What does one *class period* cost? If he knows he's losing $100 every time he skips class, he's less likely to hit snooze. (This is something I mention to my students in the first day of class. I've found it boosts attendance and punctuality.)

Really want him to feel the weight? Make him pick up at least some of the tab. One dad I know taught his children from an early age that they'd have to come up with 50 percent of any large purchase they wanted—a bicycle, a snowboard, or a college education. Because he also taught them how to shop around, assess price versus value, and diligently save, his kids developed a habit of owning their financial decisions. By college, it naturally carried over.

It doesn't have to be 50 percent, but make it something. That way your son has skin in the game and is more invested. Once you've picked a figure, help him set up a plan to raise the money through work and savings. You might establish a "reward system" whereby better grades earn a little extra money from Mom and Dad (toward tuition). Or throw in an interest-free loan, but with the understanding that it must be paid off within a year after graduation.

The key is getting him involved so he's not passively going along for the ride.

In conversation 2 we talked about the importance of recreation being measured (rather than impulsive) and restorative (rather than distracting). Here we need to observe that recreation should be *economical* rather than *expensive*, given a college student's limited income. The mountains, the ocean, or a nearby lake represent wonderfully refreshing (and *free*) venues within God's creation. An hour of basketball with friends provides social and physical benefits (again, *free*). Campus clubs and student societies offer a variety of enjoyable outings at reasonable prices. Many local establishments offer student or group discounts.

There's also value in limiting recreational activities. If your teens enjoy eating out, a medium-priced restaurant every two weeks might run them 30 or 40 dollars a month, but dining out every other night could run them as high as $300 a month (and that's if they don't hit the upscale joints). Weekend getaways and other trips can be fun but if pursued too often can leave a student broke or in debt.

Recreation and relationships are essential. Jesus himself promoted merriment with his first miracle (see John 2:1-11). But teach your teens to avoid being mastered by whatever they find fun and to move away from activities that absorb too much time (to the detriment of their academic and other responsibilities) or cost too much money (to the detriment of their essential expenses and their biblically required giving). If your teens are intentional about not spending a fortune, they'll be surprised at how many things they can enjoy on a shoestring budget.

EARNING MONEY WHILE IN COLLEGE

Having looked at some ways students can save money while in college, let's talk about whether they should be earning any. This is an issue on which there has been significant generational change. In 1980, about half of high school graduates immediately pursued college. Today that figure is closer to 70 percent. During this stretch, the price tag at a four-year public university has risen three and a half times faster than the rate of inflation. Prefer a private four-year college? The price tag at those has only gone up two and a half times faster than the inflation rate.[11] From 2000 to 2010 alone, four-year college tuition shot up by 70 percent while household incomes were mostly stagnant or in decline.[12]

The result is that while more high school graduates are going to college, more of them need to rely on scholarships and grants but also outside work or student loans to supplement any personal or family savings. Let's talk first about students having outside work. Seven out of 10 undergraduate students were working in 2011. Of that figure, half put in 20 to 35 hours per week, and about one in five put in *over* 35 hours per week.[13] How is all this work impacting their academics?

On the one hand, it's possible to go to college part-time—to enroll in one or two classes a semester—while working full-time. The advantage of such a plan (assuming the job pays well enough) is that students are more likely to stay debt-free throughout their experience. The disadvantages, however, are twofold. First, logistics: it's often challenging to schedule classes around full-time job duties. Many campuses don't offer lectures in the evening, so students might wind up taking online classes. And evening or online classes make it harder to access professors, most of whom hold their office hours during the day. But the other disadvantage is that it would take six to eight years to get most bachelor's degrees this way. That's a long time. Just think about how many life-altering circumstances could come about in that period, preventing students from completing their degree.

Okay, so what about going to college full time but working 20 to 35 hours per week? You typically pay the same amount to take 18 units per semester as you do to take 15 units, which is why many students attempt a full load. And of course, graduation comes faster that way (assuming students pass their classes). But that's the problem: college classes are demanding. For every hour in class, a student needs to plan on two hours of out-of-class work. That means 18 hours per week of class time translates into 36 hours per week of out-of-class work, or a 54-hour academic week. Maybe your teens are above average students (aren't they all?) or they take at least one easy class so they can get away with putting in a 45- to 50-hour academic week. That still doesn't leave much time for a side job.

Here's what often happens, unfortunately, when full-time students try taking on a demanding side job. They faithfully clock in their work hours, since the alternative is getting fired. But then they cut corners with their homework. And then they're shocked when they get a bunch of Cs and Ds for the semester. Getting a D often means repeating a class, which adds cost and time to graduation. The "three steps forward, two steps back" approach to college is not strategic.

I recommend students work primarily during the summers, when classes are out of session. If a student is going to work during the semester—and most legitimately need to—it really should be 10 to 15 hours per week, maximum, ideally in a job where they can get some studying done (for example, checking people into the school's fitness center) or even better in something related to what they're studying. Two semesters of course work take up 32 weeks each year, tops. Let's say your family takes a vacation, leaving your teens with 18 available weeks. If they put in 40 hours per week earning only 10 dollars per hour, they'll gross $7,200. Now let's say they put in 10 hours per week while classes are in session. That's another $3,200. If you figure 25 percent goes to God and government, they're still left with $650 per month (much more than the $500 we estimated earlier).

Many resourceful teens can make more than 10 dollars per hour by focusing on their skills and being entrepreneurial. My wife gave piano lessons in people's homes, earning about 20 dollars per hour (and this was in the 1990s). I tutored students in math and physics. Others have started lawn-mowing or painting businesses. As your teens move through college, they should look for internships in their chosen field. While some internships don't pay very well (if at all), they're often worth it because the experience helps students land full-time jobs after graduation.

THE PERILS OF STUDENT DEBT

A diligent student should be able to earn some money during the college years, but most are finding their earnings (combined with their parents' savings) to be insufficient. For the 2011–2012 academic year, 56 percent of full-time students and 9 percent of parents took out loans.[14] The average student loan debt for a borrower who received a bachelor's degree in 2013 was $30,000.[15] What are we to make of this?

First off, this section will not address *why* college has become so expensive or how you, as parents, can financially prepare yourselves to help shoulder the hefty burden. The latter is addressed (albeit briefly) in the appendix, and the former is a fascinating topic that's beyond the scope of this book.[16] In what follows I'm assuming that anyone considering student loans will fill out the FAFSA (which might, among other things, qualify your teen for federally-subsidized loans or need-based grants). I'm focusing on *student* loans, but the principles are similar with regard to parent loan options (addressed briefly in the appendix).

So, should you or your teens take on debt to pay for college? If so, what factors should be considered in making this decision?

Some Christians think debt is never permissible under any circumstances because of texts like Romans 13:8 ("owe no one anything") and Proverbs 22:7 ("the borrower is the slave of the lender"). If that's your family's conviction, you should certainly follow it rather than act against your conscience.

But there are other verses in the Bible that encourage lending (see Psalm 37:21, 26; 112:5), so an absolute prohibition, in my view, is a bit of a stretch.[17] Many Christians finance their homes at reasonable, fixed-interest rates and end up just fine. (In fact, because of our tax code, they come out ahead.) The danger is when we use debt to purchase something we truly can't afford and end up falling behind on our payments. Debt can deceive us, making us feel richer than we are. The acceptance of any loan involves at least some risk and should never be undertaken lightly.

Student loans are not tied to physical assets that can be considered collateral. On a home loan, the bank can repossess your house. But if someone can't make student loan payments, students have no way to "sell back" their education. And since educational loans lack bankruptcy protection, the debt follows them for life. Nevertheless, many consider such loans to be "good debt" because college graduates generally earn more than non–college graduates over the course of a lifetime. That's true collectively, but it's not true for every student individually. It's a good idea to consider every viable alternative before taking out a student loan.

Many students fail to explore their options. It's true that most students today are taking out loans, but just because others do it doesn't make it right or best for your teens. I gave some ideas earlier in this chapter on how to spend less during the college years (dramatically less if the student lives at home). Here's another: While your teens are in high school, are there ways they could earn college credit, perhaps by taking advanced placement (AP) or international baccalaureate (IB) classes or by dual-enrolling in a community college? Your son or daughter might be able to knock out a semester or two that way, drastically reducing overall tuition. This is strategic since most full-time students now take five or six years to graduate, not four, especially if they're in majors with more required units (such as microbiology or chemical engineering). And don't forget that tuition and fees tend to rise every year.

Tip

Enrolling in college courses during high school is known as *dual enrollment*. One advantage (beyond the cost savings) is that it's often available to a wider range of students than just those who qualify for AP or IB classes. It's important that the community college instructor be appropriately challenging so that your teens genuinely learn the material, as it may prove foundational for future college-level courses.[18]

Another thing to consider before taking out a loan for your incoming freshmen teens: about one in four freshmen do not immediately return as sophomores, and 44 percent of those who pursue a four-year college degree have not completed that degree even six years later.[19] They still have to pay back any loans. Of course, you're reading the right book to keep your children from being in either of those statistics. Still, given that high school students have the ability to earn college credits, given that the majority of students today change majors (most commonly during or right after their freshman year), and given the high freshman-to-sophomore dropout rate, why would you take out a loan for your children's *freshman* year of college, before they've established any sort of track record of commitment and success within a given major? Besides, if you can't pay for their first year of college without taking on debt, how much additional debt will you end up with after their subsequent three or more years? Count the cost up front.

Speaking of that first year, many of the one in four freshmen whom colleges lose would have been well advised to take a year off before college. Some lack personal discipline. And others (together with their parents) simply lack the finances. A year off means an extra year in which they—and you—can be working and saving money. Nothing wrong with that. In fact, your child can still apply to colleges and defer acceptance for a year (though consider that some schools may not hold scholarship funds without a deferral letter—see pages 349–352). Another advantage of a year off is that it gives teens more time to figure out what they want to study so that they're less likely to change majors once they get to college. Some use this year to be an apprentice (paid, usually) in a field of interest, which ends up undergirding and complementing their future academic or professional pursuits. (We'll talk more about the idea of a "gap year" between high school and college in conversation 11.)

That first year of college requires the largest adjustment

Key Points on Student Debt

- Fill out the FAFSA to maximize school aid.
- Be creative about lowering expenses.
- If necessary, encourage your teens to consider taking a year off to save money.
- Get them established in their major before taking loans.
- Treat loans as a last resort.
- Realistically consider your teens' future salary prospects.

and is therefore your teens' biggest test. Although classes thereafter do get harder, the dropout rate decreases with each successive year because students have successfully made that initial leap. Once they're established within their chosen major, once the finish line to graduation isn't so hazy, a loan represents a much smaller risk. Plus, less interest accrues before the time when they can get out, find employment, and start making payments. A loan taken out their freshman year accrues interest during their sophomore, junior, and senior years. But a loan taken out their senior year has barely any interest on it before students start working and can begin paying it off.[20]

Perhaps you're thinking, *But won't my children do better academically if they take out a loan instead of losing precious study time working a side job?* Actually, graduation rates are *higher* among students who work a modest number of hours (less than 15 per week) than those who don't work at all.[21] Young adults and too much free time are not a good combination.[22] And contributing to the expense of college makes them appreciate it more.

Remember that a loan, at the time, can feel like a gift. It's easier to spend other people's money than our own. The weight of the debt burden simply does not register until later. I've corresponded with dozens of students who've taken on $50,000–90,000 of student debt. The most common thing you'll hear is "I had no idea how much debt I was generating until I got out of school." That's because it's easy, once a student starts taking on debt, to keep taking more of it. And it's hard to keep track of just how much is being accrued (especially if a student has multiple loans with different balances and interest rates).

I'm not suggesting an absolute prohibition of student debt. I'm just saying count the costs, both short and long term, so that you and your child go in with your eyes wide open. When students graduate, land full-time jobs, and are able to repay their loans without crippling their aspirations, it works out. But sadly, many young adults feel stressed by their debt burden. They're delaying marriage, children, and home owernship because of it.[23] They're turning down jobs they'd love, and to which they feel deeply called, in favor of jobs that simply pay more. Some choose not to enter the ministry or go on the mission field as a result of their student debt. I don't want bondage to be the future for your children. I want them to graduate with the freedom to pursue their God-given ambitions. By being creative and resourceful, debt can often be minimized or even avoided.

Salary prospects should also factor into the decision to take on debt, since any debt (in the best-case scenario) is an investment on which the borrower expects to receive a return over time. A chemical engineer who graduates with $20,000 in debt is probably in a better situation than an elementary education major who graduates with a debt load of $10,000. Be realistic. Jobs in different industries pay different amounts. That's life in a Western market economy. That doesn't mean we should demean lesser-paying fields. God gifts people in different ways, and to him all legitimate human work has inherent dignity. But we should make our financial decisions in the light of day.

SUMMARY

- Financial responsibility begins with the understanding that God owns everything. We are simply God's stewards, called to manage his resources in a way that advances his interests.
- To help our teens be faithful stewards of God's money,

we must teach them basic skills like making a budget, balancing a checkbook, and tithing off the top. They also need to understand how compounding interest works and the difference between a debit card and a credit card.

- At college our teens will need to distinguish wants from needs, live within their means, and avoid consumer debt. They should look for ways to keep their housing, food, textbook, transportation, and entertainment expenses at levels they can afford.

- Our teens should plan to earn money primarily during summers and breaks while at college, prioritizing their academic work when classes are in session.

- Our teens should view student debt as a last resort and should fully count the cost before signing any loans. This includes an accurate consideration of their likelihood of success, time to graduation, and salary prospects upon graduation.

CONVERSATION STARTERS

1. Teens are naturally in the process of separating from their parents and establishing their own identities. Talk with your teens about the measure of freedom and responsibility they currently have with regard to their finances. Brainstorm ways they can take increasing ownership for their financial decisions as they move through high school and leave for college.

2. You may have already covered this in your child raising, but ask your teens what they think of tithing. What is its purpose? Is it important, and why? How would they explain and defend the practice to friends who aren't believers?

3. Ask your teens what they think (or have heard) about using student loans to pay for some of their college-related expenses. Discuss the perils of student debt, and brainstorm strategies for saving and earning in order to minimize (if not avoid) debt.

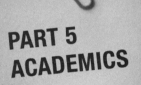

**PART 5
ACADEMICS**

CONVERSATION 8

Encouraging Teens to Work (Academically) unto the Lord

RYAN WAS A bright guy who came from an accomplished family. His parents pushed him early and often. Academic success and college readiness were a big deal in their home, though it never really had anything to do with God. Ryan went on to make his parents proud by getting accepted to one of the top universities in the nation. Once there, his life took a turn for the worse. High school had come easily for Ryan, especially with his parents cracking the whip. But he had never developed a vision for learning, and with a full plate of tougher classes, his grades promptly nose-dived.

Megan's family encouraged her to view high school as a season of preparation. School wasn't easy, but her grades got better over time, and she ended up at a moderately selective college with a partial scholarship in violin. By then Megan had become disciplined and responsible. She transitioned well to her new environment, earning a 3.5 GPA in her first year while making a few good friends in her major. Looking back, she and her parents were really happy with how things were going.

In the next two chapters, we'll focus on academic preparation for college—which some might say *is* college preparation, but I would beg to differ. There is a reason I put the character chapters first in this book. True success in life—academically, professionally, and elsewhere—is the overflow of the inner life, a person's worldview and moral character. Ryan floundered because his preparation for college had been superficial. His only motivation to study had been to keep his parents off his back. Once he left home, his true colors were revealed in the form of laziness and poor judgment. Megan's high school years weren't perfect, but she had learned to view studying as a way to honor God. As she stepped up in diligence, her parents enjoyed transitioning from taskmasters to cheerleaders. This internal transformation prepared her for college. By contrast, Ryan's high school success was purely external, a mirage built on shifting sand that would soon drift away.

As I noted in the introduction:

Worldview & Character → **Attitudes & Behaviors** → **Habits & Destiny**

A person's *worldview* (how they think) and their *character* (who they are) impact their *attitude* (what they think) and their *behavior* (what they do). Attitude and behavior, in turn, give rise to a person's habits and life trajectory.

Where do academics fit in? Under the larger umbrella of attitudes and behaviors. How can we motivate our teens to get serious about their schoolwork, not in an anxious, oh-no-what-if-I-get-a-B sort of way, but from an attitude of truly wanting to glorify God with their minds? Is that even possible? It's unlikely to happen without our coaching. There's no exact formula, and every child is different, but here are three strategies that can go a long way: modeling the goodness of work to them in the way *we* act toward and talk about our responsibilities; reminding them that schoolwork is their God-appointed work; and helping them find enjoyment in the learning process. We'll explore these three strategies in the first part of this chapter. In the second part, we'll flesh out what a teen with these values might look like.

THREE STRATEGIES FOR MOTIVATING TEENS

Modeling the Goodness of Work

In the last chapter we talked about financial stewardship: God has entrusted us with his wealth so that we can use it to advance his purposes. But stewardship applies to far more than our finances. It extends to our time, talents, and opportunities—our entire lives, really. God has put us in charge of his good world (see Genesis 1:28). Why? So that we might use our God-given faculties to accomplish good things in a way that puts God's greatness on display and makes the world increasingly serviceable for humanity.

This is all the more important after the Fall, since the human race is now in rebellion against God (see Romans 3:23; 1 John 5:19). Those who trust in Jesus are being re-created in God's likeness (see Ephesians 4:24; Colossians 3:10) so that we can get back to doing what God intended. Jesus, in essence, *recommissions* his followers in Matthew 5:16: "In the same way, let your light shine before others, so that they may see *your good works* and give glory to your Father who is in heaven" (emphasis added). Our good works don't save anyone—they aren't the gospel—but they flow from and testify to the gospel (see Titus 2:11-14) and are thus a part of our witness to what God has done in Jesus and what he offers to anyone who will accept it.

And what are these good works? Are they extraordinary acts of valor, done once in a blue moon, like selling our possessions and going to live in a remote region of Africa? Some are indeed called to make sacrifices of this sort for the name of Jesus. But good works extend to the regular, day-by-day output of a Christian's life, the discharging of duties associated with our various spheres of God-appointed responsibility (what some call vocations or callings). We're to do good "always" (1 Thessalonians 5:15), to bear "much" fruit (John 15:8), and to "abound in every good work" (2 Corinthians 9:8). Driving the kids to school, designing a new building, finalizing a financial report, teaching classes, coaching

Little League, making dinner, cleaning the house, caring for patients in a hospital—these and a thousand other tasks for Christians are good works, acts that please God and help others, assuming they're done for God's glory in the strength he supplies (see 1 Corinthians 10:31; 1 Peter 4:11).[1] So we have countless opportunities every day to model the goodness of work to our teens.

Note that motivation and attitude count. Getting things done with a grin-and-bear-it, duty-oriented demeanor doesn't cut it. When my wife graduated college, she worked for a Fortune 500 telephone company. She noticed her coworkers regularly counting down the years until retirement, as if their jobs were a burden to be endured (a little depressing for a 22-year-old just starting her career). If our teens see us display a "can't wait till Friday" mentality, they're likely to adopt the same attitude toward schoolwork.

Good works extend to the regular, day-by-day output of a Christian's life, the discharging of duties associated with our various spheres of God-appointed responsibility.

Don't get me wrong: there's a place for self-discipline and persevering under fire. We all have bad days and tasks we'd rather not do. Even Jesus "endured the cross" (motivated by a future joy—see Hebrews 12:2). But if we model a sincere gladness at the opportunity to employ our skills in the service of others, even when it's not easy, our teens are more likely to adopt that same perspective.

The question is, will they transfer this way of thinking to their schoolwork?

Helping Teens See Schoolwork as God Assigned

When parents model a positive perspective on work, one deeply rooted in their Christian faith, it's easier for teens to accept the biblical notion that work is good—a gift of God, by which we can showcase his image in us. Unfortunately, many teens who appreciate the value of work nevertheless regard schoolwork as impractical, uninteresting, and disconnected from the real world. "How does reading *Macbeth* and writing this English paper have anything to do with worshiping God or helping others?" This understandable (yet unfair) assessment can stem from misinformation on the student's part, dullness on the teacher's part, or some combination of the two. Whatever the cause, we need to acknowledge it and help our teens overcome this barrier to learning.

Encourage Teens to Have a Vision for Becoming Useful

When we think of what we want for our kids in life, many things probably come to mind: health, happiness, a good marriage, a well-paying job, children of their own. But have you ever hoped that your teens would be *useful*? That might sound strange. But remember back in conversation 2 when we talked about the importance of teens having a future-orientation? That vision for the future needs to include usefulness. God created us and has saved us that we might do good works, which glorify him and truly serve others (see Ephesians 2:8-10).

Many of us love the classic Jimmy Stewart film *It's a Wonderful Life*. It's such a vivid reminder of how many lives a single life touches. Pastor John Angell James (1785–1859), a giant of the faith, spoke of how biblical Christianity makes people "holy and useful" and of how education "enlarges the sphere of our usefulness, by raising the degree of our influence. Other things being equal, that man will be the most useful, who has the greatest measure of information."[2] Let your teens know what a wonderful thing it is to be useful, to have a positive influence in the world, to live in such a way that others benefit from their endeavors. And usefulness requires competence, and competence requires lifelong learning and continuous improvement. Starting . . . now.

I became a Christian when I was about 14 years old. Regrettably, for several years my understanding of Christian ethics was mainly one of avoidance: don't curse, don't smoke, don't drink, don't have sex, don't watch the wrong movies, and so on. These are wise admonitions for a teenager, but they're insufficient. They don't give a practical, future-oriented vision for getting up in the morning; going to school; and studying geometry, biology, English, and history. But such a vision is what's needed to propel good works in the academic realm *today*.

Teens need to appreciate that future usefulness requires good preparation, which means diligent effort. Amazingly, in a survey of more than 2,000 high school seniors in the Chicago area, sociologist James Rosenbaum found that almost half of them (46 percent) agreed with the statement "Even if I do not work hard in high school, I can still make my future plans come true."[3] Churched teens might even put a Christian spin on such wishful thinking: "It's all in God's hands."

True, but God has given us intellectual abilities along with 24 hours each day, and he calls us to be good stewards, as ones who will have to give an account.

Encourage Teens to View Schoolwork as Part of Their Spiritual Worship

The book of Proverbs tells us that "the fear of the LORD is the beginning of knowledge" and "fools despise wisdom and instruction" (Proverbs 1:7). The fear of the Lord should motivate our teens to align their hearts with God's—that is, to hate sin and pursue holiness (see Proverbs 8:13). Biblical values and habits of moral character are vital if great knowledge is to be employed toward noble ends. The Bible also tells us to work hard at learning: "Apply your heart to instruction and your ear to words of knowledge" (Proverbs 23:12). While the Bible isn't a math or science text per se, all of nature "declare[s] the glory of God" (Psalm 19:1). All truth, wherever it's found, has a unifying source in the Triune God, the creator and sustainer of "all things . . . visible and invisible" (Colossians 1:16-17).

The reason intellectual growth is both possible and desirable is that we've been made in God's image, as vice-regents of his orderly creation. Our learning is to be a stimulant to a more informed worship of God and a more competent service to others. The beauty in a good piece of music or art, the logical rigor and consistency in the laws of mathematics and science, and our sense of right and wrong in assessing historical and contemporary issues are not disconnected accidents for the Christian student. They are evidences of the beauty, goodness, intelligence, justice, and rationality of God.

Encourage Teens Not to Fear the Secular, but to Engage It

I've known some parents who take the view that the only subject their teens need to study is the Bible. That and their children's character are all that's emphasized in their homes. Everything else is secular, polluted in one way or another and unworthy of attention. While an emphasis on Christian character is crucial and studying the Bible is essential, the denigration of scholastic pursuits in other areas goes too far. The Bible presents to us a God who reigns over every aspect of his creation. He's honored when his children pursue mathematical and scientific truth: "Great are the works of the LORD, studied by all who delight in them" (Psalm 111:2). And he's honored when we play the piano, or practice singing, or create beautiful artwork as expressions of worship, even if those activities never put food on anyone's table.

I went to college in a rural part of western New York. Few who lived in the town had themselves ever gone to college. Those I met at church were friendly enough, but they believed in reading the Bible and devotional literature and not much else. From their perspective, what made work legitimate was its immediate, tangible impact in the lives of others. A farmer was doing real work—he was producing food to feed scores of families (including his own). A janitor was doing real work—if he didn't clean the halls and bathrooms, they'd become so dusty and dirty that people would

For a couple of years in junior high, when we were still homeschooling our sons, I occasionally took them (one at a time) to the office with me for a day of work. They sat quietly, read, and studied. They saw what I did, how I interacted with coworkers, that people asked my opinion. It made them see their dad in a different light. And I'd like to think I was able to model to them the importance of working unto the Lord.

We also put in occasional workdays for family friends in which my sons and I performed manual labor (mowed lawns, dug ditches, etc.). It didn't take long for them to see the contrast between using their brains versus using *sheer* brawn. I'm not dismissing trade jobs. Working in a trade can take a lot of mental acumen, but work that doesn't require thinking is more easily replaceable by someone younger, stronger, or more energetic. For a long-term career it's advisable to develop your mind—to work hard *and* smart—and this requires study, discipline, and a willingness to learn, all of which are easier when a person is young, and all of which are helpful in future white-collar or blue-collar jobs.

David

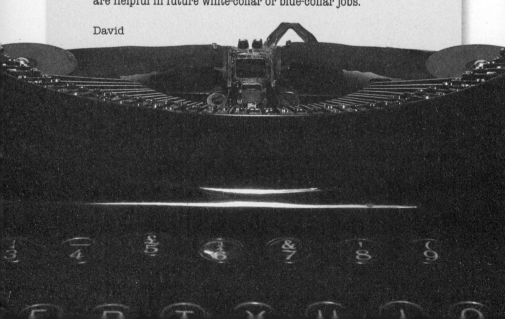

catch diseases. But me? I was studying calculus and thermo-dynamics, trying to get ready for tests the next week. What good did that do? Reading the Bible—that made sense. But Plato and Socrates? Come on.

I don't say this to insult the work of farmers or janitors. Nor do I wish to suggest that hands-on jobs don't require intelligence, skill, or training; that's a myth we'll bust in conversation 11. But these sincere Christians had gone too far in downplaying schoolwork. Reading books of cultural significance, studying science, and learning advanced math-ematics prepare our teens for many lines of valuable work. They also prepare them to engage the culture in important ways. We're not to be of the world, but we are sent into it (see John 17:14-18). That doesn't happen when we retreat into Christian cocoons, afraid of listening to what non-Christians have to say. That also belittles the God who gives gifts and insights even to those who don't yet follow him (see Matthew 5:44-45; John 1:9; Romans 1:19-21).[4]

Encourage Teens to See the Practical, Long-Term Value of Schoolwork

Some teens are ambitious, in a good way—and impatient. Like the late Steve Jobs, they want to "make a dent in the universe." They want to do big things—like fight human trafficking, alleviate extreme poverty, or develop an awesome iPhone app—and they want to do them now. They don't want to mess around with busywork that seems irrelevant to where they feel they're headed.

All of us hunger to see the relevance of what we're doing. It's deflating to be forced to do things that seem uninteresting or unimportant, especially if we have our sights on work that energizes us and seems significant. We should commend ambition in our teens. God is pleased when his children wish to imitate his greatness by accomplishing and being part of something significant. It's what he made us for. And busywork is certainly not the ideal. Academic assignments should be challenging, facilitating a deep understanding of the material. Ambitious teens are often bored; their schoolwork is too easy, or they're under teachers who don't make the content come alive and feel relevant. If this describes your teens, you might consider if they could switch into more demanding courses with new (and often better) teachers. That was my experience.

But what I also wish I'd heard in high school is that academic skills are highly transferable. Math and science courses teach students how to think analytically, how to reason so as to make an argument from A to B to C. Good philosophy or logic courses do this too. It's a skill that comes in handy when making basic financial decisions (like renting a home versus buying one) or when trying to trace a problem back to the root cause. How about literature, history, or any other class that requires reading? Even if some of the assigned topics don't tickle your teens' fancy, learning to read well is of immeasurable value. Reading makes us better thinkers and listeners because it forces us to follow what someone else is saying—and if we get lost, to go back and figure it out.

And writing—which for high schoolers usually means

Tip
How to Read a Book by Mortimer Adler and Charles Van Doren (New York: Fine Communications, 1972) is a classic resource on how to assess information. The authors describe different levels of reading and when to apply each one.

responding to something they've read—forces them to understand the author's thesis and to engage with it in an accurate, nonsuperficial manner. What many have found is that writing helps them figure out what *they* think, because it forces them to clearly string ideas together. That's certainly been the case for me. And speaking of transferability, if your children are the math and science type (the kind I teach at college), remind them they'll never escape having to give presentations or write memos, so it's worth taking the time to improve their written and oral communication skills, even if they'll never like them as much as numbers or experiments. Every employer I've spoken to puts communication skills toward the top of the list of what they're looking for in new hires.

We need to help our teens be patient and work hard, even when they can't see an immediate payoff. Encourage them to not despise "the day of small things" (Zechariah 4:10). Little acts of faithfulness now—writing an essay, doing math homework, studying for a history test—prepare them for greater feats in the years to come. No doubt some, through extracurricular involvement, will make substantial contributions even in their teen years. And that's great when it happens. But even Jesus spent 30 years in obscurity, being faithful to his parents and his carpentry work (see Luke 2:51-52). The apostle Paul spent three years in Arabia before launching his public ministry (see Galatians 1:17-18). And Daniel was trained in Babylon for three years, after which he was found "ten times better" than his Babylonian peers in "every matter of wisdom and understanding" (Daniel 1:8, 18-20). Those years got him ready for significant service to Kings Nebuchadnezzar and Belshazzar.

High school academics, pursued rightly, provide a good foundation for whatever comes next. Since teens tend to have a short horizon, and since schoolwork can be difficult, we need to help them take the long view. Because of the Fall, all work is sometimes tedious and frustrating, so they ought not be surprised. Remind them that they're young and have (in all likelihood) a long life in front of them. High school academics—the work itself and the character it develops— are directly and indirectly preparing them for every future endeavor. Nevertheless, we should do what we can to make learning engaging, enjoyable, and connected to real-world applications that our teens can appreciate.

Helping Teens Love Learning

In conversation 3 I quoted Jim Rayburn, the founder of Young Life, who said, "It's a sin to bore a kid with the gospel." Although some take this too far, Jim makes a good point. Something as important as the gospel should be presented in a winsome manner. As a professor, I feel similarly about academics. I think it's shameful when teachers are boring. We should do our best to make learning as attractive, interesting, and worthwhile as possible. And I'm not just talking to those who homeschool. We can all be genuinely excited for what our teens are learning, particularly if it's something *they're* interested in. You'd be surprised how contagious such enthusiasm can be.

Good teachers can do this too. I remember my junior-year history teacher, Mr. Pobst. One day he was teaching about World War II and how Hitler had expelled the Jews without cause. We students were incredulous: "The German people just let him do that?" Mr. Pobst explained the German reaction to the Treaty of Versailles, the psychological need for a scapegoat, and how questioning authority is easier said than done. Somewhere in that, he physically grabbed a student (Kyle) by the shoulder and told him to stand outside. I remember thinking that Kyle must have misbehaved (although I hadn't seen anything). Class resumed, with students (myself included) continuing to pontificate about how *we* would have defended the Jews had we been there. Eventually Mr. Pobst chimed in, "Like Kyle? Did anyone defend Kyle?" He had tossed Kyle out without cause, just to see if anyone would stand up for him! It was an unforgettable object lesson. (And I think Kyle eventually forgave him.)

There is no reason why new concepts and information can't be presented in a creative, captivating manner, one that draws teens into an intellectually rich discussion. To the extent possible, expose your teens to teachers like Mr. Pobst, because they make students love learning, see the practicality of it, and want to do more of it.

Active vs. Passive Learning?

The importance of students loving learning can be seen in the current trend in education toward *active learning* and away from *passive learning*. High school teachers and college professors are encouraged to integrate opportunities for interaction during their class periods, as opposed to giving unbroken lectures. Why? Research finds that even the best lecturers don't achieve the highest levels of long-term learning in their students. Approaches that require students to be involved in the discovery process often work better. At the very least, they complement well-crafted lectures. Tutorial, laboratory, and moderated discussion sessions deepen student understanding because they force *students* to wrestle with the concepts more than they would if they merely received lectures all the time.

I'm not trying to justify the distractibility of some teens. Many would do well to become better, more active listeners—a skill that can be learned. It involves picking out the main points, taking good notes, making associations, and patiently holding questions until the appropriate time. Nevertheless, the burden also falls on teachers to find ways to engage their students.

But what can you do if your teens have dull teachers who make academic work seem irrelevant? Here are some steps everyone can take:

1. *Go on family field trips.* Museums, aquariums, art institutes, planetariums, festivals, concerts, hikes, and historic tours can all provide educational value. But also think about road trips and summer vacations. Clearly, it's easier if your teens are studying US history, but maybe there's a pertinent museum exhibit you can view when your teen is studying world history.

2. *Work on a science project together.* Don't do it for them, but get involved. Encourage them to pick a topic that interests them. That's important. Then fuel the fire of their curiosity by being curious yourself. Help them find resources and focus on main issues over peripheral details. If you have a background in science, can you help them design a few simple experiments?

3. *Join their literature class.* Try reading whatever book your teens are reading. Or if the book has been made into a movie, perhaps rent the DVD and watch it together. Then discuss the major themes. In what ways was the movie faithful to the book, and what did Hollywood alter? What were the character traits of the protagonists? What did they want, and what (or who) was standing in their way? Is there an

argument or central idea about the human condition being conveyed? Is that idea or argument true?

4. *Go to public lectures.* Local colleges often have these in the evening, and they're usually free and open to the public. Topics can be all over the map, as can the perspectives presented. They won't all be good (colleges can be bastions of postmodernism and bizarre curiosities), but many will be. My wife grew up going to lectures and debates at Stanford University. I've been attending such lectures for the past 15 years on topics ranging from film studies to economics to US foreign policy.

5. *Encourage your teens to love reading.* Reading is one of those things that seems to be falling by the wayside for teens in our day. Whether it's because of the Internet or cell phones or who knows what, teens simply aren't reading, at least not at the level and frequency that they used to.[5] The 2012 Renaissance Learning Survey of books assigned to high school students found that the top 40 titles were, on average, at a sixth-grade reading level.[6] See if this is happening at your teens' school. Ask teachers to give you lists of classics that were once more commonly read by teens. There's no reason why they can't read great works by William Shakespeare, Nathaniel Hawthorne, Mark Twain, John Milton, Jane Austen, C. S. Lewis, J. R. R. Tolkien, and Fyodor Dostoyevsky.

Dr. Benjamin Carson, a retired neurosurgeon from Johns Hopkins and a bestselling author, once reflected on his childhood reading with these words: "We were very poor, but between the covers of those books, I could be anybody, I could do anything."[7] He didn't enjoy it at first, but his (illiterate) mother required him to write two book reports per week. Eventually he came to love reading. In hindsight, Dr. Carson credits reading with taking him from the bottom of the class to the top. The same could be said of many others.

It's noteworthy that God chose to reveal himself to us in a book. Those who don't wish to read will probably not read the Bible. If your teens are hooked on texting or playing silly cell phone games, prod them toward a more rewarding and mentally stimulating addiction. Of course, people have different aptitudes when it comes to books. Not everyone will become a bibliophile, and that's okay. But all teens should be encouraged to read, not only because reading will expand their horizons but because reading will strengthen their analytical and creative faculties. Those faculties, in turn, will allow them to keep learning and improving throughout their lives in whatever God calls them to do.

In summary, the love for learning that fuels academic success, rightly understood, is the overflow of teens' commitment to love God with their minds. Teens who welcome adulthood will pursue their schoolwork with vigor because it honors God and prepares them for a lifetime of usefulness. They'll do their best to enjoy learning and will persevere even when it isn't fun.

WHAT MOTIVATED TEENS LOOK LIKE

Let's explore two aspects of how this might look in practice: prioritizing learning over grades, and working smart.

Prioritizing Learning over Grades

Austin came to my office with a puzzled look on his face. I had recently handed back an exam, and on one problem he had lost about half the points. Yet he had put down the correct final answer. Like many professors, I award points based on a student's answers *and* methods, so I asked Austin to explain how he had approached the problem. He couldn't remember but was hoping I could take a look.

I stared at it and then went into professor mode. I explained that he had made two conceptual errors that ended up (fortuitously) canceling each other out, resulting in the correct answer. There were certain situations where his method would have been correct, I explained, but there were several reasons why this problem was different. I waxed eloquent (I'm sure) for about five minutes while Austin listened patiently. I thought he was interested, until he responded dejectedly, "So I'm not getting any points back?"

I'm embarrassed to admit that I was often the same way

as a student. Here's what I wish someone had told me in high school: teachers intend grades to be a by-product of learning, an assessment of a student's mastery. Students short-circuit the process when they make their grade the primary objective. This mentality leads students to prefer "easy As" to actual learning.

> Teachers intend grades to be a by-product of learning, an assessment of a student's mastery. Students short-circuit the process when they make their grade the primary objective.

The irony is that once students get to college, nobody will ever again ask them for their high school GPA. Yet when their college classes are in full swing, many look back and wish they had learned more in high school. Here's an exchange I've had many times. Me: "Did you learn this concept in high school?" Student: "Sort of. But I don't really remember anything about it. It was a super-easy course. We never had to do anything difficult." The student then sheepishly confesses that a tougher class might have been better in the long run.

Remind your teens that their GPAs (and by extension, their high school diplomas) are worth only as much as they actually signify. They're supposed to signify that a transformation has taken place in a student's mind, forever impacting the student for the better. An education happens inside a person, and when it has happened, nobody can take it away. An increased appreciation for God's majesty in his creation. An ability to read challenging passages, comprehend the author's meaning, and intelligently respond, orally or in writing. An ability to perform mathematical operations and

Q: *Our son, Joshua, was caught plagiarizing a paper using the Internet. How can we help him see this as wrong?*

A: Unfortunately, cheating has become rampant in high school and college. The Internet has blurred the lines between collaboration and cheating, making plagiarism as easy as copying and pasting. As I write, Harvard College is recovering from a huge scandal in which some 70 students were expelled for cheating.

It's one thing to do research on the Internet, citing reputable sources appropriately, but the ideas and logical flow of a paper should be the student's. It's possible he simply doesn't understand this distinction. In that case, help him see that copying things off the Internet is wrong because it deceitfully misrepresents the author of a work. It's saying "this is Joshua's work," when it's really someone else's.

In my experience, however, most students who plagiarize *know* it's wrong. But they're so caught up in the game of "needing" good grades that they violate their consciences. They fear failure. So they take the easy way out. Walk through this with Joshua: Is it really in his interest to go through school copying other people's work? A life built on such deceit is eventually exposed, resulting in humiliation.

Help Joshua see that if he prioritizes learning over grades, he can enjoy the peace and freedom that come from knowing he did his best. And in the long run that's worth more than straight As.

understand scientific principles. An accurate understanding of US and world history. These are inherently valuable, apart from any grades. Students who truly love learning would not be content with an "easy A" when they could have learned more in another class. Nor would they feel right about receiving an A without having genuinely mastered the material.

Unfortunately, too many high school teachers are willing to play along, inflating grades to the point where As and Bs become meaningless. By contrast, accurate grades are a blessing to those who prioritize learning, because they provide a true assessment of students' skill in particular subjects. Good students want to know the truth about how well they're doing; they don't want to be flattered with empty praise and inflated grades. Those just set them up for failure down the road.

The Benefits of Prioritizing Learning over Grades

Harold Abrahams and Eric Liddell were elite British runners whose stories were told in the 1981 Academy Award–winning film *Chariots of Fire*. Abrahams and Liddell had very different orientations to their running. Abrahams was talented and hardworking but insecure and unhappy. To him, a race represented "10 lonely seconds to justify my whole existence." It wasn't enough to run; Abrahams had to *win*.

Liddell was likewise talented and hardworking, but he had so much peace with who he was before God as a man and as a Christian that he could forgo a likely gold medal rather than betray his conscience by competing on Sunday. Liddell's perspective on running? "When I run, I feel his pleasure." The joy for Liddell was in the running itself, done *coram Deo* (before the face of God). It wasn't about winning or medals.

If our teens make good grades more important than learning, they'll go the way of Abrahams. It's the path of anxiety, insecurity, and jealousy. Prioritizing grades makes a student nervous, which is less enjoyable and often leads to a worse outcome. Have you ever seen athletes choke under pressure, performing well below their abilities? Chances are anxiety got in the way. When teens focus on learning, they tend to be more relaxed. Which means they are happier, learn more, and get better grades. It's a win-win-win.

Second, by prioritizing learning, teens' tendencies to live for the praise of others is weakened. They're freed (like Liddell) to live for God's praise. Elevating achievement to the place of ultimate importance is part of a broader bondage of finding dignity and worth in what we *do* rather than who we *are*.

Third, prioritizing learning makes students less competitive toward each other. In 1 Corinthians 4:7 we're reminded, "What do you have that you did not receive? If then you received it, why do you boast as if you did not receive it?" Suppose Emily is in an honors-level US history class with her friend Hannah. Emily got a B- on a recent test, while Hannah got an A. If Emily remembers that her (and Hannah's) abilities come from God, she can have peace, even though her friend got a higher score. The grade isn't the point. She did her best. God was honored; that's what matters. Emily is

Can Academics Become Too Important?

Just as some teens deprioritize academics, some teens over-prioritize academics, to the point where grades become an all-consuming idol. In both cases, parents, beware: whether it's too low or too high a view, your teen will more naturally gravitate toward whichever extreme you model in the home.

The objective of high school academics ought to be learning, but even learning is not an ultimate end. The ultimate end is a more informed worship of God resulting in a more competent love of neighbor. As the Westminster Catechism teaches, our chief end is "to glorify God and enjoy him forever." Our learning can enhance our worship, but it can also puff us up with pride (see 1 Corinthians 8:1). The longing for prestige and admiration, the desire to be on the top of the social ladder, the longing to know and understand more than anyone else—these are common idols in academia, all of which ultimately enslave and disappoint. As parents, we need to be careful not to motivate our teens toward academic excellence so that we can brag about them at neighborhood or church social events. That would only reinforce the same sort of worldliness in our teens.

freed to learn from Hannah and to help others who may have struggled more. In both cases, a *grace*-orientation trumps a *grade*-orientation. Success is redefined for Emily when she remembers her dependency on God, prioritizes learning, and works "unto the Lord" (see Colossians 3:23-24). She becomes mindful that while her teachers (rightly) look at external results, God "looks at the heart" (1 Samuel 16:7, NLT). And since it's God's praise that ultimately counts, Emily can have peace whatever the outcome.

Is Hannah simply smarter than Emily? That's a tough call to make. Assuming that both Emily and Hannah studied for their US history test, the different outcome might be the result of Hannah being naturally more gifted, but it could also be that Hannah worked harder. Or—more likely—she may have worked *smarter*.

Working Smart

It's my belief that academic performance is a function of four things: God-given talent, background, hard work, and smart work. The Bible is clear that talents are distributed unevenly, and I'm pretty sure my poor choir teacher knew it too. The distribution of talent is God's business; ours is to be faithful with what has been entrusted to us (see Matthew 25:14-30). Background—previous education or exposure to certain concepts—happened in the past, and you can't go back in time. We've talked elsewhere about the importance of working hard. If teens are undisciplined or lazy, they simply cannot do as well in the long run. Assuming Emily is disciplined in her studies, what can make a big difference is working *smarter*.

It's the only other knob she can turn, but it's a really big knob. When I finally learned how to work smart (my senior year in high school), my GPA jumped almost a full point and never went back down during college. Below are a few tips for your teens that helped me. Each of them is consistent with prioritizing learning over grades and trying to enjoy the process rather than worrying about the outcome:

- It was Jim Elliot who said, "Wherever you are, be all there." Mental focus is huge—in class and while studying. An hour of focused work can accomplish more than two hours of distracted work. Turn off the cell phone.
- In lectures, listen for the main points and look for how the subpoints relate to the main points. Don't lose the forest for the trees. Keep your eye on the big picture. Do this when studying and reading, too.
- Don't bang your head against the wall for too long. It's good to persevere, but if you can't figure something out, get help (from Mom or Dad, a classmate, or the teacher). There's no shame in it—as long as you don't let them do it all for you!
- Use the calendar feature of a cell phone (or a calendar or planner) to keep track of when things are due. Take time daily and weekly to review due dates and to schedule time to work on assignments.

Who's Right: East or West?

We're told that countries like China and South Korea push memori-zation but give short shrift to creativity. The United States values out-of-the-box thinking but deemphasizes rote learning. Who's right?

What I've found is that memorization of the fundamentals frees a student to be creative and innovative. Teens have sharp minds, and with a bit of effort and discipline, they can truly master gobs of information—facts, figures, and concepts that can later be called upon at a moment's notice.

Students are not well served when they need their calculators to perform basic arithmetic or have to consult Google to find fundamen-tal facts that a previous generation of students simply *knew*. Students should be required to do more in their heads without becoming so technology dependent. American schools often underestimate the power of memorization, especially in math, science, and foreign lan-guages. Rote learning, especially at an early age, sharpens a person's brain, making creative processes later in life more readily attainable. I saw this lived out in graduate school with my foreign classmates, whose rote knowledge *and* creativity often exceeded mine.

In short, rote learning builds a platform of knowledge—a tool chest from which students can later draw. As students get older, educators can call upon them to be innovative because they've already mastered the fundamentals.[8]

- Start the bigger or more challenging assignments early. Mishaps occur. Things take longer than you hope. And this way, you can chip away at them rather than be forced to put in all-nighters at the last minute.
- On research projects, know the difference between legitimate sources and fluff. Blogs and Wikipedia are not subject to the same review processes as technical journals and reputable periodicals.

SUMMARY

- Our teens must learn to work unto the Lord—to cultivate a vision for future usefulness, to embrace their current status as students in a season of preparation, and to take a distinctively Christian perspective on their academic studies.
- We can help our teens get there by modeling the goodness of work to them in the way *we* act toward and talk about our responsibilities, reminding them that schoolwork is their God-appointed work, and helping them find enjoyment in the learning process by showing them the relevance of learning and by challenging them intellectually.
- The purpose of academic work is learning (not grades), and the purpose of learning is a more informed worship of God, resulting in a more competent love of neighbor.
- Motivated teens prioritize learning over grades, resulting in greater peace of mind, and they work

smart, resulting in more learning and (often) better grades.

CONVERSATION STARTERS

1. Ask your teens if they ever feel like their schoolwork is disconnected from the real world. Which subjects seem disconnected, and why?

2. Ask your teens: What is the purpose of a high school education? Do you think your schoolwork is achieving this purpose? What steps can you take to get more out of school?

3. Describe your favorite teacher to your teens, and ask them about theirs. What did you (and they) like most about that teacher?

4. Discuss with your teens the link between Christianity, academic learning in general, and loving God with their minds.

CONVERSATION 9

Discovering Your Teens' Talents and Interests

JACOB GRIMACED AS his dad called him from the kitchen. "Jacob, can you come in here for a second?" His midsemester report card had come in the mail, and Jacob was nervous about how his dad might respond. Jacob walked in from the backyard. "What's up, Dad?"

"I was just looking at your report card."

"Yeah, I was afraid of that. Look, I know precalculus was bad, but I really did try."

"Actually, what stood out to me were your As in English and history. Way to go! Are you surprised to be doing that well in those classes?"

Jacob was taken aback. Dad didn't want to talk about the C in precalc? His friend Justin had been grounded for getting a C in chemistry.

"Uh . . . sort of, I guess. Those are my favorite classes. I felt good about our history test a couple weeks ago, and I've enjoyed the reading we've done so far in English this semester. I've gotten As on my essays and on my short story."

"The reason I asked," Dad responded, "is that we know you've never liked math. But all through high school you've been getting better in any class that involves reading or writing. Have you thought about what you could do with that after high school?"

Jacob replied, "Not really. But Mr. Simpson encouraged me to enter a writing contest he knows about."

"Oh, yeah?" Dad said. "That's great! You should go for it. And hey, this Saturday, why don't we go out for lunch? I want to give you some ideas for what you could do someday if you keep enjoying things like history and English."

"Um . . . sure, that works."

Wow. Jacob was delighted that his fears of parental backlash were unfounded. Now if only his precalculus fears could be so easily expelled. . . .

THE HEART OF ACADEMIC DEVELOPMENT

Some of us are natural pessimists. I don't know about you, but I pick up on deficiencies far more readily than I acknowledge strengths or a job well done. In looking at our teens (and at their report cards), it's easy to get caught up with the problem areas—the weaknesses—rather than the strengths. We look at their lower grades and tell ourselves how awful it is that (in this case) Jacob has a C in precalculus. Or perhaps we put a positive spin on it and proclaim that precalculus is a "growth opportunity." Yes, he has a C in precalc, but if Jacob were to improve in that subject, just think how much his GPA could go up!

And that's true, in a sense. There's more room for improvement in a class in which Jacob is getting a C than one in which he's getting a B. If Jacob's C is owing to laziness, there's certainly no excuse for that. Or maybe Jacob needs to work a bit smarter, like we talked about at the end of the last chapter.

But Jacob's dad is doing something very wise in this conversation. He's focusing on his son's strengths rather than his weaknesses, because ultimately Jacob's strengths reveal his talents, and his talents represent his areas of greatest potential. In all likelihood, Jacob will never be great at (or enjoy) math, numbers, equations, and all the rest. At most, his efforts to improve his grade in precalculus are damage control, an attempt to prevent his GPA from taking too much of a hit. It has to be done sometimes, of course, especially in cases where a student is in the D or F range (and graduation might be at risk). But we shouldn't confuse damage control with the heart of academic development: the discovery and nurturing of our teens' God-given talents and interests.

For some, like Jacob, it might be ideas and words. Teens like him often go on to become teachers, journalists, lawyers, editors, philosophy professors, or freelance writers. For others, it might be math and physics. They'll often go on to become engineers, computer programmers, accountants, or actuaries. For still others it might be illustration and design.

They'll go on to become graphic artists, architects, or professional animators. And of course, these are but a few of the many possibilities. Some teens have a strong affinity and level of skill for a wide variety of subjects—they're great at just about everything. It's a nice problem to have, even if it sometimes makes it harder for them to decide upon a college major.

The heart of academic development is the discovery and nurturing of our teens' God-given talents and interests.

Here's the point. In God's wisdom, he did not fashion us to be carbon copies of one another. We each have our particular blend of talents and interests to go along with our unique personal history and temperament, all of which play a role in determining the kinds of work for which we'll ultimately be best suited. To be successful, students do not have to be jacks of all trades. They need to focus on what they like—what they're willing to work hard at, what they hope to someday be really good at. And it helps if they're already showing some promise for long-term success in those areas.

The last chapter was about the importance of teens loving learning itself. This chapter is about how teens, from the strong foundation of being diligent and cheerful learners, can discover and nurture their God-given talents and academic interests. By *talents* I mean any innate tendencies in their thought, feeling, or behavior that can be channeled into academic or professional success. And by *interests*, I'm referring to desires to pursue certain types of study (for example, law, business, science, education, physical therapy) or to address specific needs (for example, inner-city youth, mothers in crisis pregnancies, children with special needs).

Though I'm primarily discussing *academic* interests in this chapter, I certainly don't want to discount teens' interests in particular social or global issues. If all your teens know about their interests is that they are passionate about a specific kind of injustice or suffering in the world, nurture that interest by looking for ways they can do something about it now—and by looking into what kind of education might be most strategic in preparing them to make a significant impact in that field down the road. For example, they might want to double major in business and global studies, with the long-term goal of assisting microenterprises in the developing world.

We want our teens to discover and nurture those things they're naturally good at (talents) and love (interests). And we'd like this discovery process to be actively unfolding while they're in high school so that they graduate ready to start college (or vocational school) with a sense of who they are and where they're going. So as you read this chapter, think about how you can best help your teens decide upon a direction for their future studies in an informed and intelligent manner.

HELPING YOUR TEENS DISCOVER THEIR TALENTS AND INTERESTS

While more high school graduates than ever are immediately pursuing college, the majority of them will change their academic major at least once. This might have been no big deal a generation ago, when the cost of college was far more manage-able, but in our day I'm concerned that such indecisiveness can come at a price in the tens of thousands of dollars. Don't get me wrong—there are definitely times when switching majors is legitimate, and if your teens think it might happen, there are ways to minimize the impact. For some students, it may be wiser to make a final decision on a major after taking a class or two at college in their possible major. That said, the more informed and self-aware we can help our teens become before they leave for college, the better.

How can we accomplish this? By doing the kind of thing Jacob's dad is doing: taking the time to kick-start our teens' thinking about what comes after high school. Jacob's dad is helping his son listen to both his heart (English and history are his favorite classes) and the objective feedback of those with expertise (his teachers). Jacob hasn't yet thought about what he wants to do, and that's not uncommon (I hadn't either at his age). Don't wait for your teens to come to you. Bring them ideas and stoke their curiosity. Make the conversation a fun interaction by combining it with lunch, ice cream, a baseball game, or even an overnight trip. It's a discussion that can happen in bits and pieces as they're grow-ing up, but it should become more intentional and focused toward the latter part of their high school years. Note that it's ideal to have college applications submitted in the early months of your teens' senior year. So their junior year (and perhaps sooner) is a good time to initiate focused dialogue on this topic.

What if your teens can't think of anything that interests them? Aim to light ambition's fire by introducing them to the needs of the world and some of the countless ways we can serve God. Encourage them to go on short-term mission trips, to volunteer for ministries or nonprofits, to read books on some of the pressing social and global needs of our day, to listen to lectures by people doing impactful work. Praise them when they do well on a test, paper, or project—positive

Assessing Teens' Interests

- Are there any constructive activities they really enjoy doing?
- What is their favorite subject at school?
- What do they talk about all the time?
- Is there any kind of work that engrosses them, making them lose track of time?
- Is there a class they wish they could take?
- If salary were irrelevant, what would they call their ideal job (their answer must include serving other people, providing them some kind of product or service—being useful)? Would they work with their hands? At a computer? With books, people, machines, or equations? In a classroom, library, theater, laboratory, or outdoors?

reinforcement can be vital, especially when it's rooted in an objective accomplishment. Recall that good works aren't some ultra-special category of actions, but the entirety of our obedience within all our realms of responsibility. William Wilberforce (1759–1833), a devout Christian whose tireless political efforts led to the abolition of the slave trade in the British empire, made this remark: "No man has a right to

Assessing Teens' Talents

- In what areas, if any, has success come to them more quickly or with greater ease than it did for their peers? In what areas have they gone further than their peers?

- Where have they found the most success (such as good grades, projects well received, volunteer work done well, music, sports)?

- Do knowledgeable, trustworthy adults ever tell you, "I could really see your teen doing (fill in the blank) when (s)he is older"?

- According to teachers, coaches, or mentors, in what kinds of situations does your teen shine?

- What kinds of jobs can *you* see them doing? Would they work with their hands? At a computer? With books, people, machines, or equations? In a classroom, library, theater, laboratory, or outdoors? On what do you base your assessment?

be idle. . . . Where is it that, in such a world as this, health, and leisure, and affluence may not find some ignorance to instruct, some wrong to redress, some want to supply, some misery to alleviate?"[1] In other words, there's so much to do; if God has given you an able body and mind, find a need that grips you, and get busy being the solution!

We've listed some questions in the sidebars to help you jump-start a conversation with your teens about their areas of potential interest and talent. Note that you, as their parents, mentors, and youth workers, might also pick up on things that they aren't aware of themselves.

WHAT ABOUT AREAS OF WEAKNESS?

Academically, teens' long-term goals should be to play to their strengths and manage their weaknesses. This is not the same as ignoring their weaknesses or allowing their weaknesses to derail them. So I'm not advocating that Jacob completely blow off precalculus or any other classes simply because he doesn't like them. He needs to persevere and do what he can but not stress out over the fact that his best may be less than someone else's. Jacob should do his math work "unto the Lord" and let the chips fall where they may. And for his senior year, instead of taking calculus, Jacob might consider a simpler course (like statistics) that would fulfill his math requirement and prove less distracting from his preferred courses, less harmful to his GPA, and perhaps even more strategic for him in the future.

And about his GPA. Yes, a C pulls it down. But one C isn't

the end of the world. Jacob needs to assess whether that C represents his best effort, all things considered, or if he could raise his precalculus grade without hurting his other grades. After all, two As and a C are better than three Bs (a 3.33 versus a 3.00). But wouldn't the C look bad on his transcript? I suppose it'd look worse than a B, but colleges will primarily look at his GPA, test scores, essays, recommendation letters, and extracurricular involvements and accomplishments. And Jacob is unlikely to be the only humanities-type guy not to have mastered precalculus.

Of course, he may not have any idea what his career options are with strong skills in reading comprehension, writing, and the understanding and interpretation of historical events. That's why it's great his dad is taking him out to lunch to begin brainstorming the possibilities with him. Suppose Jacob has an interest in fighting human trafficking. With a degree in English or history, he could write grant proposals for nonprofit organizations (perhaps while pursuing law school). Or how about journalism? He could sell articles and pursue speaking opportunities at churches and elsewhere while writing a book-length nonfiction work on the side, or perhaps even a novel to create awareness around the issue. Jacob's dad is trying to help his son catch a vision for what he can do with his life, for how he can impact the world and be useful to others. Even if our teens' ambitions are but a dim flicker, the regular, wisely imparted motivation of Mom, Dad, and other mentors can fan them into fiery flames.

What about Career Guidance Tests?

There are a number of career guidance tests and personality inventories out there. My suggestion is that while these can give some insight into teens' *dispositions*, their value in *career guidance* is fairly limited. Let them supply one piece of the puzzle, but don't rely on them exclusively. The reason is that they're generally founded on the premise that people in a particular career have strong similarities in temperament or style. And that's simply not true. Most of the students I teach are engineering majors. I have also worked in that field. My coworkers and students have had a wide variety of personalities (outgoing, quiet), learning styles (hands-on, auditory, from a book), and preferred work environments (alone, in groups). I've not found any of these traits to correlate with their future success or failure. Similarly, successful managers, pastors, ministry leaders, and even high-level executives range from introverted, analytical data crunchers to inspiring, charismatic extroverts. There are many different job types that any major feeds into. And within specific jobs, graduates can tailor the way they do them to fit their unique style. Good employers are interested in results, not in dictating how people do their jobs. So competence, desire, discipline, and the character traits discussed earlier usually end up being more important than temperament or personality.

Tip

Not sure where to start? Download the academic catalog of a large, reputable public university. Scan through the list of majors and see what pops out based on what you know about your teens. Then read those major titles and descriptions with your teens and see how they react.

ARE TALENTS AND INTERESTS ALIGNED?

In the opening illustration, Jacob both enjoys and is good at English and history.

And he both despises and is bad at math. Is it always that way, the two going together, both positively and negatively? Bestselling authors Marcus Buckingham and Donald Clifton give their take on how talent relates to enjoyment:

> Talents have not only an "I can't help it" quality to them but also an "it feels good" quality. Somehow nature has crafted you so that with your strongest connections the signals flow both ways. Your talent causes you to react in a particular way, and immediately a good feeling seems to shoot back up the T1 line. With these signals flowing smoothly back and forth, it feels as if the line is reverberating, humming. This is the feeling of using a talent.[2]

Replace "nature" with "God" (per Psalm 139), and the rest is spot on. The strong connections referred to are synaptic connections in our brains—literally, the way God has wired us, not just in the womb but in our formative early years. Each of us is unique in the kinds of things we naturally gravitate toward, do well at, and enjoy. And yes, like Jacob in our illustration, the things we enjoy are usually the things we do well. For some people, doing something well is the very thing that gives them enjoyment. Math was like that for me. When I learned multiplication at the age of five, others praised me, which made me want to do and learn more.

For others, perhaps later in their childhood, it may start with the enjoyment of the activity: they love doing it, so they end up doing it a lot, and all that practice leads to their doing it exceptionally well. Bill Gates is a classic example. While he was attending an elite private school, his mother helped raise $3,000 for the school's computer club. This was 1968, and Gates was among a handful of eighth graders on the planet to have access to a computer terminal. He quickly fell in love with programming. A few years later, when Gates was in high school, he learned that the University of Washington (within walking distance of his home) had computers in their medical center and physics department. Students had to schedule time on them, and they were fully booked—except from 3:00 to 6:00 a.m. But by this time Gates was fanatical about programming. So he'd sneak out late at night and be home in time to get back in bed to fool his parents. Later Gates was able to arrange for evening and weekend access. By the time he finished high school, he had logged countless hours programming, perhaps more than anyone else his age at that time.

The point is not that every teen is going to be as zealous about their area of interest as Gates was. It's that for all of us, to a greater or lesser degree, there's a positive feedback loop, a virtuous circle (if you will) between our enjoyment of an activity, our doing more of it, and our success, which boosts our enjoyment of the activity, and the cycle repeats itself. Looking back at his youth, Gates wrote, "It was hard to tear myself away from a machine at which I could so unambiguously demonstrate success."[3] In other words, his intense passion for programming was in part the *result* of his early success.

I mention this because teens are sometimes insecure about choosing a college major. "I just don't know if I really *love* it," they say. That's often too high a subjective, emotional bar for a 16- or 17-year-old. It's enough if they like it, are at least somewhat good at it, and (most important) are willing to put in the time and effort to get better at it.

This understanding of talents is consistent with biblical themes. We see it reflected in God's distribution of spiritual gifts (see Romans 12:3-8; 1 Corinthians 12). Everyone gets something, and nobody gets everything. That way, everyone can both serve others in unique ways and be served by others in different ways. Experience shows it's analogous in the realm of natural gifts. Everyone in the world, whether they acknowledge the Source or not, has been given specific talents, through which God ultimately calls them to certain

lines of work (or vocations). When we pray, "Give us this day our daily bread," God answers this prayer through farmers, grocers, truckers, and others along the way, all of whom are using their talents in concrete ways (and of course, we must similarly use our talents to earn the money to buy the bread).[4] In Deuteronomy 8:18, we read that God gives us the power to gain wealth. And how is it that wealth is gained? By our doing things for others with sufficient skill, for which they're willing to pay us. Does God bless only Christians in this way? Clearly not. His distribution of intellectual, athletic, mechanical, and artistic talent is as universal as it is varied.

As I explain to students in *Thriving at College*, figuring out what we should pursue vocationally is ultimately a two-way process—we pursue our interests and passions, and God confirms our direction over time through accomplishments and the positive feedback of others. In terms of getting a job someday, it's never enough to want to do something; someone else (an employer or customer) has to be willing to pay us to do it. Our word *vocation* comes from the Latin *vocatio*, meaning "a summons or a calling," not a choice. We pursue our interests, but God ultimately calls us to certain lines of work as our output is deemed worthy and more opportunities are sent our way. Good grades and test scores help get us into college. Projects done well open the doors for us to undertake more complicated ventures. Good presentation skills help us secure employment. And doing one job well can help us secure a bigger or a better job down the road. It's always a two-way process in that others must affirm us.

And so it must be for our teens. Unfortunately, problems can arise when interests and talents are not present in equal measure.

WHEN INTERESTS AND TALENTS DON'T SEEM TO ALIGN

What if teens excel at something they don't really like? In my experience, this can be corrected by giving them sufficient challenge. When something's too easy, we're prone to take it for granted, and it becomes boring. When something's too hard, we're prone to give up and look for something that feels more natural. But when we enjoy something and have a natural capacity for it, we're likely to respond well to a stretching but doable challenge, one that requires focus and effort and calls forth the best from us. We're neither bored nor overwhelmed but stimulated and engaged in our task. A doctor performing surgery, a lawyer arguing a case before a judge, a pastor preaching a sermon, a musician giving a concert—hopefully we've all experienced the pleasure of losing ourselves in our work. That high degree of mental "flow" is what propels the greatest performers in every field.

The heart is deceitful above all things, and desperately sick; who can understand it?

—JEREMIAH 17:9

The opposite scenario, though, is more common. What if a teen really likes something but isn't very good at it? We live in a "just follow your heart" culture. Here's the problem: our hearts can deceive us (see Jeremiah 17:9). Some teens are legends in their own minds. They think they're great at something when in fact they're mediocre at best. Or they think they'd love a certain line of work based on an overly glamorous understanding of what's actually involved.

About a decade ago college enrollment in forensic science sharply rose all across the country. Observers soon recognized that it was a response to the popular television program *CSI: Crime Scene Investigation.* The show has been incredibly successful at keeping viewers glued to the screen, but it (naturally) sensationalizes the crime scene investigators' role.[5]

Similarly, I've met students who wanted to be engineers because they heard there are lots of high-paying jobs out there, or maybe because they have a cool uncle and that's what he does. When they find out more about what is actually required in their coursework—lots of math, physics, programming languages, and courses with laboratory components (things they don't particularly enjoy or grasp)—they switch to another major. These are the kinds of perception adjustments we want our teens to make *before* they've invested a few semesters and a chunk of change at a university. So if they express interest in a particular field, help them find out what's really required to be successful in it, both at college and in the workforce. If you don't know, see what you can find out together and then discuss it.

In talking with our teens, we should also help them understand that every adult has hobbies—things they maybe did earlier in life on a high school or college team (or club) but now continue to do just for fun. In fact, our word *amateur* comes from the Latin *amator*, which means "lover." An amateur singer is one who sings for the love of it, not for the money. What's wrong with that? Almost nobody sings for the money! We have the phrase "Don't quit your day job" because a lot of us have things we enjoy doing, but it would be imprudent to expect that we'll ever earn a living from them.

Working with college students as a professor these last eight years, I'm convinced that the assumption of greatness, this sense that the stars will align if we just *believe* hard enough, has become something of a cultural trend (probably from watching too many Disney movies). We need future college students to understand that nothing worthwhile comes easily. But they also need to recognize that just because they love something and work hard at it doesn't mean their every dream will immediately come true.

Perhaps your son or daughter is a very talented athlete. He or she may be hoping to land a full-ride scholarship to a Division 1 university. That's a great ambition, and I hope it works out, but it's wise to have a contingency plan. What I'm pleading for is a balance between *idealism* (shooting for the stars) and *realism* (understanding and accounting for the statistical likelihood of success in certain types of ventures). For example, a student whose grades were mediocre at best once told me he chose mechanical engineering as a major because he "planned" to work for Disney as an Imagineer (a professional animator). That sounds awesome, but I hope there are other jobs that might also interest him, because I have a feeling that there will be some stiff competition for those jobs. Unfortunately, I've seen students devastated when their lofty and unrealistic expectations have gone unmet. By all means, encourage your teens to aim high and pursue excellence in whatever they do. But help them be ready for life on earth with the rest of us if they don't immediately make the leap to stratospheric greatness. The truth is that all we can do is give our best effort. The rest is in God's hands. It helps to be at peace with that (see Isaiah 26:3-4).

WAYS TO NURTURE YOUR TEENS' ACADEMIC INTERESTS

Okay, so let's say you've sat down with your teens and identified a few areas in which they have some interest and perhaps even some talent. What now? Look for ways to test things out and see what happens. Talents reveal themselves in the

Q: *Our son would rather pursue landscaping than go to college but is talented in math and loves it. Should we encourage him to pursue a math-related field?*

A: There's a big difference between mowing lawns to earn spending money and landscaping for a living. I suspect that what makes your son think he'd like landscaping is the mental relaxation that comes from being outside in nice weather, turning up the music, and mindlessly pushing the self-propelled lawn mower.

Try to get him exposed to adults in both landscaping and mathematics-related careers (accounting, actuarial work, engineering). Have them explain what training he'd need and what the natural career progression would be. This will give him a fuller picture of what's involved in being successful.

A general principle he needs to know is that people pay you to do useful things for them—things they either can't do or don't want to do for themselves. If something is hard, there will be fewer people who can do it well. If he's one of them, they'll have to pay him more. Most people are *not* mathematically inclined. If he is, he'd be wise to cultivate that talent. Once he understands more of what he can do with math, matures more, and develops intellectually, my guess is his attitude toward college will change.

crucible of experience. That might mean putting your teens into more demanding classes in particular subjects. It could mean a writing contest (as Jacob's teacher suggested), a math team, a robotics club, a community orchestra, or a school play. Note that with things like math and robotics there are also contests in which a local team, club, or individual can participate.

In the last chapter, I mentioned how my history teacher Mr. Pobst made his lessons come alive. If your teens think they might be interested in something science related, is there a scientist like Mr. Pobst at your church or among your relatives? Could your teens perhaps shadow the scientist for a day at work? Better yet, could they volunteer for a couple of months or land an internship? For example, Page Hayley was homeschooled through high school. She finished a year early and opted to take a year off rather than go directly to college. Page was interested in pursuing a science-related degree, so during that year she obtained part-time work as a research aide at a teaching hospital (where her mother was also employed).[6] How many high school students would have thought they could land a part-time job as great as that? It can happen. Brainstorm creatively and think about whom you're connected to and how they might be able to help.

For someone like Jacob, our A student in English and history, a speech and debate team could be a great fit. What's so great about speech and debate is that it teaches teens so many different skills, such as critical thinking, conducting research, and public speaking. If your teens show interest in business, encourage them to look for needs they can meet via some product or service. Help them brainstorm ways they could test out their ideas. Or might they like an investment club, where they could learn about stocks, bonds, and mutual funds? If your teens are interested in computers, encourage them to take a programming or animation course and then look for part-time work through which they could further develop their skills. Bottom line, whatever useful enterprise your children's hands (or minds) find to do, and enjoy doing, encourage them to do it with all their might.

....

Whatever your hand finds to do, do it with all your might.
—ECCLESIASTES 9:10, NIV

....

Summer programs in areas like business, engineering, art, and science are another good option. They're often hosted on college campuses, which is a great way for your teens to get a feel for those campuses (and decrease the stress of freshman year, should they end up going there). In addition to giving teens substantive training in an area of interest, these programs usually have group projects through which your teens can develop teamwork skills (something every employer is seeking). One possible downside is that programs of this sort can be expensive, as you're paying for teaching, any materials (for crafts or labs), and room and board.

A little-known and relatively inexpensive way for teens over the age of 16 to explore their interests and develop skills is through regional occupational programs. These are county-sponsored classes that combine traditional instruction with on-the-job training in selected areas based upon current and future labor market demands. In Riverside County, California (where I live), at this moment, these are some of the classes available: digital imaging, crime scene investigation, 3-D computer animation, automotive technology, and allied health occupations. For many students, these kinds of courses will be gateways to vocational careers that don't require traditional college (see conversation 11 for more). But they can also provide a way for high school students to develop the kinds of skills that allow them to earn significantly more than the minimum wage in a part-time job while they attend a traditional college. As I noted in conversation 7, college students can make better money in part-time jobs if they leverage a skill they've developed, be it piano instruction, wedding photography, computer technician work, or something else. And of course, experience in a particular sector can help teens select a college major with greater confidence.

Lastly, I may be biased, since I love books, but I think good biographies can be enormously encouraging and inspiring for anyone, perhaps especially teens. Think of biographies as a way to expose your teens to historical examples of people who, like them, had an interest in writing, science, business, politics, music, missions, or whatever and did something significant with it. In most cases, you can find examples of dedicated Christians whose life work in a specific field was the overflow of their commitment to glorify

Extracurricular Activities: Quantity or Quality?

Colleges are looking not just for extracurricular experiences but for significance of accomplishment. Doing a little bit of everything, hoping to wow admissions officers with a dizzying array of activity, is less than optimal. Better to start as a low-level assistant on the school's newspaper and rise to be senior editor of the yearbook. Or to take a few computer programming classes, master several languages, and then test out of the college's technology requirements. Focus, dedication, and achievement in specific areas show colleges that prospective students "know who they are"—which makes them more interesting as people and causes their applications to stand out. And this approach spares teens from the stress and impossibility of trying to do it all.

Another thing that stands out is leadership experience. Student government, being captain of the volleyball team, being on the ministry team of their youth group—anything that shows your teens have earned the respect of their peers and authority figures or are able to rally others around a good cause. In whatever club or activity your teens are involved with, encourage them to assume the lowest place (see Luke 14:7-11) and look for ways to help the common cause. Godly leaders lift others up. And they do it to achieve a worthwhile objective, not to gratify their egos. People of all ages assign moral authority to those who are deeply helpful, and moral authority is the basis for influence, and influence is the essence of leadership.

God. This is important, because Christian teens sometimes get the idea that the only way they can *really* serve God is in full-time ministry. That leads to the kind of disconnect between schoolwork and church life that I talked about in the last chapter. So when they meet people like Madeleine L'Engle the fiction writer, or William Wilberforce the statesman, or Truett Cathy the entrepreneur, or J. S. Bach the composer, or Robert Boyle the chemist, or Michael Faraday the physicist—all of whom pursued their callings as dedicated Christians—it rocks their assumptions.

Biographies can also provide teens with the right kind of heroes to emulate. There's no doubt that many teens have an unhealthy obsession with sports figures, rock stars, and Hollywood celebrities. But the desire for someone to admire and even imitate is normal, particularly for teens seeking to establish their identities as young adults. The apostle Paul invited it: "Be imitators of me, as I am of Christ" (1 Corinthians 11:1).[7] What our teens need are *good* role models, the kind whose public and private lives are praiseworthy. The kind who humbly seek to live out their faith and serve others in the context of their vocation. And how much better if these role models share not only our teens' Christian faith but their particular academic interests as well?

OVER-PARENTING (REVISITED)

We discussed under-parenting and over-parenting in conversation 1 because they relate to how we go about shaping the decision-making skills and moral character of our teens.

They also have particular relevance here, because when we talk about helping our teens discern and develop their interests and talents, with a view toward getting them ready for college, it's easy for us as parents to advance our agendas rather than give our teens space to pursue their own sense of God's leading. For starters, it's good to brainstorm ways your teens can assess their interests (the way Jacob's dad plans to do over lunch) and even leverage your contacts to see what might be available in terms of job shadowing or internship opportunities (the way Page's mom did). But try to have them do the final asking. This develops their social prowess and prepares them for future interviews.

Similarly, resist the urge to force them into saying yes to this or that. Perhaps you've always thought they'd make great doctors, or you have your sights set on them taking over the family business or going into ministry. Look for fruit in their lives and hearts to see if any of that makes sense. Whatever happens, remember that they are the ones who have to live with the consequences. So give them space to own these decisions.

Some teens are extra compliant and will pursue even their parents' perceived preferences. Other teens are more eager for autonomy—the most you can do is let them know you're there to help them process ideas, because if you start making suggestions, they'll feel smothered and either dig in their heels or do the *opposite* of what you suggest. Know your teens, and recognize that it's not abnormal for them to want to take the reins in this area of their lives.

I started out as a biology major, figuring I'd follow in my dad's footsteps as a dentist. I did well in college, and after graduation I worked full-time for my dad while preparing to apply to dental schools. But I ended up hating the work! My father loves his job, but I felt cooped up in the office, and I was quickly bored with teeth, mouths, and drills. I didn't think I would ever enjoy going to work in the morning. God graciously used the experience to lead me into a different career that's better suited for my gifting and passions.

My pre-dental friend Josh wasn't so lucky. He kept his head down in college, worked hard, studied for his tests, and pounded out the lab reports. And like me, he was set on following in his dad's footsteps. But he just couldn't pull the grades. After graduation he realized he wouldn't get into dental school, so he retook a bunch of classes—and didn't do any better. People were pushing him to "keep pursuing his dream." Eventually Josh realized it wasn't meant to be—he was merely chasing a dream that others had for him. He's now doing a fabulous job as a camp director and loves the work. But I wonder if he would have started doing that a lot sooner if people had done a better job of helping him discover his God-given talents and interests.

Brian

You probably know this by now, but please don't step in when things don't go your teens' way. If your daughter tries out for an elite choir (for example) and doesn't get accepted, don't call the choir director and ream her out. This only teaches your daughter that she's helpless. Don't call the choir director, but do console your daughter. Give her the strength to believe she can get back up and pursue other opportunities.

Lastly, as alluded to earlier, a change of major can result in extra time at college. I've had students sitting in my office, scared to switch majors because they think their parents are going to be upset by the implications. You can't anticipate everything, but do what you can before they leave for college to prevent this from becoming a source of friction. If there are bumps on the road once your teens start college, think creatively about ways to lower and share costs (as we discussed in conversation 7). In my experience, most students are understanding and are willing to shoulder part of the burden, especially if unforeseen changes are a result of their choices.

Of course, the cost of a college education depends on the school. From community colleges to elite private universities, the advertised tuition figures are all over the map. And for most families, cost is but one factor in the equation. Families must also consider the school's location, size, and reputation (both in general and in the subject their children are planning to declare as a major). Then there's the religious and moral climate to ponder. When it comes to selecting a college, the possibilities can seem endless—and they are, as you'll soon find out if you haven't already been flooded with college advertisements. With so many factors to consider, and so many options, how are teens and their families to go about making this supposedly momentous decision? That's what our next chapter is about.

Tip
Switching majors is doable, especially early. At some point, though, it's more cost effective for students to persevere and graduate in whatever major they've selected. The good news is that college graduates can get full-time jobs in areas unrelated to their majors if their academic performance and extracurricular accomplishments give evidence of a strong work ethic, personal responsibility, clear communication skills, an ability to work well with others, and a desire to keep learning. All employers are seeking to hire these kinds of people, and most provide on-the-job training in the specifics of their company and industry.

SUMMARY

- The heart of academic development is the discovery and nurturing of our teens' God-given talents and interests. We should help our teens play to their academic and professional strengths and mitigate their weaknesses.

- There is a virtuous feedback loop between a teen's enjoying an activity, doing it more, and doing it better. This reinforcement is particularly strong if the activity is in an area of a teen's innate talent.
- Interests and talents are not always aligned in equal measure. Some things our teens enjoy will become hobbies, not careers. They should balance idealism with realism, and strenuous effort with trust in God.
- Talents are often revealed in the crucible of experience (challenging classes, special projects, summer programs, and so on), as teens put areas of interest to the test. Teens should avail themselves of such opportunities so that they can make more informed decisions about what to pursue after high school.
- In helping your teens figure out an appropriate college/career plan, beware of pushing your preferences too strongly. You'll have legitimate insights into where they can be successful, but give them space to own their decisions, since they will have to live with the consequences.

CONVERSATION STARTERS

1. Discuss your teens' favorite school subjects and other topics that interest them. How might these interests shape what they pursue after high school? What careers might align with their interests?

2. Ask your teens what they want to do after high school. Discuss these ideas with them. Help them

discern which make the most sense based on what you know about them (grades earned; projects completed; special skills; character traits; athletic, musical, or artistic performances; and so on).

3. Identify a few ways your teens could assess and develop their interests "in the crucible of experience." Can you think of people in your network who could help your teens secure relevant opportunities (job shadowing, volunteer positions, internships, and so on)?

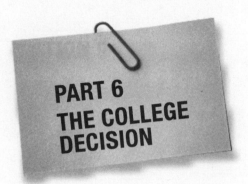

PART 6
THE COLLEGE
DECISION

CONVERSATION 10
Asking the Right Questions about College

BEFORE WE GET into discussing the college decision, a few disclaimers. I'll be using the terms *college* and *university* interchangeably.[1] I won't be referring to vocational or trade school options in this chapter. There are discipline-specific training programs out there if you want to become a dental hygienist, cosmetologist, auto mechanic, welder, electrician, and so on, but we'll discuss those options in conversation 11. I'm also not going to discuss the selection of a two-year school per se (community colleges and the like), even though many people earn associate degrees that way (another conversation 11 topic) or later transfer into four-year colleges.

Before starting the lengthy, complicated process of

selecting a college, it helps to answer a fundamental question: What do your teens hope to gain from their college experience? What are their "must-haves"? Here are a few examples:

- Madison isn't sure what she wants to major in. She really wants a great Christian education in the liberal arts tradition, and she doesn't want to be more than three hours from home.
- Danny is an accomplished athlete, and he hopes to play on a competitive Division I basketball team. A few recruiters have expressed tentative interest. Danny plans to pick a college based on the quality of its basketball program, the size of its scholarship offer, and how well he connects with the coaches and other players.
- Brandon loves biology and math. After conversations with his teachers, he's thinking about biomedical engineering. He'll focus on schools that have reputable programs in that field.

ESTABLISH A PRIORITIZED LIST OF CRITERIA

Encourage your teens to do as Madison, Danny, and Brandon did and identify the things they are looking for in a college (and what they hope to gain from the college experience). It may take some brainstorming to get their thoughts flowing. The first semester of their junior year, or as soon as possible thereafter, is a great time to start this conversation in earnest. They'll have been in high school for a couple of years and have a better sense of who they are, but there will still be plenty of time to visit and apply to colleges.

The next step is to reduce this list to a few important items. Let me be totally honest with you: finding a college where your teens can have a good time is not very hard. Even if they have great relationships at home, almost all teens relish the sense of independence that comes with getting out on their own and living with a bunch of people their own age. College campuses tend to be attractive in appearance and offer a wide assortment of recreational options. Even if your teens plan to commute, they'll still only be in class for half as many hours as they are in high school. It is the rare college student who doesn't have more open time during the week than he or she has ever had before.

That's why it's so easy for teens to choose a four-year college for superficial or sentimental reasons—things like "they have an awesome recreation center with a rock-climbing wall," or "the dining hall is amazing," or even what led me to Alfred University as an 18-year-old freshman: a good friend went there. What's wrong with that? Don't teens need good community at college? Of course they do, but college is a season for them to transition into responsible adulthood, not to perpetuate their high school social scene. Establishing *new* friendships is itself an important developmental step in their journey toward independence.

I completely understand that not everyone will have the financial means to send their teens away to college. If your family is in that boat, you are not alone. In 2013, a majority of families (57 percent) reported a student living at home or with a relative, up from 43 percent in 2010.[2] If that's your situation, then location should go on your teens' "must-have" lists. Identify relatives your teens could live with, then limit your selection to colleges that are within commuting distance from those homes.

I recommend you whittle the list down to the top five factors. That may be tough, but it's crucial that your teen eliminate the unessential. If everything is important, then nothing is important. In the space below, I submit three criteria for your consideration.

1. *Quality education.* A college that delivers an all-around high-quality education, with faculty who love teaching and care about students and whose curriculum is excellent so that graduates become strong critical thinkers, good communicators, skilled problem-solvers, and lifelong learners who can continually rise to the challenge of new professional and personal responsibilities.

2. *Job preparation.* A college that has a well-resourced, reputable program in your teens' area of interest and a track record for helping its graduates secure meaningful, full-time employment in their chosen field or continue on to related graduate studies at respected universities.

3. *Christian community.* An environment that offers opportunities for strong personal and spiritual

Q: *What about massive open online courses (MOOCs)? Don't these have the potential to dramatically lower tuition, perhaps even eliminating the need for colleges?*

A: If teens are autodidacts and love computer programming, I can envision a scenario in which they take free courses on the Internet and achieve some kind of certification sufficient to land them temporary (and perhaps eventually full-time) employment in the technology sector. But for *most* young adults in pursuit of *most* kinds of academic learning, I think a one-way interaction with a virtual talking head will leave much to be desired.

Is it better than nothing? Sure. In subjects like math, science, or computer programming, information can be powerfully conveyed via online videos and lectures, and *gifted* students will soak it up. Others won't. And the jury is still out. Most of today's MOOC participants already have college degrees and don't complete their MOOC courses. Even when courses are completed, it's hard to assess learning beyond multiple-choice tests. Excellent professors, experts who love their students, present material in an engaging manner and then *measure* student learning, giving them meaningful feedback along the way—these drive academic excellence.

I'm not saying computers can't play a role. A hybrid format (part face-to-face, part online instruction) is showing signs of promise. But an education is more than information. Actual professors—if they're good—are a huge advantage.

enrichment and for the establishment of enduring Christian friendships that can sustain and strengthen your teens during their years at college (and perhaps well into adulthood).

I'm not saying every family will rank these three in the same order. And I'm certainly not saying they are the *only* important criteria in selecting a college. For example, Danny, our aspiring Division I basketball player, will want to add "must have a good D1 basketball team" to his list. Others will have location restrictions, perhaps due to finances. And Madison will want to add "Christian liberal arts school" to her list.

I join many others in the conviction that Christian higher education (and the liberal arts in general) offers significant advantages. We'll get into these a bit later. But it's also true that many Christian students thrive at secular universities, some of which have excellent academic resources, feature first-rate instruction, and boast excellent job placement records, along with unparalleled opportunities for evangelism and learning to engage the culture. I think this is one of those areas where Christian liberty should be respected among families. There are students who would have floundered at a secular university but who come to own their faith at a Christian college. On the other hand, forcing a teen to attend a Christian college can backfire, resulting in resentment and rebellion. At either type of university, Christian students will need to be intentional about practicing and growing in their faith, which is why I consider Christian community (my third item) as essential for all.

ACCOUNTING FOR PERSONAL PREFERENCES

Since you may have already written your list of criteria, I want to comment on a few neutral factors. These can legitimately go either way, depending on the temperament and preferences of your teen.

If your children grew up in a rural area and would feel like fish out of water at an urban college (or vice versa), that's worth thinking about. If they will be really uncomfortable, it will probably have a negative impact on them academically, socially, or both. Not a problem—just add population density to your must-haves list.

Some teens put geographic or weather conditions on their list. "Must be near beach," or mountains, or snow (for skiing), and so on. If your teens are talking that way, I'd suggest gently pushing back a bit on this one. Make this sort of preference a tie-breaking factor, not a tier-one priority. College isn't vacation; it's a place of academic and professional preparation. If they love the ocean, or hiking, or whatever, maybe you can take a family trip or they can pursue an internship or even full-time work in such places after graduation.

Then again, most teens (about 53 percent) end up going to a college within 100 miles of their home.[3] That offers clear advantages in terms of lowering travel-related expenses and having a greater sense of familiarity with the surrounding area. On the other hand, by going to college farther away, teens naturally assume a greater measure of independence and ownership for their lives. They're more likely to move beyond their high school social scene and meet new, interesting people who expand their horizons. That said, if they're dead set on going to college on the other side of the country, it's worth discussing why. It's not necessarily a bad thing, but it could be indicative of a breakdown in their relationships at home or a desire to set aside the supposed strictures of church community and related expectations.

With that, let's jump into a discussion of the items I listed as being essential for all students, starting with a quality education. Why should our teens prioritize receiving a quality education at college? Because it prepares them to be the kinds of people who can succeed not just on the job but in the totality of their lives.

THE IMPORTANCE OF A QUALITY EDUCATION

The Pros and Cons of Large and Small Universities

Institution size is in part a personal preference—some teens would feel lost at large universities; others would feel cloistered at small colleges—but there are also academic and professional factors to consider. Both large and small schools can offer a high-quality education, but it's worth exploring the pros and cons on an institution-by-institution basis.

Large universities now have, in some cases, north of 50,000 students. They've adopted a research model, with professors who teach one or two classes per semester but who are mainly researchers, working with graduate students in highly specialized subfields within larger academic departments that operate relatively independently from one another. An advantage, proponents argue, is that such faculty are up to speed with the latest developments in their field. Therefore, they can offer undergraduate students a more innovative, cutting-edge educational experience. Moreover, as undergraduates advance into their junior and senior years, having such a diverse and large faculty can translate into professional opportunities. Large universities also offer many more curricular options (including niche fields) than smaller colleges. (Brandon, who wants to study biomedical engineering, will probably not find many small universities that offer that program.) Large universities also tend to have state-of-the-art facilities (the high costs are distributed over a larger number of students). In addition, if the university is public and in your home state, there can be significant tuition savings.

Large schools also have vast networks of alumni who might assist your teens in finding employment upon graduation. Compare, for example, Pomona College to Stanford University. Both are highly selective schools, with student bodies of similar caliber, but unless you live in California, there's a good chance the only name that's familiar to you is Stanford. That's the power of having a larger number of accomplished faculty getting in the news for their research, more great alumni in the workforce, and competitive sports teams that are sometimes featured on national television. All these factors create undeniable clout, which paves the way and opens doors for future alumni.

On the other hand, large universities have some drawbacks worth considering. Note that these will negatively impact some kinds of students more than others. First, in order to free up the faculty to teach only one or two classes per semester (as opposed to three or four, the norm at teaching-oriented colleges), the university has to either hire two to three times as many full-time professors (dramatically raising their costs), increase their class sizes (not always possible for specialized junior- or senior-level courses), or rely on inexpensive part-time instructors and graduate students to teach a greater share of the courses than at smaller, teaching-oriented colleges. Remember what I said in conversation 7 about one in four freshmen failing to advance to their sophomore year? It's easy for students to get lost in huge lecture halls with part-time instructors who are relatively unavailable outside of class because the school didn't give them an office and they're working two or three jobs to make ends meet.

Professors are attracted to research-oriented universities because they're passionate about their area of specialization. Their heart is usually in their research—they're hoping to rise in stature by publishing, serving on national committees, and participating in other activities that take their focus away from teaching lowly undergraduate students. Moreover, research productivity is how they're evaluated by their management. The presence of accomplished researchers raises the prestige of a university, but what good does it do your teens if they can't interact with them? In fairness, when I was a graduate student at UC Berkeley (a school of about 35,000 students), I took a few classes from professors who were amazingly knowledgeable and gifted communicators. But even to me, a graduate student, they weren't available for much interaction outside of class.

In an effort to cut costs during the post-2008 economic downturn, many universities have been increasing their dependency on part-time instructors and graduate students (arguably at the expense of quality). So when you're looking at colleges—large and small—don't just look at the student-faculty ratio. It doesn't tell you how likely your child is to

Small or Large University?

Key Strengths of Small Schools:

- More interaction with faculty
- Professors who teach more
- More likely to have curricular cohesion (interdisciplinary connections)

Key Strengths of Large Schools:

- More program and course offerings
- Faculty keep up with latest research
- Wider "brand" recognition

receive instruction from full-time professors or how much their professors actually care about teaching. Ask these kinds of questions: How many courses do full-time faculty teach per semester? What percentage of the undergraduate courses, laboratories, and discussion sections are taught by part-timers and graduate students, and are they required to hold office hours?[4] Note that the more courses a typical faculty member teaches (four per semester, or 12 units, is common at teaching-oriented institutions), the more emphasis the university places on teaching when evaluating faculty performance.

One caveat: every university uses part-time (or adjunct) professors to some extent. What you want to know is how often your teen would have classes with them and how accessible they are when students need help. Some adjunct professors are really good, particularly ones who are retired from previous careers and now teach to stay active. (If you get their names, you can even check out their public profiles on LinkedIn.com.)

Now let's talk about small schools. The academic advantages include smaller class sizes, professors who teach more, professors who are more likely to advise and mentor students, access to faculty outside of class, and more opportunities to participate in class discussions. At many small schools, there's a greater commitment to helping students make cross-disciplinary connections and giving every student a broad-based liberal arts education (even if they major in a pre-professional field). The main disadvantages are that small schools might not have the academic programs that

> **Tip**
>
> At the National Center for Education Statistics College Navigator (http://nces.ed.gov/collegenavigator), you can find, for any college or university, a numerical breakdown of the number of full-time faculty and part-time faculty. You can also see how many full-time and part-time faculty are "instructional" (meaning they teach) versus "research and public service" (meaning they don't).

your teens want to pursue, they certainly won't have as many course offerings, and they might not have the reputational clout of some larger schools with lots of alumni.

Personally, I benefited profoundly from going to a smaller university for my undergraduate degree. My memory may be fuzzy, but I don't believe I received *any* instruction from part-time professors. All my professors conducted some research, but they were accessible and helpful outside of class. I think that's the only reason I did as well as I did and was later able to get into a top graduate program in my field.

The Intrinsic Value of the Liberal Arts

Let's come back to this issue of giving every student a "broad-based liberal arts education." Perhaps you're wondering what that phrase means and whether your teens need such an education. I think a strong liberal arts education would enhance your teens' academic experience—even if they major in a professional field (for example, engineering, nursing, or business), as I did.

The liberal arts originated in ancient Greece, where free persons were to be skilled in grammar, rhetoric, and logic (the *Trivium*) in order to participate meaningfully in civic life. In medieval times and thereafter, subjects such as mathematics, music, astronomy, philosophy, theology, history, and literature were added. These subjects were believed to have *intrinsic* value apart from any particular utilitarian or vocational use. In other words, they train students not just for certain occupations but for the totality of their lives. They impart what Matthew Arnold called "the best which has been thought and said"—the greatest writings, the most significant cultural and historical insights—giving students a vantage point from which to assess their own culture and thus "liberating" them.[5] When colleges were first established in the United States, their purpose reflected this broad-based view of education because their founders recognized that a well-functioning democracy required an educated and virtuous citizenry.

> The liberal arts train students not just for certain occupations but for the totality of their lives. They impart what Matthew Arnold called "the best which has been thought and said."

When done well, a liberal arts education teaches a student how to think critically, communicate clearly, and solve complicated problems. These foundational competencies allow students to grow and adapt throughout their careers and take on broader responsibilities over time, which is why they are precisely the qualities employers like Raytheon, Boston Scientific, and Principal Financial are seeking in graduates.[6] If you think about it, part of what it means to be a well-educated person is being *conversant* in a wide range of topics and *fluent* in a narrower range of subjects.[7] Teens today will probably go through a variety of jobs over the course of their careers, and being well-rounded, broadly educated, cultivated adults will strengthen them not just as employees but as citizens, friends, neighbors, spouses, and parents.[8]

I know what some of you are thinking. A liberal arts degree leads to unemployment or low wages. It's true that the job market is currently favoring degrees in science, technology, engineering, and math-related fields (the STEM disciplines), along with other applied majors such as accounting, economics, and finance. I'm not saying everyone needs to major in the liberal arts. I'm saying everyone benefits from having a liberal arts component to their education because of the internal transformation such courses produce in the hearts and minds of students. If your teens love subjects within the liberal arts, one thing they can do to distinguish themselves for the job market is to major in a discipline such as English, history, or philosophy but pick up a minor in an applied field (say, business). They can also look for internships during their college years to help them stand out when they graduate. And they can periodically talk with their professors and the career services office at their college about potential career tracks in their major (something surprisingly few students do).

But besides a reputation for dismal employment prospects, there's another critique of the liberal arts in our day. The humanities departments at many universities have strayed from the original vision for liberal arts studies. These departments are run by scholars who came of age in the late 1960s counterculture movement. They've rejected the Judeo-Christian values of previous generations and have come to view the history, great books, and cultural heritage of Western civilization not as a legacy to be preserved and examined but as a burden to be "deconstructed" and overcome. They tend to view "the study of literature and history as a melodrama of race, class, and gender oppression."[9] Consequently, they've set aside the requirement that students acquire a working familiarity with the most influential writings of antiquity— the Bible, Homer, Plato, Augustine, Locke, Shakespeare, the Declaration of Independence, and the like—on the premise that such works are either racist, sexist, elitist, or simply outdated and insufficiently representative of the multicultural society we've become, allowing students to fulfill what was once a Western civilization requirement with one of several activist courses instead (gender studies, ethnic studies, and so on).

Assessing the Educational Quality of a College

Liberal arts education in this country began with lofty aims, but the reality today is less than grand in some cases. So what should you do about it? Check out the core curriculum at any prospective college or university, especially if your teens are considering a major within the liberal arts. The core curriculum (sometimes known as "general education") is a set of mandatory courses or (more commonly) a set of subject areas in which students must take a specified number of courses. What's required? What isn't? Can you get the syllabi of the courses and see what textbooks are used? Do the courses have an overt bias?

Some colleges let students take virtually any courses they want to satisfy these requirements. A question worth asking on a campus tour is "How hard is it to get exceptions to the requirements?" If exceptions are always granted, then the rules are meaningless. My own view is that those who have traveled farther down the road of life should guide those with less experience. A liberal arts education should be well structured and prepare all graduates not just for a particular job but for a successful life. A college that has put little thought into this foundational aspect of its curriculum is likely to fall short in other areas as well.[10]

In addition to examining the core requirements, also check out the learning culture of the institution. Your teens can look for this when they sit in on classes during a college visit. How do the students behave? Are they sitting up, alert, taking notes, raising their hands, and making intelligent contributions? Or are they slouched over, sending text messages, and otherwise disengaged? The question your teens should try to answer is this: How likely am I to find classmates at this college who will spur me on in the love of learning?

As a youth pastor, I've seen wave after wave of students go through the college-selection process. I've observed that much of the pressure they feel has to do with the mistaken view that when it comes to choosing a college, there is only one right answer. Should they pick the "right" school, a rewarding experience awaits them, with a dream job, wonderful spouse, and happy life on the other side. Should they pick any other school, they'll spend the next four years wondering what could have been.

I've seen this lead to crippling anxiety and the paralysis of overanalysis. And it's unnecessary and unbiblical. God has revealed that we should grow in the likeness of Jesus and develop our talents and interests so that we can successfully (and enjoyably) earn a living, support our families, and be generous with others. He calls us to pray about the college decision (including whether to go), to rationally consider the pros and cons, and then to make the best decision we can, using our sanctified intelligence and knowing that God is more interested in our following him than we are. This liberates students and their families to jot down their "short list" of college criteria, do their research, visit a few schools, and then make an informed choice. A much more pleasant process! Oh, and after they get to campus, they're less likely to second-guess themselves if they realize that *every* college has its pluses and minuses.

Dan

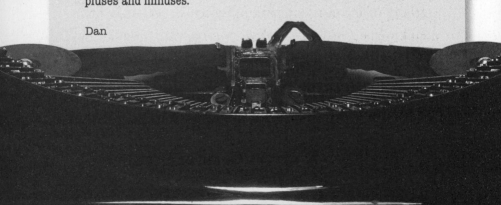

And don't forget the professors. Encourage your teens to talk to them. I know this will require courage, but your teens should aim to get to know at least one professor during a campus visit. It's best to set up these kinds of appointments in advance. If the professors show no interest in your teens when they're prospective students, they're not likely to show much interest after they're enrolled.

Admittedly, a campus visit gives you just a snapshot. Depending on the size of the campus, it can be a very limited picture. Prospective students can sometimes get overly mystical, as if they're waiting for God to speak audibly, "Pick this college!" While not advocating for such an extreme, I do think campus visits are an important aspect of the college-assessment process. Especially at smaller colleges, there is often an overarching ethos among the students that can be detected in person. At larger colleges, the ethos is less discernible because the school is going to have all types of students. It may take initiative and focus, but there's a good chance your teens can find kindred spirits among tens of thousands. Nevertheless, a campus visit lets your teens take in the lay of the land.

There are lots of college catalogs out there, as well as a plethora of inconsistent ranking systems. I strongly commend to you *Choosing the Right College*, which is published every two years by the Intercollegiate Studies Institute.[11] It evaluates the academic life, student life, and campus politics of about 150 colleges and universities (the most sought-after schools, but also what they deem as the better low-cost colleges in every state). It delves into details like the percentage of students who receive need-based financial aid and the average student loan debt of a recent graduating class. And it tells you how strong and historic the college's core curriculum is, even giving an eight-course "suggested core" so your children can receive the best possible general education should they choose to go there.[12]

Choosing the Right College also tells you which professors are particularly good—and which ones to avoid. Under student life, it tells you what percentage of students are in a fraternity or sorority, which schools have non-coed dorm options, and whether colleges are characterized by a pervasive "party atmosphere." Under campus politics, it offers red, yellow, or green ratings on each school: red for the ones that most heavily indoctrinate students to toe the "politically correct" line on intellectual, cultural, and religious issues, and green for the ones that respect a wide range of opinions and practice "true tolerance" (as we discussed in conversation 4) toward those who believe in absolute truths and hold to a Christian worldview. Even if your children don't plan to attend one of the 150 schools that *Choosing the Right College* evaluates, this catalog equips you to ask the right kinds of questions of whatever your children's prospective colleges happen to be.

Regardless of your teens' majors or how you decide to approach liberal arts requirements, our second consideration will probably be important: How on earth are your teens going to support themselves after college?

THE IMPORTANCE OF JOB PREPARATION

Over the last 40 years there has been a massive shift in what students look for in a college education. In 1967, more than 82 percent of incoming freshmen said that "developing a meaningful philosophy of life" was a very important goal in their pursuit of a college education. Such a goal is consistent with the historic view of college as a place for life training (not just job training), for seeing how different subjects are interconnected within a coherent whole, and for becoming a cultivated human being. But by 2012, "developing a meaningful philosophy of life" was important to only 45 percent of incoming freshmen. Contrast that downward trend with the percentage of incoming freshmen for whom "being very well off financially" is a very important objective. In 1967, about 45 percent of incoming freshmen said that was true for them. But by 2012, a whopping 81 percent affirmed it, with an even greater number (88 percent) saying that "getting a better job" was a very important factor in their deciding to go to college.[13]

Why would there be an almost reversal in these priorities, between "developing a meaningful philosophy of life" and "being very well off financially"? Before bemoaning the mercenary tendencies of youth today, we should acknowledge that there are two legitimate reasons for this new emphasis on job preparation and making money:

1. Most of the new jobs created over the last 30 years have required college-level training. A Georgetown

university economic study reported that 63 million jobs were added to the economy from 1973 to 2007—while those requiring only a high school degree or less fell by two million. The authors predicted that between 2007 and 2018, the labor market will grow by about 12 million jobs, with less than 3 percent of this increase going to jobs which require a high school degree or less.[14] Not coincidentally, college graduates find it easier to secure employment than high school graduates. For the last 20 years, the unemployment rate for college graduates has been about *half* the unemployment rate of those without college training, in good times and bad.[15]

2. The earnings premium (additional money earned by college graduates as compared with high school graduates) has been steadily rising for the last 30 years, especially for some majors (engineering, computer science, economics, finance, and nursing are among the highest). For example, someone with a bachelor's degree in electrical engineering earns about $2.50 for every dollar earned by someone with only a high school degree working an equivalent number of hours.[16] That adds up over time and has contributed to a huge disparity between the wealthy and the not so wealthy. Former US Secretary of Education William Bennett and David Wilezol note that "starting around 1970, nearly all of the income

gains in the United States have gone to those in the upper 50 percent of income distribution—those preponderantly holding college degrees, working in sectors like finance, law, communications, and technology."[17]

Here's the upshot: drastic changes in our economy over a long period of time have led an institution originally founded to equip the *whole* person, with the goal of forming capable and cultivated human beings, to become mainly a means of career preparation. My view is that you need both. In fact, I'd argue that career preparation is best when it's built upon the foundation of students becoming broadly educated, cultured, and virtuous people. But it's undeniable that students today, on the whole, are more interested in getting trained to earn a living than they are in being prepared to live a good and noble life. They're more interested in literal riches than in being personally, spiritually, and culturally enriched.

It's foolish to deny that the changes in our economy over the last few generations have been vast and irreversible. Job preparation has become a more important component of college, and that's here to stay. My plea is simply that students keep professional considerations in perspective. "Developing a meaningful philosophy of life" is frankly a really good idea, and college is a great time and place to do it. When I majored in engineering at college, I loved my courses in literature, philosophy, and music appreciation. There is intrinsic value in becoming a cultivated person, in preparing not just for a job but for a life. In fact, in a world where people will be changing jobs throughout their careers and where many of the future jobs are as yet uncreated, it may be more important now than ever.

What Influences a College Graduate's Job Prospects?

Very few families can afford to shell out tens of thousands of dollars so their kids can learn for the sake of learning, independent of any career or financial aspirations. This is a major issue in a slow-growth economy in which experienced employees are faring substantially better than new graduates.[18] A 2013 McKinsey & Company survey found that almost half (45 percent) of recent college graduates were working in jobs that do not require a college degree. A third said they didn't think college had fully prepared them to enter the working world. And the vast majority did not use career services offered by their colleges or tap into alumni networks to find jobs.[19]

It's wise to consider the job prospects for whatever academic major your teens are considering. It's not always the case, but majors often line students up for specific kinds of jobs or for certain industries. The point isn't necessarily to push teens away from lower-paying professional aspirations to ones that are more lucrative. It's to help all college-bound teens have a realistic sense of what they're getting themselves into so they can make wise, informed decisions on matters such as how to pay for college. Disappointment and regret are often avoidable when people enter new ventures with accurate expectations.

The job prospects of college graduates depend primarily on the quality of the graduates themselves—the skills they master, along with their extracurricular professional experiences and how they present themselves. Drop teens into the best college learning environment in the nation, and unless they have the disposition, desire, and discipline to learn, they won't. Conversely, teens with these positive character qualities can succeed at just about any college that accepts them. That said, it's wise to assess the instructional resources of a university, particularly in your children's desired major. Is the program accredited? How many units will your teens be required to take? How does that figure compare with the number of units required for that major at other institutions? What online tools will be available? Will students develop an electronic portfolio of their work (important to many employers)? Check out the library. If the school has a state-of-the-art recreation center but dilapidated academic buildings, that could be an indication of misplaced priorities. If one of your children plans to pursue a major within the sciences, look at the quality of both the classrooms and the laboratories.

You should also explore the job placement record of the university—again, particularly in the area of your teens' desired majors. What are the statistics on students working internships while matriculated? Do employers come on the campus to interview and recruit students? Which ones came last year? How have alumni fared in their search for employment? What is the average starting salary of recent graduates, and what is their unemployment rate? How long after graduation does it take them to secure a job? What lines of work are they entering? What percentage are going on to graduate school? Ask these questions of the dean of the academic program into which your son or daughter would be entering. Most are now collecting this kind of data (and if they aren't, they should be).

What does all this mean to a high school junior looking for a college? Look for schools that provide robust job preparation but that also provide an exciting learning environment, with engaging professors and motivated students. Teens should plan to spend significant time *learning*, not just getting a bunch of "easy As" on the shortest path to a degree. Such a degree, I fear, might be worth as little as the time they put into it.

Safety, Match, and Reach Colleges

If your teens love learning and are naturally gifted, they will probably be happier around like-minded teens of similar ability and inclination. A great place to get comparative data for colleges is the National Center for Education Statistics College Navigator. You can get some idea for the quality of a school's students by looking at the 25th and 75th percentile scores on the ACT and SAT. If your teens did better on these tests than 75 percent of the college's current students, they can consider it a "safety" school.

Resources for Assessing Employment and Salary Prospects

A McKinsey & Company survey of over 5,000 new college graduates found that half of them (53 percent) would now choose a different major or a different school. Employability and earnings were common sources of regret. Four in ten hadn't looked at job-placement or salary records. Graduates in STEM subjects were most likely to be in jobs that require four-year degrees (75 percent). The McKinsey survey is available online (http://mckinseyonsociety.com/voice-of-the-graduate). Here are a few other resources:

1. Anthony Carnevale, Ban Cheah, and Jeff Strohl, "Hard Times, College Majors, Unemployment and Earnings 2013: Not All College Degrees Are Created Equal," Georgetown University Center on Education and the Workforce, May 2013. This report gives unemployment rates and earnings of recent and experienced graduates in 16 different fields.

2. Three times per year the National Association of Colleges and Employers produces a salary survey for new college graduates in eight disciplines (www.naceweb.org/salary-survey-data).

3. The *Wall Street Journal* has a tool that compares starting and mid-career salaries for graduates from different colleges by region, type of college, and college major (http://online.wsj.com/public/resources/documents/info-Degrees_that_Pay_you_Back-sort.html).[20]

For those unfamiliar with the terms, a *safety* school is one where your teens' academic credentials are above the school's range for the average freshman. A *match* school is one where your teens' academic credentials fall within the school's range for the average freshman. And a *reach* school is one where your teens' academic credentials fall below the school's range for the average freshman.

Here are a few thoughts on the pros and cons of safety, match, and reach schools. At a safety school, your teens have a chance to stand out from the pack and be among the top students. That can lead to research, mentoring, or internship opportunities—all of which can help your teens land full-time jobs or get into top graduate programs. If your teens go on to pursue an advanced degree, the reputation of their graduate-level institution ends up mattering much more than that of their undergraduate school. The disadvantage of a safety school is that your teens may not feel challenged by their peers, which could cause them to get bored and tune out. At a match school, your teens will be somewhere in the middle. The advantage is that they're guaranteed to have many peers at their level. That would be my preference, personally. At a reach school, your teens would be on the lower end of the spectrum, which can be stressful. If professors grade on a curve, your teens may consistently find themselves toward the bottom of the distribution. That said, there are some students who were fairly lazy in high school but who grow up and really rise to the occasion in college—and a rising tide lifts their boat, so to speak. And of course, a reach school may have a strong reputation with employers.

The larger problem with a reach school could be financial. Reach schools may ask you to pay more, since only the best students at a particular college get offered scholarship discounts (another advantage of safety schools). If the choice is between taking out a bunch of loans to get into a reach school or attending an affordable match school with solid curricula, I would generally suggest the latter unless your teens are pursuing (and have the discipline to succeed in) majors like chemical engineering that would in all likelihood drop them into a high-paying job.[21] Even then, here's a possible rule of thumb: your teens could aim to graduate from college in four years with no more total debt than half the current median annual salary for the line of work they (reasonably) hope to enter with their choice of college major. Alternatively, from an estimate of what their total debt would be at graduation, determine their monthly payment (assuming a ten-year amortization). What percentage of their gross salary would that be, assuming they're earning the current median starting salary for the line of work they're pursuing? Anything more than 10 to 15 percent might be onerous. (Websites like Finaid.org have loan calculators.)

THE IMPORTANCE OF CHRISTIAN COMMUNITY

We've talked about the importance of colleges delivering quality education along with strong job prospects. Now for the third item on my short list: the value of Christian community. This is something you'll need to assess at both Christian and secular schools.

Some would argue that the biggest advantage of a Christian college is the Christian community. But the advantages extend to the classroom, in my opinion. Here are a few specifics:

1. At Christian colleges, there's generally a greater commitment on the part of the staff and faculty to the cultivation of the whole person. We're not just filling minds but shaping hearts. We want capable graduates, of course, but we also want them to be men and women of virtue and honor—consistent with the original purpose of higher education. I have seen this have direct bearing on the marketability of graduates. Employers want skilled people, but they also want employees who are trustworthy, hardworking, and honest.

2. At Christian colleges, faculty are encouraged to integrate their faith into their courses, to show how mathematics and science (for example) make sense from within a Christian worldview. All truth has its origin in God, the Creator and Sustainer of the universe. And all learning has worship and service as its end. As John Milton said, "The end then of learning is to repair the ruins of our first parents by regaining to know God aright, and out of that

knowledge to love him, to imitate him, to be like him."[22]

3. At Christian colleges, students are surrounded by a community that can help them wrestle with the Christian faith and really make it their own. They'll find more fellow Christians with whom to form potentially lifelong friendships. If they live in the dorms, there will be guidelines that encourage sexual purity and mutual respect.

It's worth noting that not all Christian colleges place equal emphasis on the above items. If any of these advantages is important to you, check out each prospective college with care. Are faculty and staff required to sign a statement of faith, to maintain Christian conduct, and to be active in a local church? Does a Christian worldview pervade the curricula, or are faith matters treated as peripheral to academic pursuits?

Similarly, at a secular university, you and your teens should evaluate the potential for Christian community. Here are a few suggested questions to explore:

1. What Christian groups are on the campus, and how well attended are their meetings? That a ministry is listed on a university's website doesn't necessarily mean it's active. If possible, contact someone by phone and, even better, arrange to meet them during a campus visit.

2. What's the culture like in the dorms (assuming your teens will be living in one)? Are there quiet floors? Are there unisex floors, or are there only coed options? You've probably heard that coed bathrooms are increasingly in vogue. I'd rather die than have my daughter live in such an environment, but that's just me. Plenty of college women are uncomfortable with this arrangement but feel pressure to stay silent. (Check the discussion threads on sites like CollegeConfidential.com.) Be informed.

3. Look at the churches in the area (*with* your teens, not *for* your teens). Ask your pastor or others you trust if they have any recommendations. Utilize any denominational connections. Listen to the sermons, and check out their beliefs and what ministries they have. Do any look like they'd be good matches for your teens? Do any have a student ministry to the campus? It's possible that a college that would otherwise be a suitable choice has no good churches nearby and needs to be crossed off your list.

A lot of this research can be done remotely, which can make your campus visits more effective. Include visiting a church as part of your campus visits (this applies to Christian colleges too). Your teens will see what it's like, and the inertia that often hinders a first visit will be out of the way. The idea of church involvement while at college is one more thing to talk about on the way home.

Colleges tend to mirror the religious demographics of the surrounding vicinity. Universities in the Northeast tend to be more secular than those in the Southeast. The Midwest tends to be more religious than the West Coast. That said, on the whole, young adults are the least religious segment of the population, and some are happy to explore the "wild side" at college. So help your teens set a game plan on how they're going to find iron-sharpening-iron friendships once they arrive (especially if they're naturally more inclined to follow than to lead). Having in mind specific Christian people, churches, and campus ministries—with whom they have already met and connected—is helpful. That first month or two when they arrive at college is crucial in terms of forming habits of church attendance and Christian community.

SUMMARY

- Teens should avoid selecting a college for superficial or sentimental reasons. They should likewise avoid the excessive anxiety that accompanies the opposite error—thinking that there's only one right college.
- That said, the college decision is worth making in a deliberate, intentional, and prayerful manner. Three things worth looking for are high-quality education, strong job preparation, and vibrant Christian community.
- A broad-based liberal arts education, an environment conducive to learning, motivated classmates and peers, well-equipped instructional facilities, and informed,

engaging professors are the ingredients for a high-quality education—the kind that prepares students not just for a profession but for the totality of their lives.

- Teens should realistically assess their job prospects based on the skills they'll acquire in their courses, academic major, and extracurricular activities. They should also consider the job placement record of prospective colleges and the specific departments in which they would be enrolled.
- Teens (together with their parents) should assess the Christian community available at prospective colleges by exploring the campus ministries and the churches in the area. They should also consider the social ethos of the dorm life, the Greek system (if any), and the campus in general.

CONVERSATION STARTERS

1. Identify with your teens a short list of no more than five "must have" criteria they're seeking in a college. Discuss what a college with these traits might look like.

2. Talk through various personal preferences (location, population density, and so on), the pros and cons of small versus large schools, and whether you'll be looking at Christian or secular colleges (or both).

3. After your teens have taken the SAT and ACT, aided by your short list of "must haves," your interaction

on personal preferences, and tools like the National Center for Education Statistics College Navigator, identify a handful of "match" schools, at least one "safety" school, and at least one "reach" school. Make plans to visit these schools, and then apply to the ones that seem interesting.

4. If you haven't already done so, start discussing how much money you and your spouse are able to contribute toward your teens' college experience. Together with your teens, set the framework for a financial strategy (including how much, if anything, you're willing to borrow to pay for college).

CONVERSATION 11
Considering Associate Degrees or Trade Schools

JUSTIN GREW UP with a knack for working with his hands. Ever since he was given his first Lego set as a child, he has been a tinkerer. As an eight-year-old, he saw a robotics kit in a store, and it became an obsession. Soon afterward an uncle gave him some tools. He began taking apart the doorknobs in the house, examining them, and (after several requests) even putting them back on.

One day he saw his dad adding windshield wiper fluid to the car. He was engrossed in what he saw: a beautiful array of equipment, all designed to work together. Dad got him a book from the library full of schematics and explanations. He soon could be found in the driveway after school, messing around under the hood. When he was 16, he combined a few hundred dollars of savings with birthday money to purchase an old car. And that got him poking around junkyards, seeing what auto parts he could scrounge up. He started talking to body shops in the area and eventually landed a part-time job.

At school, Justin was not particularly successful. It's not that he was rebellious; he tried to stay engaged, but he just didn't find his classes to be very stimulating. He wanted to do something with his hands—real work, as he saw it, not just sitting around. Justin struggled to get a few Bs but mostly earned Cs. During his junior year, as mail from colleges piled up, his parents began bugging him.

"Justin, have you thought about where you want to go to college?" they asked. "Or about what you want to major in?"

Justin had no idea what to say, so he said nothing. The topic was both overwhelming and uninteresting. So his parents nagged. And nagged. Eventually, Justin talked to the high school guidance counselor. His grades weren't good, his SAT score was below the national average, and there were only a few college options near home.

Justin reluctantly applied to three colleges and was accepted at just one. His financial aid package was mostly loans. He studied business administration, hoping to wind up as a manager in an auto dealership or service shop. But his college grades were lackluster, and when he finally graduated (five years after starting), the economy was weak and his student debt load was just over $60,000.

Unable to find an entry-level management position

Q: *What if a young woman really wants to be a stay-at-home mother and wife? How should that desire impact her college decision?*

A: That's a noble aspiration, and one I think many share (if quietly). But very rarely is this a question of either/or. I still think academic or professional development at the intersection of her talents and interests makes sense (whether or not it's a four-year college). A well-trained mind and a set of marketable skills will come in handy if, in the uncertainty of life, she needs to earn a living for a season or later return to work part-time. Even if she immediately marries and has children, God can be trusted to use the totality of her training to make her a valuable asset to her husband, children, local church, and community. My Stanford-educated wife (and former telephone company manager) has been my editor and research assistant and our tax preparer, all while homeschooling three children.

I would encourage her to avoid or minimize student loan debt in order to maximize her financial freedom down the road, especially if she prefers to exit the workforce entirely within a few years after graduation. I'd likewise encourage her to give particular emphasis to building (or preserving) a strong Christian support network (friends, mentors, parents, pastors, and so on). This network, along with any family who live locally, can lend godly wisdom and accountability to her relational decisions.

elsewhere, Justin went back to the body shop where he'd worked part-time since high school. They had given him 10 hours per week all through college. After college, they gave him 30 hours per week on the condition that he'd enroll in a local evening school to become a certified auto mechanic. Living rent-free with his parents, he was finally able to make headway on his student loan payments.

In a few years, Justin completed his certification, got bumped up to 40 hours per week, and soon earned a promotion with a substantial pay raise. He moved out of his parents' house and finished paying off his student loans. Today he's happily married, with two kids and a modest home. Not bad, considering that he was, after all, a few years behind in starting any serious savings. Justin's family is not wealthy, but nobody goes hungry. In the back of Justin's mind, he often wonders: *So why did I go to college?*

THE INVESTMENT (AND RISK) OF COLLEGE

Justin represents a large tribe of college graduates who (along with a growing cohort of college dropouts) question the investment. Let's start with the McKinsey & Company report I mentioned in the last chapter. It found that almost half (45 percent) of recent graduates believed they were working in jobs that didn't require a college degree. Granted, unemployment has been high since the recession, with economic growth tepid at best for the last few years. But add to the mix three more troubling facts. One, approximately seven out of ten 2013 college graduates accrued some form of debt (including money owed to family members), totaling an average of $35,200.[1] About $30,000 was student loan debt.[2] Two, about 44 percent of those entering a four-year college or university do not graduate in six years.[3] And three, among freshmen who attend four-year colleges after graduating in the bottom 40 percent of their high school class (like Justin), the Department of Education says that *three-fourths* (76 percent) won't graduate even if given eight and a half years.[4] It's clear that if college is an investment, it's also a risk—and one that doesn't work out for everyone.

I realize Justin's story and the last paragraph paint a gloomy picture, but there is an important lesson we can take away. High school performance turns out to be a fairly good predictor of college performance, at least at the high and low extremes. Colleges tend to use SAT and ACT test scores as a measure of intellectual potential (fairly or unfairly), and they use candidates' high school GPAs to get a sense of their personal discipline and work ethic. So warning lights come on when admissions officers see either one of them being too low. The reason is that, to be blunt, students who are weak in high school are often weaker in college. This makes sense, because the classes are more challenging, the field of peers gets stronger, and the out-of-class workload is higher, requiring that students exhibit strong personal study habits. And for many students, Mom and Dad aren't there to crack the whip.

Bottom line: those who did not connect well with high school academics should *not* immediately proceed to a traditional four-year college. I'm not saying they should cruise around town looking for whatever work they can find. Low-skilled jobs that require no training are indeed a dead end. That part of the economy has been shrinking for over 30 years. But it does not logically follow that the only way to get a good job is to earn a bachelor's degree. There are other forms of training that can help our young people launch into rewarding careers. That's what this chapter is about.

> *Those who did not connect well with high school academics should not immediately proceed to a traditional four-year college.*

HANDS-ON WORK IS NOT MINDLESS

Let's get one thing clear: Justin *is* an intelligent guy. He's not a dunce, and he has never been lazy. Schoolwork simply did not interest him. Other work did—the kind that involved both his brain *and* his hands. Many of us unconsciously hold to a false dichotomy between "mental" work and "manual" work, as if the two were like oil and water. The truth is that some college graduates begin their careers doing mindless cubicle jobs (following procedures established by others), while the work of an auto mechanic (for example), trying to figure out where a strange noise is coming from in an old car, is often both physically and mentally taxing.[5]

I fear we may be losing many young men like Justin in our K–12 education system, particularly in high school. I remember taking woodworking in middle school and attending a large high school that offered vocational courses like auto shop. Financial pressures and an emphasis on college preparation have resulted in vocational arts classes mostly disappearing. But hands-on courses engage students differently than typical lectures on algebra, English literature, or history—and therefore they engage different students. I'm all for Advanced Placement and International Baccalaureate programs, but we need to rethink a mind-set that pushes away a whole category of skill development—one that our society depends on for paved roads, indoor plumbing, new buildings, reliable cars, working electricity, and a whole lot more.

The truth is that boys drop out of high school at higher rates than girls. Women now outpace men in college enrollment by a stunning ratio of 1.4 to 1, which works out to almost six in ten college students being female (58 percent). Even if they go, men (regardless of race or socioeconomic grouping) are less likely to graduate from college, and fewer do so in four or five years. Men also get worse grades than women.[6] But hands-on courses like woodworking, auto shop, and electronics disproportionally excite young men, and keeping more men connected to what they're learning means fewer of them will drop out and more of them will have legitimate career options after high school.

And it doesn't have to be academic *or* career-technical education.[7] For example, math and physics concepts are necessary for understanding the modern internal combustion engine. Why not teach them together? Hands-on *and* mind-on. That kind of pedagogy will help some students understand math and physics, perhaps even getting them excited about a career in science, technology, or engineering. Students could use their hands-on skills to pay their way through college (something an increasing number of students need to do), regardless of their major. Local repair shops are far more likely to offer part-time employment to teens who have completed an auto shop class. For others, courses like auto shop can pave the way to an apprenticeship, trade school, or even immediate employment, either in auto repair or some other hands-on trade.

A brief word to those of you who have children who are currently disconnected from high school academics: you aren't alone. If your son or daughter would be interested in a hands-on, skill-oriented course—perhaps something mechanical or artistic (for example, photography)—find a way to get him or her into one, either at high school, through a community college, or through a regional occupational program.

It's not that traditional academics can be neglected. On the contrary, mathematics and computer skills are more relevant now in the hands-on, skilled trades (including auto shop) than in previous years. But at a trade school they are presented in a highly application-oriented manner that keeps students engaged and continually using the information. Michael A. Lucas, director of the North Montco Technical Career Center, near Hatfield, Pennsylvania, said it this way: "The technical program serves as the catalyst for kids to understand math. It's the motivator. We've had kids who have had difficult times with algebra and math in the high school setting, but as soon as they make the connection here, they start to do the mathematics, because it is relevant."[8]

Do you see a man skillful in his work?
    He will stand before kings;
    he will not stand before obscure men.

—PROVERBS 22:29

My neighbor is a senior technician who has had a long career fixing trucks for UPS. He has a three-car garage, two-thirds of which is filled with tools. Whenever *anything* is wrong in my house—electrical, plumbing, the air-conditioning unit, you name it—I check with Greg before doing anything else. More than nine times out of ten he knows exactly what to do and has just the right tool (including tools I didn't know existed). I'm guessing he has saved me a few thousand dollars by now. Greg never went to college because, as he put it, "By then I was working."

So let's dispense with the notion that high school graduates who enjoy and find skill in working with their hands are somehow second class, unsophisticated, or unintelligent. As Christians, we ought to affirm that *all* legitimate work allows us to imitate and glorify God while serving our neighbors in particular ways—ways that complement the ways they serve us. We can't all be engineers, doctors, lawyers, and financial analysts. If "the eye cannot say to the hand, 'I have no need of you'" (1 Corinthians 12:21), then neither can the engineer say the same to the electrician, nor the businessperson to the beautician. Classrooms are not the only places where young adults can distinguish themselves. There are different kinds of intelligence and skill. There's no use forcing teens to pursue educational tracks that don't make sense with how God has wired them. Our message should instead be, as the poet W. H. Auden put it, "You owe it to all of us to get on with what you're good at."

WHAT ABOUT FINANCIAL CONSIDERATIONS?

I know, I know: we're concerned about our children's financial well-being. Won't not having a bachelor's degree put them in the poorhouse for life?

Not necessarily. Just because college graduates on average earn more than non–college graduates does not mean that all college graduates earn more money than if they (individually) had not gone to college. Look what happened to Justin. Think how much better off he would have been if he'd been in the labor force those five years, earning and saving money instead of racking up $60,000 in debt.

Here's the good news: there are a slew of high-paying careers that can be accessed by trade schools, apprenticeships, and two-year associate's degrees—for less than half the cost of traditional college. Manpower Group (an America-based multinational human resource consulting firm) conducts a massive annual survey to find out the jobs that employers are having the most difficulty filling. At the top of the list for four years in a row (2010–2013) is skilled trade workers—electricians, specialized technicians, welders, and so on.[9] They call this "the skills gap"—and as I write, there are an estimated three million jobs out there for the taking.[10] Mechanics and sales representatives, many of whom have at most an associate's degree, also made the top 10 on Manpower's list.

Unless something is done, the skills gap is about to get worse as Boomers retire. In 2012, 53 percent of skilled trade workers in the United States were 45 years or older, and 19 percent were between the ages of 55 and 64. In the overall labor force, only 44 percent of workers were at least 45 years old, and only 16 percent of jobs were held by the 55 to 64 demographic. So skilled trade workers tend to be on the older side. But they're not working too long into their golden years. Only about 2 percent of skilled trade employees are over 65, as compared with 5 percent in the overall labor force.[11] (You can't blame them for retiring; it's not as if they're sitting behind desks all day.) We need to get busy replacing skilled trade workers as they phase out. But replacing existing workers is only half the battle—many of the skilled trade fields are expected to see significant growth in the coming years.[12]

The state of Texas reported in May 2013 that two-year technical degrees have first-year median earnings of more than $50,000, just over $11,000 more than graduates of bachelor's degree programs across the state.[13] Think computer networkers, engineering technicians, and medical technicians who work in hospitals. Similar results have been found in Tennessee and Virginia.[14] And a two-year associate's degree is all you need to become a radiation therapist, dental hygienist, diagnostic medical sonographer, physical therapist assistant, occupational therapist assistant, or aerospace engineering and operations technician.

How did we get to the point where we have a trillion dollars in student debt, over a million unemployed or under-employed college graduates, and a few million high-paying skilled jobs going unfilled? Mike Rowe, the former host of

Jobs You Can Get with an Associate's Degree or Trade Certification[15]

JOB TITLE	AVERAGE SALARY	NUMBER OF US POSITIONS
Radiation Therapist	$80,410	18,230
Dental Hygienist	$70,700	190,290
Diagnostic Medical Sonographer	$66,360	57,700
Aerospace Engineering and Operations Technician	$61,980	9,750
Electrical and Electronics Engineering Technician	$58,070	144,460
Occupational Therapy Assistant	$53,090	29,500
Certified Electrician	$53,030	519,850
Physical Therapist Assistant	$52,320	69,810

The Military Option

The military represents another viable route to a successful career. Of course, the primary mission of the military is to pursue national security objectives, which often puts its personnel in harm's way. There are many young adults who may not be able to cope with the physical and psychological challenges involved. This should be seriously considered before enlisting. Others may question the legitimacy of some of the military's engagements. Nevertheless, the armed forces undeniably help their recruits transition into adulthood, and they provide generous educational and career development benefits for those who serve. Joining the military is an honorable path to a well-paying career or a means of getting the training to launch a career in civilian life. Almost all the college students I've known with a military background have been marked by a positive attitude and a can-do spirit that propels them to graduation and future success. And they're happy to have Uncle Sam covering their tuition and paying them a stipend as they earn their degree.

Discovery Channel's *Dirty Jobs* and now a leading advocate for skilled labor, says it this way: "We are lending money that we don't have, to kids who will never be able to pay it back, to educate them for jobs that no longer exist."[16] Here's what Manpower's 2012 Talent Shortage Survey report says:

> As educational systems around the world have focused on four-year university education, this has resulted in the decline of vocational/technical programs—both curricula and enrollments have eroded over the past several decades. In addition, with fewer new workers to offset current retirements in the skilled trades, many economies will face continued shortages in the future.[17]

You see what's happened? The massive increase in traditional college enrollment has come at the expense of trade school enrollment. The fact that many college graduates are holding jobs that don't require four-year degrees suggests there may currently be a glut in the market. The McKinsey & Company report also noted that "more than 15 percent of taxi drivers and firefighters have a college degree today; only 1 to 2 percent had one in 1970."[18] However great their college experience was in terms of intangible benefits, we can forgive these cab drivers and firefighters if they find themselves questioning its value. There *are* other ways to become a more cultivated person. Meanwhile, skilled tradesmen are retiring faster than they're being replaced.

GETTING STARTED

Okay, so let's suppose one of your teens is sold. He or she wants to learn a trade. How does he or she go about doing it, and what's the typical career progression? It depends on the specialization, but there are three "standard" ways to get started:

1. *Trade schools and certification programs.* You can find these all over the country, each offering a different set of specialized tracks (or possibly just one track, like a school of culinary arts). I'm also thinking of career programs at community colleges that grant associate's degrees in fields like dental hygiene, cardiovascular technology, or medical sonography. All these kinds of programs tend to have a strong hands-on (or work experience) component to their training, so graduates leave with objective, tangible skills in a particular area, which becomes their basis for employability. Since some of these programs last no more than two years, it's wise to get a sense of who the prospective employers are right from the get-go.

   You should assess a trade school, certification program, or career-specific associate degree program in concrete ways, not unlike our discussion in the last chapter. It should have good teachers who impart real-world skills and whose graduates (for the most part) receive immediate gainful employment. The tuition should be reasonable, and it ought not have an alarmingly low graduation rate or a wildly high student loan default rate (check these carefully, especially in the for-profit institutions). The school should also be accredited with the appropriate accrediting agency.

2. *Apprenticeships.* An apprenticeship combines academic instruction with paid, supervised, on-the-job training. The duration of an apprenticeship ranges from one to six years, but the majority are about four years in length (including at least a year's worth of coursework). If your child is interested, it's best that they choose one of the over 21,000 registered apprenticeship programs across the nation. The Office of Apprenticeship (OA) works in conjunction with independent State Apprenticeship Agencies (SAAs) to administer the Registered Apprenticeship program (under the Employment and Training Administration (ETA) within the US Department of Labor).[19] The OA and SAAs monitor and ensure the program's quality as well as the safety of some 350,000 participants.

More than half (56 percent) of apprentices work in trades related to the construction industry (for example, electricians, carpenters, or plumbers). But the apprenticeship route can also be used to become an aircraft mechanic, an HVACR (heating, ventilation, air conditioning, and refrigeration) technician, or to access many other such fields. Eligibility usually begins at either 16 or 18 years of age. The majority of apprentices are men (about 95 percent).[20]

3. *On-the-job training.* Photographers, insurance agents, real estate agents, and drywall tapers are a few of the professionals who access their careers with on-the-job training. (Agents do have to pass a licensure exam in their field.) This kind of arrangement can work well in a father-son situation or with a friend-of-the-family connection. For example, my wife and I know a homeschooled girl finishing high school. A talented photographer, she plans to assist an experienced photographer for about a year. She'll learn how to take and edit better pictures, of course, but she'll also learn how to book clients, plan different kinds of photo shoots, track expenses and revenue, and attend to other aspects of running a small business. The experience she'll gain will allow her to either keep working as an assistant or start her own venture. The drawback of an on-the-job training situation is that if something goes south in the employer employee relationship, the novice does not have a credential to fall back on.

Want to learn more? Alabama and Georgia have established public relations initiatives to draw attention to high-paying career options in skilled trades. Their websites (GoBuildAlabama.com and GoBuildGeorgia.com) are full of information about the skilled trades, what training is needed to get started, and the typical salaries that skilled trade jobs pay. And Mike Rowe, whom I mentioned earlier, has created several websites and a foundation that provides scholarships to help students who are paying their way through an accredited trade school or apprenticeship program.[21]

JOE'S STORY, IN HIS OWN WORDS

From as early as I can remember, I always liked building things. My favorite toys were Legos and Lincoln Logs. Much to my mother's despair, I had an intense curiosity about how things worked and how they were put together. So I would often take things apart—clocks, electric motors, and just about anything with moving parts.

When I was 10 years old, I got my first taste of making something out of wood. My cousin took me into his wood shop and showed me how to make a few decorative pieces for my mom. I learned how to use the equipment and the importance of detail. I was immediately hooked. From that point on, every time my dad was doing anything around the house, I wanted to be part of it.

When I was going into the eleventh grade, I told my guidance counselor I wanted to take carpentry at the career center. She told me I was too smart for that and needed to prepare for college. Thankfully, my mother was supportive of my decision. The carpentry class was full, so I took a different class, where I learned the plaster, drywall, wall-covering, and painting trades. This allowed me to get a high-paying summer job in apartment-complex maintenance. I continued to work for this company through my senior year, and when I graduated, they offered me a job as an assistant maintenance manager. So that was my main driving factor for not pursuing college. I was already making decent money, and I loved what I was doing.

I worked in apartment-complex maintenance for two years. It didn't take long to realize the hands-on trades I had learned were more valuable to me than continuing in apartment maintenance. I enrolled at Western Carolina University and attended classes there for a year. Not knowing if I would actually be able to afford four years, I again went against my adviser by taking mainly technical courses I knew would help me. The next year I went back to work in the construction field and shortly thereafter landed an opportunity to train as an estimator. Within three years I had made some great contacts and was being trained to manage commercial construction projects. This has been my passion for the last 27 years now.

CONSIDER A GAP YEAR

In conversation 7, I brought up the possibility of your teens taking a year off between high school and college if they lack personal discipline, have insufficient finances, or simply aren't ready for the workload of college. Many people refer to this practice as taking a "gap year." The idea of a gap year originated in Europe, where it has been a long-standing tradition for high school graduates to travel extensively, volunteer (in exchange for free food and housing), or pursue other personal interests for a year before starting college. The concept of taking a year off before college is gaining popularity here in the States but is by no means widespread. What teens do with this year varies widely.

A gap year can be a good idea for teens who lack the maturity for college or don't know what they want to do, but for it to be effective, the year cannot be a free-for-all dominated by unstructured pursuits. It must be filled with purposeful activity designed to increase a teen's maturity, work ethic, and self-awareness regarding his or her talents, interests, and associated aspirations (see conversation 9). And this self-awareness should not merely be a deeper level of introspection. Rather, talents are revealed and confirmed in the crucible of experience. Students might take classes at a community college to increase their study skills and personal discipline while better learning which subjects they enjoy and at which they excel. They might volunteer or land an internship in an area of interest, as Page Hayley (from conversation 9) did when she worked in a laboratory before pursuing a science-related major at college. Along the lines of what we discussed earlier, your teens might pursue on-the-job training in a skilled trade and later enroll in an accredited trade school.

But won't they just "lose" a year of their lives? Not if the year is spent with focus and intentionality, as I'm describing. Although more than eight of ten incoming college students expect to graduate in four years, less than half actually will.[22] Perhaps if they began their studies with a clearer idea of what they were trying to accomplish and were more disciplined in their pursuits, more could graduate sooner. For many teens college will, ultimately, be the best path, but they just need a little more time to mentally, emotionally, and financially prepare to benefit from the experience.

As a professor, I've noticed that some of my most successful students are a bit older. They've had more years to mature, and they're disciplined, humble, teachable, and eager to succeed. Some have military, even combat, experience. Others have held full-time jobs and are now working part time to maintain an income stream.

Perhaps your teens have an interest in missions work, global studies, or issues of international public policy and social justice. They can design a service-oriented gap year, perhaps teaching English overseas or volunteering at a healthcare clinic in an impoverished region of the world (strengthening a future application for medical school). And it doesn't have to be a full year; programs vary in length.

There are explicitly Christian gap year programs. As I write, there are 14 listed at the Center for Parent/Youth Understanding (www.cpyu.org/gapyear). Most combine apologetics, evangelism, and missions training to prepare Christian students to withstand the onslaught of anti-Christian propaganda they often encounter at secular universities. Some focus more on personal discipleship, theological training, developing life skills in the context of community, and serving alongside missionaries overseas. All of these are unquestionably important areas, but I'm not sure they help teens assess whether their talents and interests suggest they should major in business, engineering, or something in the liberal arts. Even if they don't, that's not meant as a strike against these gap year programs. It just means that it'd be wise for teens going into such programs to maintain dialogue with their parents and other academic or vocational mentors about such matters or to have decided on a college major beforehand.

Perhaps you're wondering, *Can one of my teens apply to colleges, get accepted, pick one, and then take a gap year?* The answer is yes. Once they've picked their college, they would simply request a one-year deferral (with a letter to the college admissions office explaining their plans for the year). Such deferrals are usually granted, but note that this may impact any scholarship offers (and regardless, you would need to fill out the FAFSA again the following year).

SUMMARY

- All legitimate work has dignity in God's eyes. And as a society we *need* all kinds of workers. The skilled trades extend beyond "dirty" jobs and include professionals such as dental hygienists, occupational therapy assistants, and medical technicians, among others.
- Help your teens discover the intersection of their interests and talents and then pursue a viable path that's appropriate for them. Avoid the temptation to seek your own social mileage from their college or career path. Using our children is the antithesis of loving them. God has put us in their lives to shepherd them into adulthood.
- If a teen opts for a gap year before college, he or she

should spend that time in purposeful, focused activity designed to develop maturity, strengthen character, bolster faith, and increase awareness of how God has wired him or her and where he may be leading.

CONVERSATION STARTERS

1. Talk to your teens about whether there might be any "practical skills" they'd like to learn, and brainstorm ways to make that happen. If any of your teens are more bookish, consider asking them to join you the next time you do some basic home maintenance. Ideally they'll learn a different kind of skill and become more balanced. If nothing else, they should at least gain an appreciation for those who are mechanically oriented.

2. Talk to your teens about whether they feel pressure to attend a four-year college. If so, why?

3. If you have reasons to think a four-year college might not be best for one of your teens, share those reasons with your son or daughter, and then discuss some of the other options presented in this chapter.

CONCLUSION
Marks of College-Ready Teens

TO PREPARE YOUR teens for college is to prepare them for adulthood. It's to build foundational character qualities into their lives that equip them to live well: the fear of God, an accurate self-awareness, a commitment to lifelong learning, and the desire to make a difference in the world. It's not about them having all the answers and never needing help. None of us is ever independent in that sense. It's about them knowing when they need help and taking the initiative to get it, rather than our having to take the lead for them. It's about their assuming responsibility for their lives, but with an awareness of their dependence on God and their need for accountability and community. It's about their having a strong foundation from which to make responsible decisions and build lives that have a positive ripple effect on others.

Together we've explored 11 conversations for you and your teens covering issues of character, faith, relationships, finances, academics, and the college decision itself. The goal has been to help you raise young men and women who are ready to leave home for college. Let's conclude by describing Zachary and Samantha, a pair of teens who exemplify the essence of college readiness. Disclaimer: these are fictional and *idealized* depictions. The goal is to illustrate what a "perfect 10" looks like—so that we know what we're aiming for. (As I said in conversation 2, teens don't rise above the expectations of those who most closely influence them.)

As you read these descriptions, think about where you are with your teens. But please don't get discouraged. Every teen is a work in progress; for some, that progress come in fits and starts. God never leaves his throne, so change is always possible.

MARK #1: AN ACCURATE UNDERSTANDING OF THE BIBLICAL MESSAGE

Samantha is leaving her parents' home for her freshman dorm having responded affirmatively to the saving message of Jesus Christ and having cultivated the fear of the Lord, which is "the beginning of wisdom" (Proverbs 9:10). Her parents took her to church, read her the Bible, encouraged her to attend youth group, and exposed her to a variety of Christian influences, all with one end in view: that she would repent of her sins, trust in Jesus Christ, and live a Spirit-empowered life of increasing obedience to God.

We know that the God-mastered life is the best life, in college and elsewhere, because God's ways cohere with how we were made to live. The themes in this book—taking initiative, accepting correction, delaying gratification, being tolerant without compromising moral convictions, practicing financial stewardship, establishing faith-sustaining friendships, exhibiting purity and intentionality with the opposite sex, working unto the Lord, discovering and nurturing academic talents and interests—are best understood as aspects of Christian discipleship and part of our "spiritual worship" (Romans 12:1). And discipleship begins with being born again, being made alive to God, becoming a true Christian.

What do we do, then, if our teens reach the age of 18, graduate high school, but have never owned the Christian faith for themselves? Is all lost? No. We can still do our best to make them aware of the biblical themes of God/Creation, sin/Fall, and Jesus Christ/Redemption. We can steep their minds (if not their hearts) in Scripture. We can pray that God will use this knowledge to prick their consciences after they leave home. As in the parable of the Prodigal Son, God can orchestrate circumstances to bring them to their senses. We can do our part to plant the knowledge of the Bible and the offer of salvation through Jesus Christ so deeply into the soil of their minds that they find it "hard . . . to kick against the goads" (Acts 26:14). Don't underestimate what a biblically informed conscience can do in a young adult over time.

That and regular prayer have been the means of conversion for many adults. Meanwhile, we have the opportunity to model the grace and patience of God to them.

MARK #2: A COMMITMENT TO PUT AWAY CHILDISHNESS AND EMBRACE ADULTHOOD

Even if our children are not yet Christians, there are great blessings that flow from living in accordance with biblical principles. We all reap what we sow. Taking initiative, delaying gratification, and having a future-orientation will help *any* young adult be more successful (and not just at college). But behind all the character qualities we've discussed, there is one foundational prerequisite: a willingness to put away childishness and embrace adulthood. This is absolutely essential for success when your teens leave home for a dorm room, makeshift apartment, military base, or wherever.

The youth culture in the media and elsewhere teaches teens to aim for endless adolescence—a happy, intermediate no-man's-land of freedom without obligations, somewhere between childhood and adulthood. Many consider having a childish lack of responsibility combined with the body and mind of a grown-up to be the best of both worlds. College-ready teens resist this mind-set at every pass.

While progressing through high school, Zachary increasingly associated freedom with responsibility. And he increasingly opposed any sense of entitlement. He's willing to earn his success, in areas small and great, rather than expect that it be handed to him. He does not entertain delusions about achieving lofty aspirations apart from hard work. He does not think of himself more highly than his accomplishments merit (see Romans 12:3), and even then he recognizes that his talents are God-given and never grounds for boasting (see 1 Corinthians 4:7). He understands that "to whom much was given, of him much will be required" (Luke 12:48).

When he's working on anything (homework, chores, basketball practice, a part-time job), he does it with all his might. He doesn't view certain tasks as beneath him. Instead, he fixes his mind on how washing dishes, sweeping floors, and mowing lawns are expressions of worship to God and love toward those he's serving. He aims for usefulness in this world and the praise of God, not a life of ease and the praise of man.

With teachers, coaches, employers, pastors, and parents, he is accustomed to showing honor to whom honor is due (see Romans 13:7). He finishes what he starts and makes good on his promises. He views recreation not as the purpose of his existence but as temporary refreshment to empower him for future labors.

MARK #3: A COMMITMENT TO PURSUE GODLY RELATIONSHIPS

Samantha has a commitment to surround herself with godly companions when she leaves home. This commitment flows from an awareness of the impact close friendships inevitably have in her life. She has internalized passages like "whoever walks with the wise becomes wise" (Proverbs 13:20) and "bad company corrupts good character" (1 Corinthians 15:33, NIV).

In conversation 10, I mentioned the importance of scoping out the Christian environment at a prospective college before deciding to enroll. Why? Because as important as it is that Samantha have a *commitment* to pursue godly companions, she must also have a *game plan* for how she's going to do it. She needs to know, going in, where she is most likely to find like-minded Christian friends. She can't just assume they'll be there—because, trust me, at some secular universities, particularly in the Northeast, there may not be too many of them.

I do think this is less of a concern at an explicitly Christian college, assuming the overwhelming majority of the students are professing believers. But even there, teens need to discern their fellow students' character and values soon after meeting them. How do they order their lives? How do they spend their time? What is their attitude toward classes, work, their parents, God, the Bible, church? What kind of entertainment do they choose, and why are they drawn to it? Do they steal music or software by making illegal digital copies? Do they enjoy sexually explicit movies?

Samantha is under no illusion that she can find perfectly sinless Christians at college. But she has a commitment and a game plan to find kindred spirits—friends who have the same love for Christ and desire to live for his glory; friends who want to kill sin, lest sin kill them; friends who can refresh her spirit and call forth the best in her.

It's not that Samantha doesn't care about non-Christians. She's committed to interacting with them in a gracious manner, displaying genuine tolerance and not expecting them to think and live the way she does. She plans to tell them about her faith in the context of regular conversations. But she knows that to be salt and light, she needs to walk to the beat of a different drum. To make a difference in a lost world, she must herself be different—not in a weird way, but in a godly way (see Philippians 2:12-15). And for that to happen, she needs friends who can stand shoulder to shoulder with her, strengthening her.

MARK #4: A COMMITMENT TO SEXUAL PURITY

Teaching teens to abstain from sexual immorality is important—and biblical—but unless we tell them why, and give them an alternative, it's a message that doesn't go far enough and is often ineffective. God doesn't ask us to refrain from sexual intimacy because it's dirty or degrading but because it's beautiful and special. It's too precious to be scattered abroad for strangers (see Proverbs 5:15-19). We refrain from it so that we can give our hearts and bodies to one person to whom we are totally and permanently committed. College-ready teens hold marriage in honor (see Hebrews 13:4) and view marrying honorably as a worthy goal and as the direction to which their desire for physical and emotional intimacy points.

Samantha fights fire with fire in the area of sexual temptation. She recognizes that flirtation, provocative behavior, or making out can deliver an immediate jolt of self-serving plea-sure, but she also knows that it's a cheap, short-lived thrill, one that makes people too big and God too small and has the potential to leave pain and brokenness in its wake. She understands that God designed physical intimacy to go with a permanent commitment, to give us greater, more lasting pleasure. Therefore, she takes pains to make her path to the altar a smooth journey with few regrets.

Zachary aims to treat women as sisters in Christ, with "all purity" (1 Timothy 5:2). He sets and maintains boundaries to protect his sexual purity and that of others. He utilizes group activities to get to know girls (and allow them to get acquainted with him) without needlessly building intimacy too quickly with any one girl. He emphasizes getting to know women as they really are, not creating idealistic images for infatuation. If he is alone with a girl, they stay in public, well-lit places, and not during the late-evening hours. He does not view such guidelines as inherently legalistic. He knows the Scriptures exhort us to exercise wisdom, not to willingly and naively put ourselves in the path of temptation.

MARK #5: A COMMITMENT TO FINANCIAL STEWARDSHIP

Zachary understands that everything belongs to God and that what has been entrusted to him comes from God, to whom he will give account. He understands that money doesn't just appear; it's earned by diligence and hard work (see Proverbs 10:4). As he transitions into adulthood, he wants to earn money and become less dependent on his parents. To do so, he is industrious and resourceful. He also recognizes the importance of giving back to God a portion of what is already his (see Deuteronomy 18:4; Psalm 24:1; Proverbs 3:9).

With regard to spending, he's neither carelessly extravagant nor miserly and stingy. He recognizes that even the ability to gain wealth comes from God (see Deuteronomy 8:18) and that our enjoyment of his bounty can be an expression of worship. But he also understands that he must live within his means and share with those in true need (see Ephesians 4:28). Therefore, he sets a budget and disciplines himself to keep it. He avoids consumer and high-interest credit card debt.

He makes wise, informed decisions with regard to student loans, knowing that they aren't free money; they must be repaid with interest. Before taking on debt, he considers the salary prospects of the jobs for which his college major is preparing him. And he makes a plan to minimize his total debt burden by graduating in a timely manner.

MARK #6: A COMMITMENT TO WORKING UNTO THE LORD

Samantha aims to love God by developing her mind as best she can. She realizes that God has saved her not *by* good works but *for* good works—works which glorify him, serve others, and make a difference in the world (see Ephesians 2:8-10 and Matthew 5:16). To best exert a positive influence, she aims to maximize her competence by working (and studying) heartily unto the Lord (see Colossians 3:23)—not neurotically, but diligently and consistently.

During high school she came to understand that God has called her to love him with all her mind. Her parents taught her that exercising her brain, like any muscle, would make it stronger. And her teachers explained that a well-trained mind would equip her not just for a particular job but for the totality of her life. This doesn't mean she enjoyed every subject equally, but she accepted that each had value because it developed her intellectual capacities in specific and complementary ways. She learned to apply her heart to instruction and her "ear to words of knowledge" (Proverbs 23:12). Over time she has become a more logical, analytical problem solver and a better reader, writer, and evaluator of ideas. She can follow arguments, detect fallacies, and differentiate facts from opinions. She now pursues learning for its own sake and not just for the grades. She understands that education is really about something intangible—an internal transformation that makes us better people, more able to fulfill our God-given functions in this world. Looking back, she realizes the question *What am I ever going to do with this stuff?* is less appropriate than *What is it doing to* me?

During high school she sought to discover and nurture her interests and talents, pursuing activities that increased her self-awareness and helped her more intelligently decide what kind of college to attend and which field to pursue. In that process she didn't merely look inside her heart (knowing that we can deceive ourselves). She also looked to the external, objective feedback of teachers, mentors, coaches, and other adults with a greater level of expertise to assess the quality of her work.

DROPPING THEM OFF

Dropping children off at college for the first time is a bittersweet sorrow unlike any other, for both you and them. It marks an important transition from which there's no turning back. They will come home again, but things won't be the same. That's because *they* won't be the same. One era will have ended and another will have begun.

This has, of course, been God's good design all along, much as we would cling to constancy. God blesses us with children and entrusts us with the task of training them. They're never really ours; they're his. We just give them back to him. We transition from being authority figures to be obeyed to colleagues and friends to be honored.

I'm not suggesting that the task of parenting comes to a screeching halt when we drop them off as new college freshmen. But our *control* over their lives—our positional authority—immeasurably declines that day and never recovers. It only diminishes as time goes on. Going forward, they will live out of the overflow of *their* worldview and *their* character—and their accountability will ultimately be to God, not to us.

We can establish legitimate requirements in exchange for any ongoing financial support. And if necessary we can set boundaries when they're in our homes. But we need to recognize and respect their unique (and changing) personalities. We ought not seek to stamp out every difference of opinion, preference, or inclination. They are becoming their own persons. They are joining us as peers in the world of adults—and we shouldn't have it any other way. We must stand next to them, not over them.

We pray for their long-term success, peace, and happiness. We affirm, encourage, counsel, and if necessary admonish them as mentors, friends, coaches, and cheerleaders—fully understanding that they will make their decisions from the overflow of who they've become (and are becoming) in their orientation toward God, work, relationships, and recreation. We'll rejoice with them in their victories. We'll weep with them in their setbacks. And in both we'll entrust them to the God whose love is stronger than ours could ever be.

Acknowledgments

A huge thank-you to Jon Cameron, Jon Grano, Amy Hall, Natalie Marini, Bill Payne, Matt Perman, Michael Sears, Dan Southam, Moses Tey, Milton Vincent, and (last but not least) Ken and Heily Young for reading drafts of chapters (in some cases the entire manuscript) and for supplying numerous insights, illustrations, and penetrating questions. I also wanted to recognize Michael Lloyd and Dawson Young, a pair of excellent former students of mine who took the time to provide illustrations from their journeys. Zac Bissonnette, Gregg Harris, Marty Nemko, Mark Regnerus, Paul Tough, Bradford Wilcox, and Bradley Wright were kind enough to correspond with me about issues related to this book. (My apologies to anyone I may have accidentally left out). And I deeply appreciate all those who took the time to review and endorse the manuscript in the midst of their very full schedules. Your interest in this project and support for the themes presented has been tremendously encouraging.

I'm grateful for Jon Farrar, who believed in this book's message from the beginning and who supported the project at every stage of the process; for Jonathan Schindler, whose exceptional editorial skill and attention to detail resulted in many improvements to the manuscript; and for all the other outstanding, dedicated people at Tyndale House Publishers, without whom this book would have never seen the light of day.

I'm extraordinarily thankful for my wife, Marni, who, in the midst of homeschooling our children, read the chapters with me numerous times and graciously interacted with me in endless late-night discussions about content, organization, and which examples to use. Your research ability and discernment are second to none. Thanks for being so helpful, honest, generous, gracious, and persevering.

I gladly acknowledge my complete dependence on my God and Father, in whom each of us lives and moves and has our being; who fills our days with undeserved blessings; who secured salvation for any who would receive it, through the death, burial, and resurrection of the Lord Jesus Christ; and who works all things together for good for those who love him. I pray this book, by God's grace, will be useful in preparing mothers, fathers, pastors, and mentors to in turn prepare their teens for a God-honoring transition into college and adulthood, filled with precious memories and few regrets.

APPENDIX
How to Plan and Save for College

IN 1968, MY FATHER-IN-LAW completed a master's degree in civil engineering and got married. With an entry-level salary, he fully supported his wife *and* covered her tuition for her junior and senior years at Stanford University. She had no scholarships and no student loans. Can you even *imagine* someone doing that today?

Times sure have changed. As I write, a year's worth of tuition at a college can run you anywhere from $13,000 for a public university to over $40,000 for a selective private university (like Stanford). And that's *not* including books, fees, or room and board. Feeling anxious? You're not alone. From 2007 to 2012, the number of parents who believed they would be able to help their children pay for their college education dropped from one in two to one in four.[1]

Wanting to help our children pay for a college education is admirable. The Bible tells us to provide for our own families and relatives (see 1 Timothy 5:8). And in Proverbs 13:22 we read, "A good man leaves an inheritance to his children's children." Godly parents carefully manage the money God has entrusted to them. Rather than squander wealth, they use it to help their children get a decent start in life.

INHERITANCE THEN AND NOW

It's important to recognize that when the book of Proverbs was written, inheritance functioned very differently than it does in the affluent 21st-century West. Randy Alcorn writes:

> In Old Testament times, passing on ownership of the land to children and grandchildren was vital. Without it, succeeding generations couldn't do their farming or raise livestock. Many people lived at a subsistence level. Most were too poor to buy land. With no inheritance they could end up enslaved or unable to care for their parents and grandparents, who normally lived on the property with them until they died.[2]

In other words *inheritance* was what you gave your children so they would have the means to provide for themselves and for *you* in your elderly years. A college or trade school education, in our day, is a lot like an inheritance in biblical times. It functions as a ticket to the professional opportunities that allow our teens to achieve financial independence, support a family of their own, and contribute to the needs of others. It makes more sense to help our children pay for college and land on their own two feet than to give them a bunch of money after we die (when they're probably well into their mid-life years and have hopefully long since achieved financial independence).

But the cost of college in our day can be overwhelming for even the most responsible among us. What are we supposed to do?

First of all, if we haven't been wise managers of the money God has entrusted to us, we ought to put an end to our wasteful spending habits. According to a 2009 survey by the FINRA Investor Education Foundation, half of all Americans do not have three months' worth of expenses set aside in case of emergency.[3] For some of us, there are good explanations: a severe illness in the family, long-term unemployment, or severe under-employment. But for the rest of us, what's our excuse? We must recognize that saving for specific events (like college) is an expression of wisdom and responsibility (see Proverbs 6:6-8; 21:20).

If we've been bad at saving, it's worth asking ourselves if there are things we can do without—expensive vacations, daily lattes—to start building the kind of savings that will allow us to better serve our teens as they enter adulthood.

We must change our habits where necessary, live within our means, and set aside what we can in advance.

Throughout this book we've talked about how to prepare your teens for the many challenges that come with college (including the financial temptations that await them). In this appendix, I want to talk about *your* financial preparation.

THE IMPORTANCE OF SHARED OWNERSHIP

Let's begin with the obvious. Almost none of us can afford to pay for four or five years of private or perhaps even public university tuition. In conversation 7, we talked about the importance of teens contributing to the expense of college, how it makes them appreciate it more and contributes to a sense of shared ownership. When should this process start? Ideally, no later than when you start the college search process. You want to help them understand that college is expensive and that the bank of Mom and Dad has its limits. Tell them you're doing your best to set aside money but that— like all parents—you don't have an infinite reservoir to pay for their every college whim.

This conversation lays the foundation for shared ownership of the college experience. Even if God has blessed you financially, you've been a wise saver, and you're able to send your teen to four years of college entirely on your dime, I would submit to you that the concept of shared ownership is still crucial to your children's success. The few students I've known who have felt nothing of the financial weight of college have been the most frivolous and least appreciative of the higher education enterprise. Having skin in the game makes students want to get their money's worth. It helps them become more financially savvy, which in turn makes them better prepared for life after college.

And when they're ready to actually start college, that's a good time for you to establish what you expect from them in return for your helping to pay for college, especially if they're planning (or hoping) to live outside the home. What actions on their part would cause you to be unwilling to continue paying for college? Do you expect them to achieve a certain minimum GPA? To maintain whatever academic scholarship their college is giving them? To attend a local church? Talk frankly about expectations and consequences.

I'd like to unpack four topics: saving money, how the Free Application for Federal Student Aid (FAFSA) works (since almost everyone fills one out), lowering the expense of college, and (parents) borrowing money to pay for college.

Earning More + Spending Less = Saving Money

The good news is that there *are* ways to send your kids to college without going broke. It may take ingenuity and discipline, but it can be done. If your teens are high school seniors, don't panic, and don't assume you need to take out a huge loan—at least not yet. What should you do if you're strapped for cash and you need money for college pronto?

Before resorting to a loan, think about how you could earn more money. Work is the God-appointed means for

us to provide for ourselves and our families (see 2 Thessalonians 3:7-10; 1 Timothy 5:8), to avoid becoming dependent on others (see 1 Thessalonians 4:11-12), and to share
with those in true need (see Ephesians 4:28). If you already
have a job, can you get overtime or an extra project? What
about freelance or consulting opportunities within your area
of expertise? Be creative. With the Internet and professional
and social networking tools like LinkedIn, Facebook, and
Twitter, it's never been easier to get connected with folks who
could benefit from your services. The key is finding needs
you can meet in exchange for remuneration.

Second, spend less. Earning more and spending less are
what make it possible for you to save more. Are there things
you could give up or reduce for a few years to lower your
expenses? Consider movies, eating out, massage therapy,
facials, smoothies, pedicures, hair coloring, golf outings,
and so on. If you lowered your spending by as little as $150
each month while your child is in high school, you'd save
$7,200 over four years. And if your teen lands a full-time
summer job after his or her junior and senior years and nets
(after taxes and tithing) as little as 10 dollars an hour over a
10-week period, that's $8,000 after two summers. Together,
you'd have $15,200. That's a good start.

Note that even after only *one* year you can generate almost
$6,000 this way. Your teen could start off at a community
college, live at home, and later transfer these credits to a
four-year school. Wouldn't that be better than going into
debt right out of the gate? As discussed in conversation 7,

borrowing money for college as a last resort makes more sense at the end of the process than at the beginning. Start off in the black; save the red (if necessary) for your teens' junior or senior year, when they're closer to graduating and less likely to drop out or change majors.

Third, sell stuff. Craigslist and eBay can be amazing. You'd be surprised at the hundreds, if not thousands, of dollars you can generate by selling the junk you've been storing at the back of your closet or in the corner of your basement. Bonus: your house will be cleaner when you're done.

Financial discipline now and throughout your teens' college years will go a long way. The sooner you start, the more you can take advantage of compounding interest. Speaking of which, let me explain some of the more popular tax-advantaged saving vehicles out there: Coverdell Education Savings Accounts (ESA), Uniform Gifts to Minors Act (UGMA) accounts, Uniform Transfers to Minors Act (UTMA) accounts, and 529 plans.

COVERDELL ACCOUNTS, GIFTS TO MINORS, AND 529 PLANS

These aren't the only tax-advantaged vehicles out there, but they're the most common plans used specifically by parents saving money for college. And of course you can accrue interest on taxable accounts that contain a mix of money markets, CDs, bonds, mutual funds, and stocks. The benefit of taxable accounts is their flexibility—you don't have to use them for educational expenses.[4] The disadvantage, of course, is the taxes!

A Coverdell ESA is a way to set aside up to $2,000 per year per child. The money you put into this account is not tax-deductible, but the growth is tax-free, provided the funds are used for "qualified educational expenses" such as the tuition, fees, books, and room and board of one of your dependents. Coverdell account funds can be used not only at colleges but also at elementary schools and high schools (including Christian schools), provided the institution is eligible to participate in a student aid program administered by the Department of Education. (Just ask the school if you aren't sure.)

UGMA accounts and UTMA accounts are similar to each other.[5] You (the donor) give or transfer assets to your child (the minor, or beneficiary), but they are held in a trust (controlled by a custodian) until the minor reaches the age of majority (usually 18 or 21, depending on state law). The transfer of assets is *irrevocable*: you can't get the money back. The main advantage of these accounts is their flexibility. The assets don't have to go toward education-related expenses. Most parents (myself included) also consider that a showstopping *dis*advantage: the child can turn 18 or 21 and decide to buy a sports car or a new wardrobe instead of going to college. The other disadvantage is that as far as the FAFSA is concerned, your child has a greater net worth, and therefore colleges will expect him or her to pay more.

Individual 529 plans are like Coverdell savings accounts,

except the annual cap is much higher than $2,000 per child and the funds can only be used for college-related expenses (including graduate or professional degrees).[6] Plans are operated at the state level but handled by investment management firms like Vanguard, TIAA-CREF, and Fidelity. The majority of these plans are open to anyone—you aren't locked into the one in your state. They work like a 401(k): you choose from a variety of investment options, ranging from aggressive to conservative. You invest after-tax dollars, but the growth is tax-free, provided you ultimately use the funds for qualified college-related expenses at an eligible institution (otherwise you pay a penalty on the earnings).[7]

Unlike with UGMAs and UTMAs, the funds in a 529 account are considered yours, not your child's. And you aren't paying taxes on the growth. If you put in $5,000 today and it grows to $15,000 by the time your child needs it for college, the $10,000 gain is tax-free. And having the money in your name is advantageous when it comes to the FAFSA. The FAFSA expects your teens to spend a bigger chunk of *their* net worth on college expenses than it expects of their parents. This is part of the mysterious FAFSA formula that spits out an expected family contribution (EFC). Let's take a closer look.

BREAKING DOWN THE FAFSA

FAFSA stands for Free Application for Federal Student Aid. Not all colleges and career schools participate in federal student aid programs, but most do, especially if they're accredited. If you want a need-based tuition discount, *you absolutely must complete the FAFSA*, and do so *annually*. The rules change slightly every year, as will (in all likelihood) your income situation. The FAFSA asks a lot of questions about your income and savings as well as your college-bound child's. Using a complicated formula, it then produces an expected family contribution (EFC). Generally, a college's financial aid office will expect you to pay at least this much. How much is it going to be? You can get a rough estimate in a few minutes using your most recent tax return and the EFC Calculator at www.finaid.org.

At a superficial level, the process makes sense. The FAFSA takes into account your age, adjusted gross income, and any savings (cash, stocks, mutual funds, bonds) not including retirement savings (for example, IRAs, employer-sponsored plans). It also considers your children's income and personal savings—which usually aren't much, but the government expects a much larger percentage of their income (if they have any) to go toward college. But there are a few anomalies to keep in mind:

1. The FAFSA doesn't take into account the particulars of your personal budget. It doesn't recognize if you have the added expense of taking care of your elderly mother. Or if you're paid on commission and that, while the past year was great, there's no guarantee that next year will be equally strong. Or if you were out of work most of last year and are just now

paying off some large bills. Credit card debt is not considered at all—if you owe $10,000 to Visa, the FAFSA does not pity you.

2. The FAFSA doesn't take into account your home equity or your retirement assets.[8] Two families can both have annual incomes of $80,000, but one could have $200,000 more in retirement savings and an extra $200,000 in home equity. Colleges will think both families are equally able to pay the tuition. Some people make extra payments on their mortgage or store away more in their 401(k) before their children get to be seniors in high school.

3. If you sell appreciated investments (such as stocks or mutual funds) to pay for your children's freshman year in college, you'll get hit with capital gains taxes *and* you'll hurt your ability to qualify for financial aid, because your income for that year will appear high. If you plan to pay for college this way, you're better off selling the stocks their junior year in high school.

A lot of colleges will advertise that they "meet 100 percent of a student's demonstrated financial need." Here's the problem. One of the ways—quite possibly the *major* way—they do that is by making student loans available. It's a bit unfortunate that universities can treat loans as a form of financial aid, because it's misleading. Yes, they are "helping" your teens go to college, but loans have to be paid back, unlike scholarships or grants or work-study positions (by which students earn money).

Here's the upshot: whatever amount the FAFSA says you should pay, plan on colleges expecting you to pay at least that much. But that doesn't mean it's prudent for you to pay that much. Nor is it necessarily prudent to borrow the rest of the money simply because somebody will loan it to you. In fact, the wiser course of action is often to first look for ways to lower your expenses—to get as much educational value as possible for your limited college dollars.

LOWERING THE EXPENSE OF COLLEGE

Merit scholarships are easier to earn if your children are among the better students at a particular college. Therefore, one of the best ways to lower the expense of college is to encourage your children to apply to universities where they are likely to be among the better students ("safety" schools— see pages 320–322).

Here are some other ways to lower the expense of college:

1. *Negotiate with the college of your choice, especially if it's a private college.* In May 2013, the *Wall Street Journal* reported that private US colleges were offering "record financial assistance to keep classrooms full."[9] The "discount rate" (reductions due to grants and scholarships) at private colleges has climbed for seven years in a row. According to a survey conducted by the National Association of College and University

Business Officers, the average tuition discount rate for incoming freshmen in 2012 was 45 percent.

President Obama's administration has launched a website called College Scorecard (www.whitehouse .gov/issues/education/higher-education/college-score -card). You type in the name of a college, and it gives you the average net price (after scholarships and grants) at that college. If an average net price is $10,000 (for example) and the college's list price is $20,000, that means the tuition discount rate is 50 percent. The College Scorecard information is a couple of years old, so you'll have to compare, for example, the 2010 list price to the 2010 net price to determine what a particular college's discount rate was in 2010. Then you can compare this 2010 average discount rate to whatever discount rate the college in question is offering your child. Negotiating power will come from having more competitive offers at other schools.

2. *Consider work-study offers or part-time jobs near campus.* I think there are benefits to focusing entirely on classes during the academic year. If students confine their paid work to 40 (or, if necessary, 50) hours per week over 12 weeks in the summer, they can earn plenty of money to cover incidental expenses throughout the entire 12-month year.

But for many college students, too much unstructured time results not in more studying but in greater mischief. As noted in conversation 7, students benefit academically and financially from the extra responsibility of a part-time job. It not only forces them to be more disciplined, which usually leads to better grades, it also puts more money in their pockets— money which can even pay down tuition. Work-study jobs can be particularly strategic, because they are on campus. Even though these jobs pay minimum wage, students don't lose time or gas money commuting to and from work, and they may even be able to get some studying done on the job.

3. *Consider a community college or online program for general education classes.* In conversation 10 I spelled out the benefits (tangible and intangible) of having a high-quality, well-rounded general education, regardless of a student's major. That said, every family will have to decide if this is something they can afford. If your teens take their general education courses online or at a community college and then transfer the units to the four-year college of their choice, that will probably save money.

Your teens should check in advance to make sure the credits will transfer (it's best to get it in writing). Some states allow high school juniors or seniors to take courses via dual enrollment—an arrangement whereby a student simultaneously earns high school and college credit.[10] Such a strategy could help your child complete college a semester or two early, resulting in substantial tuition savings.

4. *Consider keeping your teens at home or having them stay with nearby relatives.* This can save you thousands of dollars each year in room and board expenses. Granted, living on campus can be a big part of the social experience of college. But friendships can be formed even if your teens commute. They'll have to go out of their way a bit more, but it's definitely doable. And it's a lot better than going into deep debt over a four- to six-year period.

5. *Consider having your teens work for a year before starting college.* You'll still want them to apply to colleges their senior year of high school. Then, request a one-year deferral so that your teen can earn money to afford college. In your deferral request letter, highlight that your teen will grow in maturity and character over the course of the year and will come to college far more prepared to excel academically. It's very likely such a deferral would be granted.

   The downside is that your teen will look "richer" on the FAFSA, which could cause your EFC to rise. On the other hand, an extra year for your teen also means an extra year for you to save money for college. The pros might outweigh the cons.

WHAT ABOUT PARENTS BORROWING MONEY?

Most of the principles discussed in conversation 7 regarding student loans apply to the popular parent loan vehicles available. First, consider the fact that most freshmen today change majors and take an average of five years to graduate. Is it really worth taking out debt in their first year of college when their path to graduation is anything but straight or certain?

Borrowing for college should be a last resort. If you have to do it, start with extended family members. Could Grandpa and Grandma chip in? Next, check out Federal Stafford loans (subsidized, if you qualify, otherwise unsubsidized). They have the lowest interest rate as I write (although it's a variable rate based on the ten-year Treasury note, the rate is capped at 8.25 percent for undergraduate students). And even though a Stafford loan would be in your child's name, there's no reason you, or any other relatives, can't help pay it down.[11]

With regard to the parent loan products, the main ones are mortgage and home equity loans (or home equity lines of credit) and the Parent PLUS loan. Fixed-rate loans are usually preferable to variable-rate loans, in my view, because the monthly payment is predictable and cannot increase. The Parent PLUS loan strikes me as a bad deal because the interest rate is high compared to what you could probably get on a cash-out refinance of a home mortgage. With a cash-out refinance, you would refinance your home loan for a *higher* amount. For example, supposing you owed $100,000 on your home, you might refinance that loan for $150,000. The lender would pay off the $100,000 mortgage, give you $50,000 in cash, and open up a *new* mortgage in the amount of $150,000. In this scenario, the monthly payments on your home would likely increase substantially (depending on what interest rate you receive), and the amortization clock would start all over. But if you have equity in your home, this method is probably the least painful way to borrow money for college.

Another way to go about paying for college would be to use money you've already saved for retirement in an IRA or employer-sponsored plan. At least on an IRA, as long as you use the funds for your teens' qualified educational costs (tuition, fees, books, supplies), you generally do not have to pay the customary early withdrawal penalty.[12] But you'll still have to pay income taxes on at least some of these funds (as if you had earned them on your job) *and* they will be regarded as income when you fill out the FAFSA next year. Considering how little many of us have saved for retirement, raiding those funds to pay for college might not be the wisest course. But some families will prefer this approach to increasing their level of debt.

Notes

INTRODUCTION: THE QUESTIONS EVERY PARENT IS ASKING

1. The Bureau of Labor Statistics releases data annually on "College Enrollment and Work Activity of High School Graduates." For October 2012, 66 percent of high school graduates from June 2012 were enrolled at either a two-year or a four-year college. In October 2011, the figure was 68 percent. October 2009 represented an all-time high (70 percent). In 1980, it was only 49.3 percent.

2. National Center for Education Statistics, "Digest of Education Statistics," Table 214, http://nces.ed.gov/programs/digest/d11/tables/dt11_214.asp.

3. Harvard Graduate School of Education, "Pathways to Prosperity Project," February 2011, 2, www.gse.harvard.edu/news_events/features/2011/Pathways_to_Prosperity_Feb2011.pdf.

4. Anthony Carnevale, Nicole Smith, Jeff Strohl, "Help Wanted: Projections of Jobs and Education Requirements through 2018," Georgetown University Center on Education and the Workforce, June 2010, www9.georgetown.edu/grad/gppi/hpi/cew/pdfs/FullReport.pdf.

5. College Board, Trends in College Pricing, 2012, figure 5 on page 14,

http://trends.collegeboard.org/sites/default/files/college-pricing-2012-full-report-121203.pdf.

6. Douglas Belkin, "Parents Shell Out Less for Kids in College," *Wall Street Journal*, July 23, 2013.

7. College Board, Trends in Student Aid, 2011, 4, 18, accessed 6/10/2012, http://trends.collegeboard.org/downloads/Student_Aid_2011.pdf.

8. Sheryl Nance-Nash, "The Student Loan Crisis Is Crippling America's Families—Is the Economy Next?," *Forbes*, February 7, 2012.

9. According to a Fidelity survey of 750 college graduates, reported in CNN Money on May 17, 2013, http://money.cnn.com/2013/05/17/pf/college/student-debt/index.html. This figure includes credit card debt.

10. Phil Izzo, "Number of the Week: Class of 2013, Most Indebted Ever," *Wall Street Journal*, May 18, 2013.

11. Mandi Woodruff, "Student Loan Debt Shot up Nearly 300% in the Past Decade," *Business Insider*, June 1, 2012. Figure is according to the Federal Reserve Bank of New York's *Quarterly Report on Household Debt and Credit*.

12. Cory Weinberg, "Federal Student-Loan Debt Crosses $1-Trillion Threshold," *Chronicle of Higher Education*, July 17, 2013.

13. Hope Yen, "1 in 2 New Graduates Are Jobless or Underemployed," *Associated Press*, April 23, 2012.

14. Kathy Kristof, "Older workers snapping up all the jobs," CBS News Moneywatch, June 25, 2012. Kristof writes: "Of the 4.3 million jobs created in the past three years, nearly 3 million have gone to people over the age of 55."

15. National Center for Education Statistics, IPEDS Fall 2010 Enrollment Retention Rate File, www.higheredinfo.org/dbrowser/index.php?measure=92.

16. Association of American Colleges and Universities, "It Takes More than a Major: Employer Priorities for College Learning and Student Success," April 10, 2013, www.aacu.org/leap/documents/2013_EmployerSurvey.pdf.

17. Data from Harvard Graduate School of Education, "Pathways to Prosperity Project," February 2011, 11, www.gse.harvard.edu/news_events/features/2011/Pathways_to_Prosperity_Feb2011.pdf and US Census Bureau, "Statistical Abstract of the U.S. 2012," table 231, Educational Attainment by Selected Characteristics: 2010, www.census.gov/prod/2011pubs/12statab/educ.pdf.

18. James Rosenbaum, *Beyond College for All: Career Paths for the Forgotten Half* (New York: Russell Sage Foundation, 2001), 59–62.

19. Jean M. Twenge and W. Keith Campbell, *The Narcissism Epidemic* (New York: Free Press, 2009), 40–56.

20. According to Sallie Mae, only about one in three (35 percent) college students had a credit card in 2012. (Sallie Mae's "How America Pays for College 2012," 23–24, www.salliemae.com/assets/Core/how-America-pays/HowAmericaPays2012.pdf). Other studies give higher figures for credit card usage and monthly balances, but most of their actual data comes from before 2009. For examples, Marty Ludlum, Kris Tilker, David Ritter, Tammy Cowart, Weichu Xu, and Brittany Christine Smith, "Financial Literacy and Credit Cards: A Multi Campus Survey," *International Journal of Business and Social Science*, 3, no. 7 (April 2012): 25–33. The 2009 Credit Card Responsibility and Disclosure Act has been credited for lowering credit card use among students.

21. Sallie Mae's "How America Pays for College 2012," 23–24, www.salliemae.com/assets/Core/how-America-pays/HowAmericaPays2012.pdf.

CONVERSATION 1: TEACHING RESPONSIBILITY

1. J. C. Ryle, *Thoughts for Young Men* (Amityville, NY: Calvary Press, 2000), 10.

2. Under-parenting can also happen at church, with similarly negative consequences, because it's not what teens need or (at their deepest level) truly want. Unfortunately, some youth pastors emphasize recreation at the expense of Bible teaching in an attempt to stay relevant and attract large numbers of teens. Years later, many of these teens have left the faith. The sad truth is that if you attract teens with fun and games, you have to keep attracting them that way. Once more entertaining options present themselves, they're gone. We'll address this more in conversation 3.

3. This is the same theme that Amy Chua laid out, albeit in a sometimes over-the-top way, in her much-discussed book *Battle Hymn of the Tiger Mother* (New York: Penguin, 2011).

4. Paul David Tripp, *Age of Opportunity: A Biblical Guide to Parenting Teens* (Phillipsburg, NJ: Presbyterian & Reformed Publishing, 1997), 15.

5. The Ethics and Religious Liberty Commission of the Southern Baptist Convention, accessed May 11, 2013, http://erlc.com/issues/quick-facts/por/. Older boys (14 to 15 years old) are more likely to seek porn on the web.

6. Stephen R. Covey, *The Seven Habits of Highly Effective People*, (New York: Free Press, 2004).

7. Dorothy Sayers, "Why Work?" in *Creed or Chaos* (New York: Harcourt Brace, 1947).

8. Jean M. Twenge and W. Keith Campbell, *The Narcissism Epidemic: Living in the Age of Entitlement* (New York: Free Press, 2009), 34.

CONVERSATION 2: TRAINING TEENS TO BE FUTURE-ORIENTED

1. Robert Epstein, "The Myth of the Teen Brain," *Scientific American Mind* (April/May 2007): 58.
2. Ibid.
3. Ibid., 58–59.
4. Ibid., 59.
5. National Endowment for Financial Education, "Nearly 60 Percent of Parents Financially Supporting Adult Children," May 26, 2011, www.nefe .org/press-room/news/parents-financially-supporting-adult-children.aspx.
6. United States Census Bureau (www.census.gov/hhes/families/files /graphics/MS-2.pdf), raw data: www.census.gov/hhes/families/files /ms2.csv.
7. A. Berger, *Child Trends' Analysis of National Vital Statistics System Birth Data* (Washington, DC: Child Trends), cited in "Trends in Marriage and Fertility," http://blog.childtrends.org/2011/12/.
8. Entertainment Software Association, Industry Facts, www.theesa.com /facts/index.asp.
9. For an excellent articulation of these principles, I would commend to you Alex and Brett Harris's fine book *Do Hard Things* (Colorado Springs: Multnomah, 2008). Every teen would benefit from reading this book.
10. Kevin G. Hall, McClatchy Washington Bureau, "Teen Employment Hits Record Lows," August 29, 2013, www.mcclatchydc.com /2013/08/29/200769/teen-employment-hits-record-lows.html.
11. Brittany Smith, "Pastors Conference Explores Manhood through Fatherhood," *Christian Post*, January 31, 2012, www.christianpost.com /news/pastors-conference-explores-manhood-through-fatherhood-68369/.
12. W. Mischel, Y. Shoda, and M. I. Rodriguez, "Delay of Gratification in Children," *Science*, 244, no. 4907 (May 26, 1989): 933–38.
13. For a book-length articulation of this principle and its practical application in myriad areas, see John Piper, *Future Grace*, rev. ed. (Colorado Springs: Multnomah, 2012).
14. Finding from the Nielsen Company, June 2009, and cited in the *New York Times* and elsewhere. This data is in flux, so the number may be higher by now. I've seen figures north of 3,000 texts per month.
15. Katie Hafner, "Texting May Be Taking a Toll," *New York Times*, May 25, 2009.
16. Morley Safer, "Strategic Default: Walking Away from Mortgages," CBS

News, May 9, 2010, www.cbsnews.com/stories/2010/05/06/60minutes /main6466484.shtml.

17. For example, see Paul Tough, *How Children Succeed: Grit, Curiosity, and the Hidden Power of Character* (New York: Houghton Mifflin Harcourt, 2012).

CONVERSATION 3: RAISING TEENS WHO INTERNALIZE THEIR FAITH

1. Andrew Hess and Glenn T. Stanton, "Millennial Faith Participation and Retention," August 2013, www.focusonthefamily.com/about_us /focus-findings/religion-and-culture/-/media/images/about-us/focus -findings/FF%20-%20Millenial%20Faith%20Retention%20FINAL.ashx.

2. Barna Group, "Evangelism Is Most Effective among Kids," October 11, 2004, www.barna.org/barna-update/article/5-barna-update /196-evangelism-is-most-effective-among-kids#.Uhy3Az-ourY.

3. Christian Smith, *Soul Searching* (New York: Oxford University Press, 2005) and *Souls in Transition* (New York: Oxford University Press, 2009).

4. See, for example, S. Michael Craven, "Fathers: Key to Their Children's Faith," *The Christian Post*, June 19, 2011.

5. Lillian Kwon, "Survey: High School Seniors 'Graduating from God,'" *The Christian Post*, August 10, 2006.

6. Bertrand Russell, *Autobiography*, vol. 2 (London: George Allen and Unwin, 1968), 159.

7. C. S. Lewis, "Is Theology Poetry?" in *The Weight of Glory and Other Addresses* (New York: HarperOne, 1980), 140.

8. If your teens aren't experiencing the false dichotomy of science or faith, they probably will at secular universities. As I showed in *Thriving at College*, teens are far more likely to meet atheists and agnostics on the faculty of a secular university than anywhere else in society.

9. David Kinnaman, *You Lost Me* (Grand Rapids, MI: Baker Books, 2011), 52.

10. Ibid., 117.

11. Ibid., 140.

12. For a helpful overview of the compatibility of science and faith, see C. John Collins, *Science and Faith: Friends or Foes?* (Wheaton, IL: Crossway, 2003).

13. For further study, see books like F. F. Bruce, *The New Testament Documents: Are They Reliable?* (Grand Rapids, MI: Eerdmans, 1974). The Stand to Reason website (www.str.org) has several helpful short essays dealing with the authority of the Bible and the integrity of our English translations.

14. See Mark Kelly, "LifeWay Research Finds Parents Churches Can Help

Teens Stay in Church," August 7, 2007, Kevin A. Miller, "From Relevant Dude to Spiritual Father," *Leadership Journal*, Summer 2011, and Erik Tryggestad, "What teens want," *The Christian Chronicle*, June 1, 2009. See also Larry Alex Taunton, "Listening to Young Atheists: Lessons for a Stronger Christianity," *The Atlantic*, June 6, 2013.

CONVERSATION 4: RAISING TEENS CHARACTERIZED BY CONVICTION AND TOLERANCE

1. McDowell himself acknowledged this shift over ten years ago, writing, "Fewer and fewer people are asking questions that can be answered with evidential apologetics. Yet those questions need to be asked—and answered. But in our postmodern, relativistic culture, an emphasis on 'what is true' has decreased and an interest in 'what works' has increased." Josh McDowell and Bob Hostetler, *The New Tolerance* (Carol Stream, IL: Tyndale House, 1997), 198.

2. What's ironic is that on the secular university campus today, science faculty often regard blind, undirected evolution as incontrovertible, "objective" truth—questioned only by dolts committed to "imposing their religion on science." But fields like the humanities, religious studies, and social sciences have so been taken over by postmodernism that in these circles the notion of objective truth has been completely abandoned.

3. Rick Warren, quoted in Alex Murashko, "Exclusive—Rick Warren: 'Flat Out Wrong' That Muslims, Christians View God the Same," *Christian Post*, March 2, 2012, www.christianpost.com/news/exclusive-rick-warren -flat-out-wrong-that-muslims-christians-view-god-the-same-70767/.

4. This shift in the functional definition of tolerance is explored in exquisite detail in D. A. Carson's excellent book *The Intolerance of Tolerance* (Grand Rapids, MI: Eerdmans, 2012).

5. Someone may observe that mass murderers and psychopaths don't accept universal human dignity. The Bible explains that people can harden their consciences through habitual evil. And mental illness, like all sickness, is part of the brokenness wrought by the Fall. Nevertheless, those who commit atrocities often justify their deeds to get around their innate knowledge of human dignity. Adolf Hitler, for example, taught that the Jews were an inferior race. Likewise those who participated in the African slave trade told themselves that their chattel was subhuman.

6. Augustine, *Confessions*, book I, 1.

7. Aleksandr Solzhenitsyn, *The Gulag Archipelago, Part 1: The Prison Industry* (London: Collins, 1974), 168.

8. James Sire, *The Universe Next Door*, 3rd ed. (Downers Grove, IL: InterVarsity Press, 1997), 88–89.

9. Mark Mittelberg, *The Questions Christians Hope No One Will Ask* (Carol Stream, IL: Tyndale House, 2010), 239–246.

CONVERSATION 5: HELPING TEENS PURSUE QUALITY FRIENDSHIPS

1. Tim Keller, *The Freedom of Self-Forgetfulness: The Path to True Christian Joy* (Chorley, UK: 10Publishing, 2012).

2. For an excellent book, written to teens, that deals with these principles, see Edward T. Welch, *What Do You Think of Me? Why Do I Care?* (Greensboro, NC: New Growth Press, 2011).

CONVERSATION 6: HELPING TEENS PURSUE PURITY

1. Kevin Haninger and Kimberly M. Thompson, "Content and Ratings of Teen-Rated Video Games," *The Journal of the American Medical Association*, February 18, 2004.

2. Press release: http://ir.take2games.com/phoenix.zhtml?c=86428&p=irol-newsArticle&ID=1856686&highlight=.

3. Luke Rosiak, "Fathers Disappear from Households across America," *Washington Times*, December 25, 2012.

4. Jason DeParle and Sabrina Tavernise, "For Women Under 30, Most Births Occur Outside Marriage," *New York Times*, February 17, 2012.

5. www.familyfacts.org/charts/145/almost-half-of-children-in-single-mother-homes-live-with-never-married-mothers.

6. See W. Bradford Wilcox, "The Kids Are Not Really Alright," *Slate*, July 20, 2012, for example.

7. See W. Bradford Wilcox, "The Evolution of Divorce," *National Affairs*, Fall 2009, www.nationalaffairs.com/publications/detail/the-evolution-of-divorce.

8. See Mark Regnerus, "The Case for Early Marriage," *Christianity Today*, July 31, 2009. Also, Mark Regnerus, *Forbidden Fruit: Sex & Religion in the Lives of American Teenagers* (New York: Oxford University Press, 2007). While promiscuity is undoubtedly a problem among churched youth, some of the data reported is overly pessimistic because the researchers define "Christian" as "anyone who says they're a Christian." When you break it down more carefully and look at unmarried young adults (18–29) who call themselves Christians *and* attend church weekly, read their Bibles regularly, and adhere to traditional Christian beliefs, the *majority* of these individuals are virgins. Nevertheless, too many aren't, and others are creatively redefining

sex to remain "technical virgins." (See Bradley R. E. Wright, *Christians Are Hate-Filled Hypocrites . . . and Other Lies You've Been Told* [Grand Rapids, MI: Bethany House, 2010], 138–142. *Christianity Today* posted a helpful infographic on May 8, 2013: www.christianitytoday.com/ct/content/pdf/130501_spot_sexlives.pdf.)

9. For example, Family Life Today has a resource called Passport2Purity, a set of teachings designed to take place between a parent and a preteen over a weekend getaway. Focus on the Family also has a variety of resources available.

10. Timothy Keller with Kathy Keller, *The Meaning of Marriage* (New York: Dutton, 2011), 223–224.

11. Gerald Hiestand and Jay Thomas, *Sex, Dating, and Relationships* (Wheaton, IL: Crossway, 2012), 18.

12. For a more complete articulation of this perspective, see Hiestand and Thomas, *Sex, Dating, and Relationships*, 31–48.

13. I deal with these tensions in an article entitled "A Balanced View on Singleness," published by Boundless (a ministry of Focus on the Family) in September 2009, accessible here: www.boundless.org/adulthood/2009/a-balanced-view-on-singleness.

14. U.S. Census Bureau, www.census.gov/hhes/families/files/ms2.csv.

15. See Dennis Rainey, *Interviewing Your Daughter's Date: 30 Minutes Man-to-Man* (Little Rock, AR: Family Life Publishing, 2012).

16. A great resource on this is *Unprotected* by Miriam Grossman (New York: Penguin, 2007). Grossman, a psychiatrist for many years at an elite secular university campus, draws connections between sexual promiscuity and the rising number of mental health issues reported on campuses, particularly by women. The negative effects for men are equally real, though perhaps less immediately apparent. See Mark Regnerus and Jeremy Uecker, *Premarital Sex in America* (New York: Oxford University Press, 2011), 101–134.

17. For a great article on the importance of boundaries in these kinds of relationships, see Jim Newheiser, "The Tenderness Trap," *The Journal of Biblical Counseling*, 13, no. 3 (1995): 44–47, http://mail.ibcd.org/articles/60-the-tenderness-trap.)

18. Regnerus and Uecker, *Premarital Sex in America*, 101–134. The prioritization of career advancement at elite universities seems to be a driving factor as to why hook-ups are more common there than at other schools. Incidentally, it's not always clear that hook-ups are consensual. Alcohol is often a contributing factor, and sexual assault charges sometimes follow. When researching colleges, note that the Clery Act (also known

as the Campus Security Act) is a federal law requiring colleges and universities to disclose information about crime on and around their campuses, including sexual assault.

19. Regnerus and Uecker, *Premarital Sex in America*, 117–118.

CONVERSATION 7: TEACHING YOUR TEENS FINANCIAL RESPONSIBILITY

1. Sallie Mae's "How America Pays for College 2012," 23–24, www.salliemae .com/assets/Core/how-America-pays/HowAmericaPays2012.pdf. Other studies give higher figures for credit card usage and monthly balances, but their data may be old. For examples, Marty Ludlum, Kris Tilker, David Ritter, Tammy Cowart, Weichu Xu, Brittany Christine Smith, "Financial Literacy and Credit Cards: A Multi Campus Survey," *International Journal of Business and Social Science* 3, no. 7 (April 2012), 25–33. The 2009 Credit Card Accountability, Responsibility, and Disclosure Act, signed into law by President Barack Obama, has been credited for lowering credit card use among students.

2. "Household Debt in the US: 2000 to 2011," United States Census Bureau, www.census.gov/people/wealth/files/Debt%20Highlights%202011.pdf.

3. Ben Patterson, *The Grand Essentials* (Waco, TX: Word, 1987), 17. For more on stewardship, see Randy Alcorn, *Money, Possessions, and Eternity* (Carol Stream, IL: Tyndale House, 2003), especially chapters 7–11.

4. Amy Langfield, CNBC, "Today's Teens More Materialistic, Less Likely to Work Hard, Study Says," May 2, 2013. The study referred to, called "Monitoring the Future," has been examining high school seniors since 1976.

5. Individual families may establish other expectations, like whether the student will be contributing to his own auto insurance. To avoid unnecessary detail, I'm not accounting for federal or state income taxes in this simple budget.

6. April 12, 2013, "New Barna Study Explores Trends Among American Donors," www.barna.org/culture-articles/611-new-barna-study -explores-trends-among-american-donors?q=money.

7. According to the Association of College and University Housing Officers International. Quoted in a *Time* magazine Photo Special, accessible here: www.time.com/time/photogallery/0,29307,1838306,00.html. As for the trend continuing, see, for example, this May 9, 2013, article by interior designer Jill Lung, "Amenities for the New Millennials," www.studenthousingbusiness.com/voices/2398-amenities-for-the-new -millennials-student-housing.html.

8. The 2013 College Construction Report, issued by College Planning and Management, www.peterli.com/cpm/pdfs/CollegeConstruction Report2013.pdf.

9. For example, Scott Carlson, "What's the Payoff for the 'Country Club' College?," *The Chronicle of Higher Education*, January 28, 2013. And Kyle Stokes, "In College Dorms And Dining, How Nice Is Too Nice?" Indiana Public Media, August 18, 2011.

10. Beth Pinsker Gladstone, "As College Costs Rise, Students Trade Dorm for Home: Sallie Mae," Reuters News Service, reported in Huffington Post, July 16, 2012, www.huffingtonpost.com/2012/07/16/college-costs-rising -trade-dorm-for-home_n_1675132.html. In 2013, a majority (57 percent) of families reported a student living at home or with a relative, up from 43 percent in 2010. Even among families with annual household incomes of over $100,000, the share of students staying at home has *doubled* to 48 percent over just three years. Douglas Belkin, "Parents Shell Out Less for Kids in College," *Wall Street Journal*, July 23, 2013.

11. College Board, Trends in College Pricing, 2012, figure 5 on page 14, http://trends.collegeboard.org/sites/default/files/college-pricing-2012-full -report-121203.pdf.

12. Average annual college tuition from the National Center for Education Statistics, http://nces.ed.gov/fastfacts/display.asp?id=76. Family income data from the US Census Bureau, www.census.gov/hhes/www/income /data/historical/families/, table F-10, "Married-Couple Families, One or More Children Under 18 Years Old." (Note that the increase in tuition is less dramatic at two-year colleges.)

13. Laura W. Perna, "Understanding the Working College Student," *Academe*, July-August 2010, www.aaup.org/article/understanding-working-college -student#.UlMmvhBdwa8, and Lynn O'Shaughnessy, "More students working (a lot) in college," *CBS News Money Watch*, February 5, 2013.

14. National Center for Education Statistics, "2011–12 National Postsecondary Student Aid Study (NPSAS:12)," August 2013, 7, http://nces.ed.gov/pubs2013/2013165.pdf.

15. Phil Izzo, "Number of the Week: Class of 2013, Most Indebted Ever," *Wall Street Journal*, May 18, 2013.

16. For one perspective, see Robert B. Archibald and David H. Feldman, *Why Does College Cost So Much?* (Oxford University Press, 2010). The gist of their argument is that technological progress and economic growth favors more formally educated workers with higher salaries. Colleges and universities employ many such workers. Low student-to-faculty ratios are academically advantageous, but more expensive, as are state-of-the-art

laboratories that give students the training to compete for 21st-century jobs. Tuition would be even higher if it weren't for federal and state subsidies.

A different perspective has been presented over the years by scholars such as William J. Bennett and Richard Vedder. The gist of their argument is that colleges lack incentives to keep costs under control and have often become wasteful and frivolous. In 1987, Dr. Bennett first articulated The Bennett Hypothesis, which states that "the cost of college tuition will rise as long as the amount of money available in federal student-aid programs continues to increase with little to no accountability." Bennett and coauthor David Wilezol discuss this further in their provocative and engaging book *Is College Worth It?* (Nashville: Thomas Nelson, 2013), 21–70.

17. Romans 13:8, taken together with the previous verse, could just as easily mean, "Pay everyone what you owe them. If you take out a loan, make all your payments on time, in full. Honor your financial commitments."

18. For more information, see Joanne Jacobs, "Some Teens Start College Work Early via Dual Enrollment," *U.S. News & World Report*, March 9, 2012.

19. National Center for Education Statistics, IPEDS Fall 2010 Enrollment Retention Rate File, www.higheredinfo.org/dbrowser/index.php ?measure=92. Data on freshmen retention is for 2010. And Harvard Graduate School of Education, "Pathways to Prosperity," February 2011, 10. Note that these are aggregate figures. The six-year graduation rates vary wildly by institution and are often a reflection of the quality of incoming students.

20. If you qualify for a subsidized Stafford loan, the government pays the interest as long as the student is enrolled at least half-time in an accredited academic program.

21. Perna, "Understanding the Working College Student."

22. In *Thriving at College* (Carol Stream, IL: Tyndale House, 2011), I argued that it was academically advantageous for students not to work a job while classes were in session. I still think that's preferable *if* a student (a) can afford it and (b) can be disciplined to use time wisely (studying, student organizations, sports, music, volunteering, internship, and so on). But many students don't meet one or both of these conditions.

23. See Andrew Martin and Andrew W. Lehren, "A Generation Hobbled by the Soaring Cost of College," *New York Times*, May 12, 2012.

CONVERSATION 8: ENCOURAGING TEENS TO WORK (ACADEMICALLY) UNTO THE LORD

1. Non-Christians can also perform such tasks with excellence, but since these tasks aren't motivated by faith nor done for God's glory, they don't ultimately please God (although they are useful and have true value in this world). See, for example, the Westminster Confession of Faith, chapter 16, paragraph 7. Also, for an excellent treatment of why Christians should care deeply about doing good works, see Matt Perman, *What's Best Next: How the Gospel Transforms the Way You Get Things Done* (Grand Rapids, MI: Zondervan, expected 2014).

2. John Angell James, *The Christian Father's Present to His Children*, 4th American ed. (New York, 1825), 2:4.

3. James Rosenbaum, *Beyond College for All: Career Paths for the Forgotten Half* (New York: Russell Sage Foundation, 2001), 59–62.

4. Texts like the ones I've cited articulate the doctrine known as *common grace*. In the providence of God, tremendously valuable works of science, technology, and literature have been carried out by non-Christians. I think the blessing of being able to participate in such creative and impactful work is a part of God's goodness intended to lead them to repentance (see Romans 2:4). It's important to remember that while sin has marred God's image in us, it has not eviscerated it. That's also why many non-Christians have a keenly felt sense of morality and justice.

5. See Mark Bauerlein, *The Dumbest Generation: How the Digital Age Stupefies Young Americans and Jeopardizes Our Future* (New York: Penguin, 2009) for an outstanding analysis of the paucity in teen reading and its negative consequences.

6. Renaissance Learning, "What Kids Are Reading: The Book-Reading Habits of Students in American Schools," 2013 edition, 46–47, http://doc .renlearn.com/KMNet/R004101202GH426A.pdf.

7. Benjamin Carson, National Prayer Breakfast (in Washington, DC), February 7, 2013.

8. See also Joanne Lipman, "Why Tough Teachers Get Good Results," *Wall Street Journal*, September 27, 2013.

CONVERSATION 9: DISCOVERING YOUR TEENS' TALENTS AND INTERESTS

1. William Wilberforce, *A Practical View of the Prevailing Religious System of Professed Christians, in the Higher and Middle Classes in this Country, Contrasted with Real Christianity* (Glasgow, 1829), 216.

2. Marcus Buckingham and Donald O. Clifton, *Now, Discover Your Strengths*

(New York: Free Press, 2001), 61. This book explains the 34 "themes" of the StrengthsFinder talent profile.

3. Bill Gates, Nathan Myhrvold, and Peter Rinearson, *The Road Ahead: Completely Revised and Up-to-Date* (New York: Penguin, 1996), 13.

4. For a book-length articulation of this principle, see Gene Veith, *God at Work: Your Christian Vocation in All of Life* (Wheaton, IL: Crossway, 2002).

5. See Alexander Lemaine, "'CSI' Spurs Campus Forensics Scene," *Union-Tribune San Diego*, September 13, 2004.

6. Roy Hayley, "Homeschool Graduate Studies: Transitioning from Homeschool to College," *Old Schoolhouse Magazine*, December 2012.

7. See also Philippians 3:17; 4:9; 1 Thessalonians 1:6; 2 Timothy 3:10; and Hebrews 6:12. For a great contrast between inappropriate hero worship and commendable holy emulation, see John Piper, "Hero Worship and Holy Emulation," Desiring God, June 10, 2009, www.desiringgod.org /resource-library/taste-see-articles/hero-worship-and-holy-emulation.

CONVERSATION 10: ASKING THE RIGHT QUESTIONS ABOUT COLLEGE

1. In the USA, colleges typically emphasize undergraduate instruction, whereas universities confer both undergraduate and graduate degrees. But Dartmouth College, William and Mary College, Boston College, and Wheaton College are examples of "colleges" that offer advanced degrees.

2. Douglas Belkin, "Parents Shell Out Less for Kids in College," *Wall Street Journal*, July 23, 2013. Even among families with annual household incomes of over $100,000, the share of students staying at home has doubled to 48% since 2009–2010.

3. The 53 percent figure is for 2012, but it has been relatively static for about forty years. Libby Sander, "Ties to Home," *The Chronicle of Higher Education*, January 24, 2013.

4. This last question is from Samantha Stainburn in "The Case of the Vanishing Full-Time Professor," *New York Times*, January 3, 2010. According to a 2008 study by the American Federation of Teachers, graduate students teach between 16 and 32 percent of undergraduate courses at public research institutions (JBL Associates, Inc., "Reversing Course: The Troubling State of Academic Staffing and a Path Forward," www.aftface.org/storage/face/documents/reversing_course.pdf).

5. Matthew Arnold, *Culture and Anarchy: An Essay in Political and Social Criticism* (London, 1869), viii.

6. Melissa Korn, "Your College Major Is a Minor Issue, Employers Say," *Wall Street Journal*, April 10, 2013. Korn is discussing the results of a

survey of 318 employers conducted by the Association of American Colleges and Universities (AACU). In April 2013, the AACU published the results of their survey in a report entitled "It Takes More than a Major: Employer Priorities for College Learning and Student Success," www.aacu.org/leap/documents/2013_EmployerSurvey.pdf.

7. This sentiment is expressed cogently by D. Michael Lindsay, president of Gordon College, in an interview with Todd C. Ream that appeared in *Books & Culture* in the summer of 2013, www.booksandculture.com/articles/2013/julaug/evidence-of-gods-providence.html.

8. To learn more about the value of a decidedly *Christian* liberal arts education, see Gene C. Fant Jr., "The Heartbeat of Christian Higher Education: The Core Curriculum," in *Faith and Learning: A Handbook for Christian Higher Education*, ed. David S. Dockery (Nashville: B&H Publishing Group, 2012), 27–50.

9. Victor Davis Hanson, "In Defense of the Liberal Arts," *National Review Online*, December 16, 2010.

10. Those who came of age during the 1960s counterculture movement now lead the way not just in the humanities and social sciences departments but in many universities as a whole. Those who cast aside the traditions and values of their predecessors naturally look askance at the notion of administrators standing in *loco parentis*, telling bright undergraduates that they must study this or that subject in order to be truly educated. Similarly, the pressure to increase revenue can prompt universities to exchange high standards for high enrollment by letting students take whatever they want to get their degree.

11. John Zmirak, ed., *Choosing the Right College 2014–2015: The Inside Scoop on Elite Schools and Outstanding Lesser-Known Institutions* (Wilmington, DE: Intercollegiate Studies Institute, 2013).

12. They suggest a particular course in each of these eight critical subjects: classical literature in translation (Homer, Cicero, Caesar), ancient philosophy (Plato, Aristotle, all the way up through Boethius), the Bible, Christian thought before 1500 (Augustine, Aquinas), modern political theory (Hobbes, Rousseau, Marx, Mill, Burke, *The Federalist Papers*), Shakespeare, US history before 1865, and 19th-century European intellectual history.

13. *The American Freshman: Twenty-Five Year Trends, 1966–1990* (Los Angeles: Higher Education Research Institute, UCLA, 1991), www.heri.ucla.edu/PDFs/pubs/TFS/Trends/Monographs/TheAmericanFreshman25YearTrends.pdf. And *The American Freshman: National Norms Fall 2012*

(Los Angeles: Higher Education Research Institute, UCLA, 2013),
www.heri.ucla.edu/monographs/TheAmericanFreshman2012.pdf.

14. Anthony Carnevale, Nicole Smith, et al., "Help Wanted: Projections
of Jobs and Education Requirements through 2018," Georgetown
University Center on Education and the Workforce, June 2010, 14,
www9.georgetown.edu/grad/gppi/hpi/cew/pdfs/FullReport.pdf.

15. For June 2013, the figures were 3.9 percent unemployment (college grads)
versus 7.6 percent (high school graduates with no college). Bureau of
Labor Statistics (BLS), News Release, "The Unemployment Situation—
June 2013," 4, www.bls.gov/news.release/archives/empsit_07052013 *Faith
and Learning: A Handbook for Christian Higher Education*.pdf. Data is for
adults 25 and older—so experienced college graduates are mixed in with
new college graduates. New college graduates have higher unemployment
rates than experienced ones, and the unemployment rate varies by major
(see note 14). The BLS classifies persons as unemployed if they do not
have a job, have actively looked for work in the prior four weeks, and are
currently available for work.

16. Jonathan James, "The College Wage Premium," Federal Reserve Bank of
Cleveland, August 8, 2012, www.clevelandfed.org/research/commentary
/2012/2012-10.cfm.

17. William Bennett and David Wilezol, *Is College Worth It?* (Nashville:
Thomas Nelson, 2013), 72–73.

18. Anthony Carnevale, Ban Cheah, and Jeff Strohl, "Hard Times, College
Majors, Unemployment and Earnings 2013: Not All College Degrees Are
Created Equal," Georgetown University Center on Education and the
Workforce, May 2013, 7. www9.georgetown.edu/grad/gppi/hpi/cew/pdfs
/HardTimes.2013.2.pdf

19. McKinsey & Company, in collaboration with Chegg, Inc., "Voice of the
Graduate," May 2013, http://mckinseyonsociety.com/voice-of-the-graduate.

20. The data for this tool was voluntarily self-reported by employees and
collected by PayScale Inc., which some say makes the figures less reliable.
For information on PayScale's methodology, go here: www.payscale.com/
hr/innovations/methodology.

The federal government is seeking to increase accountability and
transparency in the higher education sector. For example, the Obama
administration has launched a website called College Scorecard: www.
whitehouse.gov/issues/education/higher-education/college-score-card.
You put in the name of a college, and it gives you the average net price
(after scholarships and grants) to attend the school for one year, how that

price varied over a recent three-year span, the six-year graduation rate, the student loan default rate, and the median level of student borrowing.

21. PayScale.com has launched a tool that compares the 30-year net return on investment of about one thousand colleges (www.payscale.com/college-education-value-2013). Basically, they're comparing how much money college graduates from a particular school make over 30 years (minus their cost to attend college) to what high school graduates would make if they worked 34 to 36 years (since by choosing to attend college, graduates give up four to six years of income they could have received had they gone straight to work after high school). Again, some are skeptical about PayScale's numbers, since they're self-reported (see previous note).

22. John Milton, *Tractate on Education*, 1673.

CONVERSATION 11: CONSIDERING ASSOCIATE DEGREES OR TRADE SCHOOLS

1. According to a Fidelity survey of 750 college graduates, reported in CNN Money on May 17, 2013: http://money.cnn.com/2013/05/17/pf/college/student-debt/index.html. This figure includes credit card debt.

2. Phil Izzo, "Number of the Week: Class of 2013, Most Indebted Ever," *Wall Street Journal*, May 18, 2013.

3. And it's a minority of students who graduate in four years. Harvard Graduate School of Education, "Pathways to Prosperity," February 2011, 10, www.gse.harvard.edu/news_events/features/2011/Pathways_to_Prosperity_Feb2011.pdf.

4. Marty Nemko, "America's Most Overrated Product: The Bachelor's Degree," *The Chronicle of Higher Education*, May 2, 2008. Based on US Department of Education, "The Toolbox Revisited: Paths to Degree Completion from High School through College," February 2006, 35–36 www2.ed.gov/rschstat/research/pubs/toolboxrevisit/toolbox.pdf.

5. For those wanting to explore this theme further, see Matthew B. Crawford's thought-provoking *New York Times* bestseller *Shop Class as Soulcraft: An Inquiry into the Value of Work* (New York: Penguin, 2009).

6. See, for example, Tamar Lewin, "At Colleges, Women Are Leaving Men in the Dust," *New York Times*, July 9, 2006.

7. ConnectEd: The California Center for College and Career is an example of an organization trying to encourage more high schools to combine academic and career-technical courses.

8. Jane M. Von Bergen, "Manufacturers Struggle to Preserve 'Shop Math' Skills," *The Philadelphia Inquirer*, March 29, 2012.

9. Manpower Group, "2013 Talent Shortage Survey Research Results," 39,

www.manpowergroup.us/campaigns/talent-shortage-2013/pdf/2013
_Talent_Shortage_Survey_Results_US_lo_0510.pdf. The survey examines
work shortages not just in the US but all over the world. Skilled trades
workers were also the most in-demand category worldwide.

10. For example, see Byron Pitts, "Three Million Open Jobs in U.S., but
Who's Qualified?" *60 Minutes*, November 11, 2012, www.cbsnews.com
/8301-18560_162-57547342/three-million-open-jobs-in-u.s-but-whos
-qualified/.

11. Joshua Wright, "America's Skilled Trades Dilemma: Shortages Loom as
Most-In-Demand Group of Workers Ages," *Forbes*, March 7, 2013.

12. To see a list of occupations with the fastest projected growth (2010–2020),
go here: www.bls.gov/ooh/About/Projections-Overview.htm.

13. The Texas Higher Education Coordinating Board (THECB) and College
Measures, "Two-Year Technical Degree Grads in Texas Have Higher First-
Year Median Earnings than Bachelor Grads," May 7, 2013.

   For Tennessee: "Depending on the program and school, some
certificate-program graduates enjoy initial earnings of more than $40,000.
Graduates with a certificate in construction trades from Nashville State
Community College earned more than $66,000 during their first year in
the workforce, and certificate holders who studied health professions at
Columbia State Community College earned more than $50,000" (www
.collegemeasures.org/post/2012/09/Big-Gaps-in-Earnings-for-Tennessee
-College-Grads--Study-Shows-Wage-Disparities-Between-Degree
-Programs-and-Schools.aspx).

14. For Virginia: "Graduates of occupational/technical associate's degree
programs, with an average salary of just under $40,000, out-earned not
only nonoccupational associate's degree graduates—by about $6,000—
but also bachelor's degree graduates by almost $2,500 statewide" (www
.collegemeasures.org/post/2012/11/Analysis-Finds-Wide-Wage-Disparities
-Among-Virginia-College-Grads.aspx).

15. All figures are according to the Bureau of Labor Statistics (BLS),
"Occupational Employment Statistics," www.bls.gov/oes/home.htm, as of
May 2012. The number of US positions does not include self-employed
workers. Starting salaries tend to be lower than average (as in any field),
but as workers gain experience, earnings can rise substantially higher
than the values shown here. In addition, the BLS expects over 40-percent
growth in diagnostic medical sonographer, occupational therapy assistant,
and physical therapist assistant positions. This is consistent with what is
widely reported: health care and technology-related jobs pay relatively well,
and the number of available positions is expected to rise.

16. Mike Rowe, interview by Mike Huckabee, *Huckabee*, Fox News, August 4, 2013, http://foxnewsinsider. com/2013/08/04/mike-rowe-dirty-jobs-alternative-college-degree.

17. Manpower Group, "2012 Talent Shortage Survey Research Results," 5, www.manpowergroup.us/campaigns/talent-shortage-2012/pdf/2012 _Talent_Shortage_Survey_Results_US_FINALFINAL.pdf.

18. McKinsey & Company, in collaboration with Chegg, Inc., "Voice of the Graduate," May 2013, 6, http://mckinseyonsociety .com/voice-of-the-graduate.

19. Their website is www.doleta.gov/oa.

20. Anthony P. Carnevale, Tamara Jayasundera, and Andrew R. Hanson, *Career and Technical Education: Five Ways That Pay along the Way to the B.A.* (Washington, DC: The Georgetown University Center on Education and the Workforce, 2012), 22–26, www9.georgetown.edu/grad/gppi/hpi /cew/pdfs/CTE.FiveWays.FullReport.pdf.

21. In 2013, there was $250,000 in scholarship money available: www .mikeroweworks.com/2013/03/mikeroweworks-foundation-education -scholarship-program. Mike Rowe has also set up a jobs database for skilled trade employment: www.mikeroweworks.com/job-site/jobs.

22. *The American Freshman: National Norms Fall 2012* (Los Angeles: Higher Education Research Institute, UCLA, 2013), 5.

APPENDIX: HOW TO PLAN AND SAVE FOR COLLEGE

1. Kayla Webley, "Sorry, Kids: Your Parents Feel Less Able to Help Pay for College," *Time*, March 29, 2012, http://business.time.com/2012/03/29 /sorry-kids-your-parents-feel-less-able-to-help-pay-for-college/.

2. Randy Alcorn, *Money, Possessions, and Eternity* (Carol Stream, IL: Tyndale House, 1989), 367–368.

3. From the FINRA Foundation's website, accessed August 17, 2012, www .finrafoundation.org/web/groups/foundation/@foundation/documents /foundation/p120535.pdf.

4. As I write, the American Opportunity Tax Credit allows you to receive $2,500 each year if you pay for $4,000 of your child's educational costs from a taxable account. This credit is reduced if your modified adjusted gross income exceeds $80,000 ($160,000 for joint filers). Check the IRS website to see if you qualify. This credit is set to expire at the end of 2017 but could be extended by Congress.

5. Some types of assets that can be transferred with a UTMA cannot be gifted with a UGMA.

6. The number "529" comes from Section 529 of the Internal Revenue code.

I chose not to cover 529 prepaid tuition plans because, as I write, the prepaid tuition plans of several states have been closed to new enrollment. Parents who select prepaid plans *are* taking on risk in most cases, as few plans are truly guaranteed by the state. And the disadvantage of prepaid plans is that they limit your children to specific colleges and universities.

7. The penalty for a "nonqualified distribution" is 10 percent as of 2013. The phrase "eligible educational institution" refers to any college, university, vocational school, or other postsecondary educational institution eligible to participate in a student aid program administered by the US Department of Education.

8. The College Scholarship Service or CSS Financial Aid PROFILE is an alternative form that determines how much a family should be expected to pay for college. It uses an "Institutional Methodology" for determining a family's expected family contribution rather than the "Federal Methodology." The difference? The CSS does take home equity and retirement assets into account. The CSS Financial Aid PROFILE is preferred over the FAFSA by some of the more selective (and expensive) private colleges and universities.

9. Ruth Simon, "Colleges Cut Prices by Providing More Financial Aid," *Wall Street Journal*, May 6, 2013.

10. Dual enrollment policies vary by state. More information is available from the Department of Education at www2.ed.gov/about/offices/list/ovae/pi /hsinit/papers/dual.pdf.

11. Families with a high degree of demonstrated financial need also qualify for the Perkins loan, which (as I write) has a slightly higher interest rate than the Stafford loan products.

12. For an IRA withdrawal, check the appropriate IRS document: www.irs .gov/publications/p970/ch09.html. With an employer-sponsored plan, it is different—and complicated. Additional fees may apply. Check with your retirement plan's custodian and your tax adviser.

Do-able. Daily. Devotions.

START ANY DAY THE ONE YEAR WAY.

FOR STUDENTS

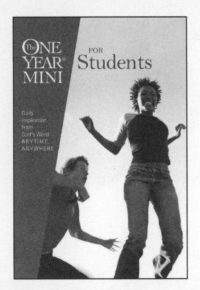

*The One Year® Mini
for Students*

*The One Year® Alive
Devotions for Students*